Just The facts101
Textbook Key Facts

Isle of Man Labor Laws and Regulations Handbook: Strategic Information and Basic Laws

by Cram101
Textbook NOT Included

Table of Contents

Title Page

Copyright

Foundations of Business

Management

Business law

Finance

Human resource management

Information systems

Marketing

Manufacturing

Commerce

Business ethics

Accounting

Index: Answers

Just The Facts101

Exam Prep for

Isle of Man Labor Laws and Regulations Handbook: Strategic Information and Basic Laws

Just The Facts101 Exam Prep is your link from
the textbook and lecture to your exams.

**Just The Facts101 Exam Preps are unauthorized and comprehensive reviews
of your textbooks.**

All material provided by CTI Publications (c) 2019

Textbook publishers and textbook authors do not participate in or contribute to these reviews.

Just The Facts101 Exam Prep

Copyright © 2019 by CTI Publications. All rights reserved.

eAIN 438664

Foundations of Business

A business, also known as an enterprise, agency or a firm, is an entity involved in the provision of goods and/or services to consumers. Businesses are prevalent in capitalist economies, where most of them are privately owned and provide goods and services to customers in exchange for other goods, services, or money.

:: Budgets ::

A _____ is a financial plan for a defined period, often one year. It may also include planned sales volumes and revenues, resource quantities, costs and expenses, assets, liabilities and cash flows. Companies, governments, families and other organizations use it to express strategic plans of activities or events in measurable terms.

Exam Probability: **High**

1. *Answer choices:*

(see index for correct answer)

- a. Link budget
- b. Marginal budgeting for bottlenecks
- c. Budget
- d. Zero budget

Guidance: level 1

:: Money ::

In economics, _____ is money in the physical form of currency, such as banknotes and coins. In bookkeeping and finance, _____ is current assets comprising currency or currency equivalents that can be accessed immediately or near-immediately . _____ is seen either as a reserve for payments, in case of a structural or incidental negative _____ flow or as a way to avoid a downturn on financial markets.

Exam Probability: **Medium**

2. *Answer choices:*

(see index for correct answer)

- a. World Money Fair
- b. Mammon
- c. Cash
- d. Purse bid

Guidance: level 1

:: Treaties ::

An _____ is a relationship among people, groups, or states that have joined together for mutual benefit or to achieve some common purpose, whether or not explicit agreement has been worked out among them. Members of an _____ are called allies. _____s form in many settings, including political _____s, military _____s, and business _____s. When the term is used in the context of war or armed struggle, such associations may also be called allied powers, especially when discussing World War I or World War II.

Exam Probability: **Low**

3. *Answer choices:*

(see index for correct answer)

- a. Guillotine clause
- b. Multilateral treaty

- c. Alliance
- d. Reservation

Guidance: level 1

:: Macroeconomics ::

A foreign _____ is an investment in the form of a controlling ownership in a business in one country by an entity based in another country. It is thus distinguished from a foreign portfolio investment by a notion of direct control.

Exam Probability: **Medium**

4. *Answer choices:*
(see index for correct answer)

- a. Direct investment
- b. Business cycle accounting
- c. Austrian business cycle theory
- d. Value added

Guidance: level 1

:: Systems theory ::

A _____ is a set of policies, processes and procedures used by an organization to ensure that it can fulfill the tasks required to achieve its objectives. These objectives cover many aspects of the organization's operations. For instance, an environmental _____ enables organizations to improve their environmental performance and an occupational health and safety _____ enables an organization to control its occupational health and safety risks, etc.

Exam Probability: **Medium**

5. *Answer choices:*

(see index for correct answer)

- a. Management system
- b. transient state
- c. decentralized system
- d. equifinality

Guidance: level 1

:: Stock market ::

A _____, equity market or share market is the aggregation of buyers and sellers of stocks, which represent ownership claims on businesses; these may include securities listed on a public stock exchange, as well as stock that is only traded privately. Examples of the latter include shares of private companies which are sold to investors through equity crowdfunding platforms. Stock exchanges list shares of common equity as well as other security types, e.g. corporate bonds and convertible bonds.

Exam Probability: **Low**

6. *Answer choices:*

(see index for correct answer)

- a. Stock market
- b. Red chip
- c. Profit warning
- d. Automated trading system

Guidance: level 1

:: Marketing ::

A _____ is something that is necessary for an organism to live a healthy life. _____ s are distinguished from wants in that, in the case of a _____ , a deficiency causes a clear adverse outcome: a dysfunction or death. In other words, a _____ is something required for a safe, stable and healthy life while a want is a desire, wish or aspiration. When _____ s or wants are backed by purchasing power, they have the potential to become economic demands.

Exam Probability: **Low**

7. *Answer choices:*

(see index for correct answer)

- a. Franchise fee

- b. Cause-related loyalty marketing
- c. Need
- d. Profit chart

Guidance: level 1

:: Marketing ::

_____ is based on a marketing concept which can be adopted by an organization as a strategy for business expansion. Where implemented, a franchisor licenses its know-how, procedures, intellectual property, use of its business model, brand, and rights to sell its branded products and services to a franchisee. In return the franchisee pays certain fees and agrees to comply with certain obligations, typically set out in a Franchise Agreement.

Exam Probability: **Low**

8. *Answer choices:*
(see index for correct answer)

- a. Patronage concentration
- b. Market sector
- c. Immersion marketing
- d. Franchising

Guidance: level 1

:: Evaluation ::

A _____ is an evaluation of a publication, service, or company such as a movie, video game, musical composition, book ; a piece of hardware like a car, home appliance, or computer; or an event or performance, such as a live music concert, play, musical theater show, dance show, or art exhibition. In addition to a critical evaluation, the _____ 's author may assign the work a rating to indicate its relative merit. More loosely, an author may _____ current events, trends, or items in the news. A compilation of _____ s may itself be called a _____ . The New York _____ of Books, for instance, is a collection of essays on literature, culture, and current affairs. National _____ , founded by William F. Buckley, Jr., is an influential conservative magazine, and Monthly _____ is a long-running socialist periodical.

Exam Probability: **Low**

9. *Answer choices:*

(see index for correct answer)

- a. Server Efficiency Rating Tool
- b. Educational assessment
- c. Program evaluation
- d. Review

Guidance: level 1

:: Identity management ::

_____ is the ability of an individual or group to seclude themselves, or information about themselves, and thereby express themselves selectively. The boundaries and content of what is considered private differ among cultures and individuals, but share common themes. When something is private to a person, it usually means that something is inherently special or sensitive to them. The domain of _____ partially overlaps with security, which can include the concepts of appropriate use, as well as protection of information. _____ may also take the form of bodily integrity.

Exam Probability: **Low**

10. *Answer choices:*

(see index for correct answer)

- a. Directory information tree
- b. Oracle Identity Management
- c. Privacy
- d. Common Indexing Protocol

Guidance: level 1

:: ::

An _____ is the production of goods or related services within an economy. The major source of revenue of a group or company is the indicator of its relevant _____. When a large group has multiple sources of revenue generation, it is considered to be working in different industries. Manufacturing _____ became a key sector of production and labour in European and North American countries during the Industrial Revolution, upsetting previous mercantile and feudal economies. This came through many successive rapid advances in technology, such as the production of steel and coal.

Exam Probability: **Medium**

11. *Answer choices:*

(see index for correct answer)

- a. process perspective
- b. Industry
- c. open system
- d. imperative

Guidance: level 1

:: Decision theory ::

Within economics the concept of _____ is used to model worth or value, but its usage has evolved significantly over time. The term was introduced initially as a measure of pleasure or satisfaction within the theory of utilitarianism by moral philosophers such as Jeremy Bentham and John Stuart Mill. But the term has been adapted and reapplied within neoclassical economics, which dominates modern economic theory, as a _____ function that represents a consumer's preference ordering over a choice set. As such, it is devoid of its original interpretation as a measurement of the pleasure or satisfaction obtained by the consumer from that choice.

Exam Probability: **Medium**

12. *Answer choices:*

(see index for correct answer)

- a. Option grid
- b. Policy
- c. Decision-matrix method
- d. Litmus test

Guidance: level 1

:: Regression analysis ::

A _____ often refers to a set of documented requirements to be satisfied by a material, design, product, or service. A _____ is often a type of technical standard.

Exam Probability: **Low**

13. *Answer choices:*

(see index for correct answer)

- a. Partition of sums of squares
- b. Specification
- c. Sobel test
- d. Standardized coefficient

Guidance: level 1

:: Goods ::

In most contexts, the concept of _____ denotes the conduct that should be preferred when posed with a choice between possible actions. _____ is generally considered to be the opposite of evil, and is of interest in the study of morality, ethics, religion and philosophy. The specific meaning and etymology of the term and its associated translations among ancient and contemporary languages show substantial variation in its inflection and meaning depending on circumstances of place, history, religious, or philosophical context.

Exam Probability: **Medium**

14. *Answer choices:*

(see index for correct answer)

- a. Good
- b. Demerit good
- c. Inferior good
- d. Bad

Guidance: level 1

:: Management ::

In business, a _____ is the attribute that allows an organization to outperform its competitors. A _____ may include access to natural resources, such as high-grade ores or a low-cost power source, highly skilled labor, geographic location, high entry barriers, and access to new technology.

Exam Probability: **Medium**

15. *Answer choices:*

(see index for correct answer)

- a. Business process improvement
- b. Organizational hologram
- c. Competitive advantage
- d. SimulTrain

Guidance: level 1

:: Marketing ::

_____ comes from the Latin neg and otsia referring to businessmen who, unlike the patricians, had no leisure time in their industriousness; it held the meaning of business until the 17th century when it took on the diplomatic connotation as a dialogue between two or more people or parties intended to reach a beneficial outcome over one or more issues where a conflict exists with respect to at least one of these issues. Thus, _____ is a process of combining divergent positions into a joint agreement under a decision rule of unanimity.

Exam Probability: **High**

16. *Answer choices:*
(see index for correct answer)

- a. The International Customer Service Institute
- b. Negotiation
- c. Prommercial
- d. Gladvertising

Guidance: level 1

:: Marketing ::

_____ or stock is the goods and materials that a business holds for the ultimate goal of resale.

Exam Probability: **Low**

17. *Answer choices:*

(see index for correct answer)

- a. Movement marketing
- b. Marketing spending
- c. Inventory
- d. Product sabotage

Guidance: level 1

:: Occupations ::

An _____ is a person who has a position of authority in a hierarchical organization. The term derives from the late Latin from officiarius, meaning "official".

Exam Probability: **Low**

18. *Answer choices:*

(see index for correct answer)

- a. Occupational closure
- b. Clockmaker
- c. Officer
- d. Housebreaker

Guidance: level 1

:: Management ::

A _____ describes the rationale of how an organization creates, delivers, and captures value, in economic, social, cultural or other contexts. The process of _____ construction and modification is also called _____ innovation and forms a part of business strategy.

Exam Probability: **Medium**

19. *Answer choices:*

(see index for correct answer)

- a. Relational view
- b. Business model
- c. Investment control
- d. Porter five forces analysis

Guidance: level 1

:: Business ethics ::

_____ is a type of harassment technique that relates to a sexual nature and the unwelcome or inappropriate promise of rewards in exchange for sexual favors. _____ includes a range of actions from mild transgressions to sexual abuse or assault. Harassment can occur in many different social settings such as the workplace, the home, school, churches, etc. Harassers or victims may be of any gender.

Exam Probability: **Medium**

20. *Answer choices:*

(see index for correct answer)

- a. Burson-Marsteller
- b. Ethical corporate social responsibility
- c. Minecode
- d. Precarious work

Guidance: level 1

:: Management ::

A _____ is a formal written document containing business goals, the methods on how these goals can be attained, and the time frame within which these goals need to be achieved. It also describes the nature of the business, background information on the organization, the organization's financial projections, and the strategies it intends to implement to achieve the stated targets. In its entirety, this document serves as a road map that provides direction to the business.

Exam Probability: **Medium**

21. *Answer choices:*

(see index for correct answer)

- a. Manager Tools Podcast
- b. Business plan
- c. Target culture
- d. Project management

Guidance: level 1

:: Real estate ::

_____ s serve several societal needs – primarily as shelter from weather, security, living space, privacy, to store belongings, and to comfortably live and work. A _____ as a shelter represents a physical division of the human habitat and the outside .

Exam Probability: **Low**

22. *Answer choices:*

(see index for correct answer)

- a. Building
- b. Cadastre
- c. Slumlord

- d. Estate agent

Guidance: level 1

:: Information science ::

A _____ is a written, drawn, presented, or memorialized representation of thought. a _____ is a form, or written piece that trains a line of thought or as in history, a significant event. The word originates from the Latin _____ um, which denotes a "teaching" or "lesson": the verb doceo denotes "to teach". In the past, the word was usually used to denote a written proof useful as evidence of a truth or fact. In the computer age, "_____" usually denotes a primarily textual computer file, including its structure and format, e.g. fonts, colors, and images. Contemporarily, "_____" is not defined by its transmission medium, e.g., paper, given the existence of electronic _____ s. "_____ ation" is distinct because it has more denotations than "_____". _____ s are also distinguished from "realia", which are three-dimensional objects that would otherwise satisfy the definition of "_____" because they memorialize or represent thought; _____ s are considered more as 2 dimensional representations. While _____ s are able to have large varieties of customization, all _____ s are able to be shared freely, and have the right to do so, creativity can be represented by _____ s, also. History, events, examples, opinion, etc. all can be expressed in _____ s.

Exam Probability: **High**

23. *Answer choices:*
(see index for correct answer)

- a. Interviewer effect

- b. Informationist
- c. Document
- d. POSC Caesar

Guidance: level 1

:: Industry ::

_____ describes various measures of the efficiency of production. Often, a _____ measure is expressed as the ratio of an aggregate output to a single input or an aggregate input used in a production process, i.e. output per unit of input. Most common example is the labour _____ measure, e.g., such as GDP per worker. There are many different definitions of _____ and the choice among them depends on the purpose of the _____ measurement and/or data availability. The key source of difference between various _____ measures is also usually related to how the outputs and the inputs are aggregated into scalars to obtain such a ratio-type measure of _____ .

Exam Probability: **Medium**

24. *Answer choices:*

(see index for correct answer)

- a. Productivity
- b. Consciousness Industry
- c. Recommended exposure limit
- d. Reindustrialization

Guidance: level 1

:: Financial markets ::

A _____ is a financial market in which long-term debt or equity-backed securities are bought and sold. _____ s channel the wealth of savers to those who can put it to long-term productive use, such as companies or governments making long-term investments. Financial regulators like the Bank of England and the U.S. Securities and Exchange Commission oversee _____ s to protect investors against fraud, among other duties.

Exam Probability: **Low**

25. *Answer choices:*

(see index for correct answer)

- a. Lit pool
- b. Shelf registration
- c. Spot contract
- d. Market distortion

Guidance: level 1

:: Employment ::

The _____ is an individual's metaphorical "journey" through learning, work and other aspects of life. There are a number of ways to define _____ and the term is used in a variety of ways.

Exam Probability: **Medium**

26. *Answer choices:*

(see index for correct answer)

- a. Monster Employment Index
- b. Employment Development Department
- c. Extreme Blue
- d. Job shadow

Guidance: level 1

:: Management ::

A _____ is an idea of the future or desired result that a person or a group of people envisions, plans and commits to achieve. People endeavor to reach _____ s within a finite time by setting deadlines.

Exam Probability: **Low**

27. *Answer choices:*

(see index for correct answer)

- a. Dynamic enterprise modeling
- b. Kata
- c. Facilitator
- d. Goal

Guidance: level 1

:: Planning ::

_____ is a high level plan to achieve one or more goals under conditions of uncertainty. In the sense of the "art of the general," which included several subsets of skills including tactics, siegecraft, logistics etc., the term came into use in the 6th century C.E. in East Roman terminology, and was translated into Western vernacular languages only in the 18th century. From then until the 20th century, the word " _____ " came to denote "a comprehensive way to try to pursue political ends, including the threat or actual use of force, in a dialectic of wills" in a military conflict, in which both adversaries interact.

Exam Probability: **High**

28. *Answer choices:*

(see index for correct answer)

- a. Enterprise architecture planning
- b. Cross-cultural differences in decision-making
- c. Strategy
- d. Group information management

Guidance: level 1

:: Elementary arithmetic ::

In mathematics, a _____ is a number or ratio expressed as a fraction of 100. It is often denoted using the percent sign, "%", or the abbreviations "pct.", "pct"; sometimes the abbreviation "pc" is also used. A _____ is a dimensionless number.

Exam Probability: **Medium**

29. *Answer choices:*

(see index for correct answer)

- a. Fifth power
- b. Number bond
- c. Percentage
- d. Division

Guidance: level 1

:: Production and manufacturing ::

_____ is a set of techniques and tools for process improvement. Though as a shortened form it may be found written as 6S, it should not be confused with the methodology known as 6S.

Exam Probability: **High**

30. *Answer choices:*

(see index for correct answer)

- a. Digital prototyping
- b. Advanced product quality planning
- c. Six Sigma
- d. Nondestructive testing

Guidance: level 1

:: Semiconductor companies ::

_____ Corporation is a Japanese multinational conglomerate corporation headquartered in Konan, Minato, Tokyo. Its diversified business includes consumer and professional electronics, gaming, entertainment and financial services. The company owns the largest music entertainment business in the world, the largest video game console business and one of the largest video game publishing businesses, and is one of the leading manufacturers of electronic products for the consumer and professional markets, and a leading player in the film and television entertainment industry. _____ was ranked 97th on the 2018 Fortune Global 500 list.

31. *Answer choices:*

(see index for correct answer)

- a. VeriSilicon
- b. Intersil
- c. Sony
- d. Everspin Technologies

Guidance: level 1

:: Reputation management ::

_____ or image of a social entity is an opinion about that entity, typically as a result of social evaluation on a set of criteria.

Exam Probability: **Low**

32. *Answer choices:*

(see index for correct answer)

- a. Star
- b. Reputation
- c. Reputation system
- d. Trust metric

Guidance: level 1

:: Human resource management ::

_____ encompasses values and behaviors that contribute to the unique social and psychological environment of a business. The _____ influences the way people interact, the context within which knowledge is created, the resistance they will have towards certain changes, and ultimately the way they share knowledge. _____ represents the collective values, beliefs and principles of organizational members and is a product of factors such as history, product, market, technology, strategy, type of employees, management style, and national culture; culture includes the organization's vision, values, norms, systems, symbols, language, assumptions, environment, location, beliefs and habits.

Exam Probability: **Medium**

33. *Answer choices:*

(see index for correct answer)

- a. Employeeship
- b. Four-day week
- c. Perceived organizational support
- d. Organizational culture

Guidance: level 1

:: Service industries ::

_____ are the economic services provided by the finance industry, which encompasses a broad range of businesses that manage money, including credit unions, banks, credit-card companies, insurance companies, accountancy companies, consumer-finance companies, stock brokerages, investment funds, individual managers and some government-sponsored enterprises. _____ companies are present in all economically developed geographic locations and tend to cluster in local, national, regional and international financial centers such as London, New York City, and Tokyo.

Exam Probability: **Medium**

34. *Answer choices:*

(see index for correct answer)

- a. Financial services
- b. Financial services in South Korea
- c. Language industry
- d. Financial services in Japan

Guidance: level 1

:: Business law ::

A _____ is an arrangement where parties, known as partners, agree to cooperate to advance their mutual interests. The partners in a _____ may be individuals, businesses, interest-based organizations, schools, governments or combinations. Organizations may partner to increase the likelihood of each achieving their mission and to amplify their reach. A _____ may result in issuing and holding equity or may be only governed by a contract.

Exam Probability: **Medium**

35. *Answer choices:*

(see index for correct answer)

- a. Business license
- b. Unfair Commercial Practices Directive
- c. Partnership
- d. Starting a Business Index

Guidance: level 1

:: Production economics ::

_____ is the joint use of a resource or space. It is also the process of dividing and distributing. In its narrow sense, it refers to joint or alternating use of inherently finite goods, such as a common pasture or a shared residence. Still more loosely, "_____" can actually mean giving something as an outright gift: for example, to "share" one's food really means to give some of it as a gift. _____ is a basic component of human interaction, and is responsible for strengthening social ties and ensuring a person's well-being.

Exam Probability: **Low**

36. *Answer choices:*

(see index for correct answer)

- a. Robinson Crusoe economy
- b. Isoquant
- c. Sharing
- d. Productivity Alpha

Guidance: level 1

:: Export and import control ::

" _____ " means the Government Service which is responsible for the administration of _____ law and the collection of duties and taxes and which also has the responsibility for the application of other laws and regulations relating to the importation, exportation, movement or storage of goods.

Exam Probability: **Low**

37. *Answer choices:*
(see index for correct answer)

- a. Customs Modernization Act
- b. Export Control Classification Number
- c. Export of cryptography
- d. Customs valuation

Guidance: level 1

:: Loans ::

In finance, a _____ is the lending of money by one or more individuals, organizations, or other entities to other individuals, organizations etc. The recipient incurs a debt, and is usually liable to pay interest on that debt until it is repaid, and also to repay the principal amount borrowed.

Exam Probability: **Medium**

38. *Answer choices:*

(see index for correct answer)

- a. Gross loan
- b. Loan
- c. Call money
- d. International lender of last resort

Guidance: level 1

:: Market research ::

_____ is "the process or set of processes that links the producers, customers, and end users to the marketer through information used to identify and define marketing opportunities and problems; generate, refine, and evaluate marketing actions; monitor marketing performance; and improve understanding of marketing as a process. _____ specifies the information required to address these issues, designs the method for collecting information, manages and implements the data collection process, analyzes the results, and communicates the findings and their implications."

Exam Probability: **High**

39. *Answer choices:*

(see index for correct answer)

- a. Indian Readership Survey
- b. Marketing research
- c. Customer advisory council
- d. Product Intelligence

Guidance: level 1

:: Marketing techniques ::

_____ is the activity of dividing a broad consumer or business market, normally consisting of existing and potential customers, into sub-groups of consumers based on some type of shared characteristics. In dividing or segmenting markets, researchers typically look for common characteristics such as shared needs, common interests, similar lifestyles or even similar demographic profiles. The overall aim of segmentation is to identify high yield segments – that is, those segments that are likely to be the most profitable or that have growth potential – so that these can be selected for special attention.

Exam Probability: **Medium**

40. *Answer choices:*

(see index for correct answer)

- a. market segment
- b. Micromarketing
- c. Faith-based marketing
- d. Unique perceived benefit

Guidance: level 1

:: ::

Some scenarios associate "this kind of planning" with learning "life skills". Schedules are necessary, or at least useful, in situations where individuals need to know what time they must be at a specific location to receive a specific service, and where people need to accomplish a set of goals within a set time period.

Exam Probability: **Medium**

41. *Answer choices:*

(see index for correct answer)

- a. corporate values
- b. process perspective
- c. Scheduling
- d. open system

Guidance: level 1

:: Asset ::

In financial accounting, an _____ is any resource owned by the business. Anything tangible or intangible that can be owned or controlled to produce value and that is held by a company to produce positive economic value is an _____. Simply stated, _____ s represent value of ownership that can be converted into cash . The balance sheet of a firm records the monetary value of the _____ s owned by that firm. It covers money and other valuables belonging to an individual or to a business.

Exam Probability: **Low**

42. *Answer choices:*

(see index for correct answer)

- a. Current asset

- b. Fixed asset

Guidance: level 1

:: Data collection ::

A _____ is an utterance which typically functions as a request for information. _____ s can thus be understood as a kind of illocutionary act in the field of pragmatics or as special kinds of propositions in frameworks of formal semantics such as alternative semantics or inquisitive semantics. The information requested is expected to be provided in the form of an answer. _____ s are often conflated with interrogatives, which are the grammatical forms typically used to achieve them. Rhetorical _____ s, for example, are interrogative in form but may not be considered true _____ s as they are not expected to be answered. Conversely, non-interrogative grammatical structures may be considered _____ s as in the case of the imperative sentence "tell me your name".

Exam Probability: **Medium**

43. *Answer choices:*

(see index for correct answer)

- a. ScraperWiki
- b. Public survey
- c. North Atlantic Population Project
- d. Flow tracer

Guidance: level 1

:: Shareholders ::

A _____ is a payment made by a corporation to its shareholders, usually as a distribution of profits. When a corporation earns a profit or surplus, the corporation is able to re-invest the profit in the business and pay a proportion of the profit as a _____ to shareholders. Distribution to shareholders may be in cash or, if the corporation has a _____ reinvestment plan, the amount can be paid by the issue of further shares or share repurchase. When _____ s are paid, shareholders typically must pay income taxes, and the corporation does not receive a corporate income tax deduction for the _____ payments.

Exam Probability: **High**

44. *Answer choices:*

(see index for correct answer)

- a. Activist shareholder
- b. Shareholder ownership value
- c. Shareholder yield
- d. Dividend

Guidance: level 1

:: Contract law ::

A _____ is a legally-binding agreement which recognises and governs the rights and duties of the parties to the agreement. A _____ is legally enforceable because it meets the requirements and approval of the law. An agreement typically involves the exchange of goods, services, money, or promises of any of those. In the event of breach of _____ , the law awards the injured party access to legal remedies such as damages and cancellation.

Exam Probability: **Medium**

45. *Answer choices:*

(see index for correct answer)

- a. Contract
- b. Pre-existing duty rule
- c. Firm commitment
- d. Domicilium citandi et executandi

Guidance: level 1

:: Graphic design ::

An _____ is an artifact that depicts visual perception, such as a photograph or other two-dimensional picture, that resembles a subject—usually a physical object—and thus provides a depiction of it. In the context of signal processing, an _____ is a distributed amplitude of color.

Exam Probability: **High**

46. *Answer choices:*

(see index for correct answer)

- a. Image
- b. Graphic charter
- c. AutoCollage 2008
- d. Spartan

Guidance: level 1

:: Fraud ::

In law, _____ is intentional deception to secure unfair or unlawful gain, or to deprive a victim of a legal right. _____ can violate civil law, a criminal law, or it may cause no loss of money, property or legal right but still be an element of another civil or criminal wrong. The purpose of _____ may be monetary gain or other benefits, for example by obtaining a passport, travel document, or driver's license, or mortgage _____, where the perpetrator may attempt to qualify for a mortgage by way of false statements.

Exam Probability: **Low**

47. *Answer choices:*

(see index for correct answer)

- a. Romance scam
- b. Medicare fraud

- c. Accreditation mill
- d. Visa fraud

Guidance: level 1

:: Interest rates ::

An _____ is the amount of interest due per period, as a proportion of the amount lent, deposited or borrowed . The total interest on an amount lent or borrowed depends on the principal sum, the _____ , the compounding frequency, and the length of time over which it is lent, deposited or borrowed.

Exam Probability: **Medium**

48. *Answer choices:*

(see index for correct answer)

- a. Annual percentage yield
- b. Amortising swap
- c. Zero interest-rate policy
- d. Notional amount

Guidance: level 1

:: Scientific method ::

In the social sciences and life sciences, a _____ is a research method involving an up-close, in-depth, and detailed examination of a subject of study, as well as its related contextual conditions.

Exam Probability: **Low**

49. *Answer choices:*

(see index for correct answer)

- a. Case study
- b. Preference test
- c. pilot project
- d. Causal research

Guidance: level 1

:: Management ::

The _____ is a strategy performance management tool – a semi-standard structured report, that can be used by managers to keep track of the execution of activities by the staff within their control and to monitor the consequences arising from these actions.

Exam Probability: **High**

50. *Answer choices:*

(see index for correct answer)

- a. Corticon
- b. Balanced scorecard
- c. Task-oriented and relationship-oriented leadership
- d. Economic production quantity

Guidance: level 1

:: Euthenics ::

_____ is an ethical framework and suggests that an entity, be it an organization or individual, has an obligation to act for the benefit of society at large. _____ is a duty every individual has to perform so as to maintain a balance between the economy and the ecosystems. A trade-off may exist between economic development, in the material sense, and the welfare of the society and environment, though this has been challenged by many reports over the past decade. _____ means sustaining the equilibrium between the two. It pertains not only to business organizations but also to everyone whose any action impacts the environment. This responsibility can be passive, by avoiding engaging in socially harmful acts, or active, by performing activities that directly advance social goals. _____ must be intergenerational since the actions of one generation have consequences on those following.

Exam Probability: **High**

51. *Answer choices:*

(see index for correct answer)

- a. Family and consumer science

- b. Euthenics
- c. Social responsibility
- d. Home economics

Guidance: level 1

:: Management ::

_____ is the practice of initiating, planning, executing, controlling, and closing the work of a team to achieve specific goals and meet specific success criteria at the specified time.

Exam Probability: **Low**

52. *Answer choices:*
(see index for correct answer)

- a. Reverse innovation
- b. Shrinkage
- c. Tacit knowledge
- d. Project management

Guidance: level 1

:: Business models ::

A _____, _____ company or daughter company is a company that is owned or controlled by another company, which is called the parent company, parent, or holding company. The _____ can be a company, corporation, or limited liability company. In some cases it is a government or state-owned enterprise. In some cases, particularly in the music and book publishing industries, subsidiaries are referred to as imprints.

Exam Probability: **High**

53. *Answer choices:*

(see index for correct answer)

- a. Revenue model
- b. Small business
- c. Defensive patent aggregation
- d. Subsidiary

Guidance: level 1

:: Business planning ::

_____ is an organization's process of defining its strategy, or direction, and making decisions on allocating its resources to pursue this strategy. It may also extend to control mechanisms for guiding the implementation of the strategy. _____ became prominent in corporations during the 1960s and remains an important aspect of strategic management. It is executed by strategic planners or strategists, who involve many parties and research sources in their analysis of the organization and its relationship to the environment in which it competes.

Exam Probability: **Low**

54. *Answer choices:*

(see index for correct answer)

- a. Stakeholder management
- b. Customer Demand Planning
- c. Gap analysis
- d. Strategic planning

Guidance: level 1

:: National accounts ::

_____ is a monetary measure of the market value of all the final goods and services produced in a period of time, often annually. GDP per capita does not, however, reflect differences in the cost of living and the inflation rates of the countries; therefore using a basis of GDP per capita at purchasing power parity is arguably more useful when comparing differences in living standards between nations.

Exam Probability: **High**

55. *Answer choices:*

(see index for correct answer)

- a. National Income
- b. Fixed capital

- c. capital formation

Guidance: level 1

:: Management ::

_____ is the identification, evaluation, and prioritization of risks followed by coordinated and economical application of resources to minimize, monitor, and control the probability or impact of unfortunate events or to maximize the realization of opportunities.

Exam Probability: **High**

56. *Answer choices:*

(see index for correct answer)

- a. Shrinkage
- b. Downstream
- c. Risk management
- d. Success-oriented management

Guidance: level 1

:: Business law ::

A _____ is a business entity created by two or more parties, generally characterized by shared ownership, shared returns and risks, and shared governance. Companies typically pursue _____s for one of four reasons: to access a new market, particularly emerging markets; to gain scale efficiencies by combining assets and operations; to share risk for major investments or projects; or to access skills and capabilities.

Exam Probability: **High**

57. *Answer choices:*

(see index for correct answer)

- a. Product defect
- b. Official Assignee
- c. Joint venture
- d. Forward-looking statement

Guidance: level 1

:: Project management ::

In political science, an _____ is a means by which a petition signed by a certain minimum number of registered voters can force a government to choose to either enact a law or hold a public vote in parliament in what is called indirect _____, or under direct _____, the proposition is immediately put to a plebiscite or referendum, in what is called a Popular initiated Referendum or citizen-initiated referendum).

Exam Probability: **Medium**

58. *Answer choices:*

(see index for correct answer)

- a. Defense Acquisition Guide
- b. Initiative
- c. Sunk costs
- d. Deployment Plan

Guidance: level 1

:: Statistical terminology ::

_____ is the magnitude or dimensions of a thing. _____ can be measured as length, width, height, diameter, perimeter, area, volume, or mass.

Exam Probability: **Low**

59. *Answer choices:*

(see index for correct answer)

- a. Size
- b. Gompertz function
- c. dependent variable
- d. Collectively exhaustive

Guidance: level 1

Management

   Management is the administration of an organization, whether it is a business, a not-for-profit organization, or government body. Management includes the activities of setting the strategy of an organization and coordinating the efforts of its employees (or of volunteers) to accomplish its objectives through the application of available resources, such as financial, natural, technological, and human resources.

:: Commercial item transport and distribution ::

In commerce, supply-chain management, the management of the flow of goods and services, involves the movement and storage of raw materials, of work-in-process inventory, and of finished goods from point of origin to point of consumption. Interconnected or interlinked networks, channels and node businesses combine in the provision of products and services required by end customers in a supply chain. Supply-chain management has been defined as the "design, planning, execution, control, and monitoring of supply-chain activities with the objective of creating net value, building a competitive infrastructure, leveraging worldwide logistics, synchronizing supply with demand and measuring performance globally." SCM practice draws heavily from the areas of industrial engineering, systems engineering, operations management, logistics, procurement, information technology, and marketing and strives for an integrated approach. Marketing channels play an important role in supply-chain management. Current research in supply-chain management is concerned with topics related to sustainability and risk management, among others. Some suggest that the "people dimension" of SCM, ethical issues, internal integration, transparency/visibility, and human capital/talent management are topics that have, so far, been underrepresented on the research agenda.

Exam Probability: **Low**

1. *Answer choices:*

(see index for correct answer)

- a. Humanitarian Logistics
- b. Supply chain management
- c. Container crane
- d. Freight interline system

Guidance: level 1

:: ::

> An _____ is a process where candidates are examined to determine their suitability for specific types of employment, especially management or military command. The candidates' personality and aptitudes are determined by techniques including interviews, group exercises, presentations, examinations and psychometric testing.

Exam Probability: **Low**

2. *Answer choices:*

(see index for correct answer)

- a. imperative
- b. surface-level diversity
- c. corporate values
- d. Assessment center

Guidance: level 1

:: Production and manufacturing ::

_____ consists of organization-wide efforts to "install and make permanent climate where employees continuously improve their ability to provide on demand products and services that customers will find of particular value." "Total" emphasizes that departments in addition to production are obligated to improve their operations; "management" emphasizes that executives are obligated to actively manage quality through funding, training, staffing, and goal setting. While there is no widely agreed-upon approach, TQM efforts typically draw heavily on the previously developed tools and techniques of quality control. TQM enjoyed widespread attention during the late 1980s and early 1990s before being overshadowed by ISO 9000, Lean manufacturing, and Six Sigma.

Exam Probability: **Low**

3. *Answer choices:*

(see index for correct answer)

- a. Engineering validation test
- b. ERPNEXT
- c. Six Sigma
- d. Highly accelerated life test

Guidance: level 1

The _____ or labour force is the labour pool in employment. It is generally used to describe those working for a single company or industry, but can also apply to a geographic region like a city, state, or country. Within a company, its value can be labelled as its "_____ in Place". The _____ of a country includes both the employed and the unemployed. The labour force participation rate, LFPR, is the ratio between the labour force and the overall size of their cohort. The term generally excludes the employers or management, and can imply those involved in manual labour. It may also mean all those who are available for work.

Exam Probability: **Medium**

4. *Answer choices:*

(see index for correct answer)

- a. functional perspective
- b. Workforce
- c. hierarchical perspective
- d. Character

Guidance: level 1

:: Human resource management ::

_____ is a core function of human resource management and it is related to the specification of contents, methods and relationship of jobs in order to satisfy technological and organizational requirements as well as the social and personal requirements of the job holder or the employee. Its principles are geared towards how the nature of a person's job affects their attitudes and behavior at work, particularly relating to characteristics such as skill variety and autonomy. The aim of a _____ is to improve job satisfaction, to improve through-put, to improve quality and to reduce employee problems.

Exam Probability: **Medium**

5. *Answer choices:*

(see index for correct answer)

- a. E-HRM
- b. Selection ratio
- c. Job enrichment
- d. Individual development plan

Guidance: level 1

:: Free trade agreements ::

A _____ is a wide-ranging taxes, tariff and trade treaty that often includes investment guarantees. It exists when two or more countries agree on terms that helps them trade with each other. The most common _____ s are of the preferential and free trade types are concluded in order to reduce tariffs, quotas and other trade restrictions on items traded between the signatories.

Exam Probability: **Medium**

6. *Answer choices:*

(see index for correct answer)

- a. Asia-Pacific Trade Agreement
- b. South Asian Free Trade Area
- c. Trade agreement
- d. Central Asian Union

Guidance: level 1

:: ::

_____ is the administration of an organization, whether it is a business, a not-for-profit organization, or government body. _____ includes the activities of setting the strategy of an organization and coordinating the efforts of its employees to accomplish its objectives through the application of available resources, such as financial, natural, technological, and human resources. The term " _____ " may also refer to those people who manage an organization.

Exam Probability: **Medium**

7. *Answer choices:*

(see index for correct answer)

- a. co-culture
- b. corporate values
- c. Management
- d. interpersonal communication

Guidance: level 1

:: Strategic alliances ::

A _____ is an agreement between two or more parties to pursue a set of agreed upon objectives needed while remaining independent organizations. A _____ will usually fall short of a legal partnership entity, agency, or corporate affiliate relationship. Typically, two companies form a _____ when each possesses one or more business assets or have expertise that will help the other by enhancing their businesses. _____ s can develop in outsourcing relationships where the parties desire to achieve long-term win-win benefits and innovation based on mutually desired outcomes.

Exam Probability: **Medium**

8. *Answer choices:*

(see index for correct answer)

- a. Management contract
- b. Strategic alliance
- c. International joint venture
- d. Cross-licensing

Guidance: level 1

:: ::

_____ or haggling is a type of negotiation in which the buyer and seller of a good or service debate the price and exact nature of a transaction. If the _____ produces agreement on terms, the transaction takes place. _____ is an alternative pricing strategy to fixed prices. Optimally, if it costs the retailer nothing to engage and allow _____ , s/he can divine the buyer's willingness to spend. It allows for capturing more consumer surplus as it allows price discrimination, a process whereby a seller can charge a higher price to one buyer who is more eager . Haggling has largely disappeared in parts of the world where the cost to haggle exceeds the gain to retailers for most common retail items. However, for expensive goods sold to uninformed buyers such as automobiles, _____ can remain commonplace.

Exam Probability: **Low**

9. *Answer choices:*

(see index for correct answer)

- a. co-culture
- b. interpersonal communication
- c. deep-level diversity

- d. surface-level diversity

Guidance: level 1

:: Personality tests ::

> The Myers–Briggs Type Indicator is an introspective self-report questionnaire with the purpose of indicating differing psychological preferences in how people perceive the world around them and make decisions. . Though the test superficially resembles some psychological theories it is commonly classified as pseudoscience, especially as pertains to its supposed predictive abilities.

Exam Probability: **Low**

10. *Answer choices:*
(see index for correct answer)

- a. Myers-Briggs type
- b. personality quiz
- c. Myers-Briggs Type Indicator
- d. Keirsey Temperament Sorter

Guidance: level 1

:: Management ::

In business, a _____ is the attribute that allows an organization to outperform its competitors. A _____ may include access to natural resources, such as high-grade ores or a low-cost power source, highly skilled labor, geographic location, high entry barriers, and access to new technology.

Exam Probability: **Low**

11. *Answer choices:*

(see index for correct answer)

- a. DMSMS
- b. Director
- c. Competitive advantage
- d. Cynefin

Guidance: level 1

:: Management ::

_____ is a set of activities that ensure goals are met in an effective and efficient manner. _____ can focus on the performance of an organization, a department, an employee, or the processes in place to manage particular tasks. _____ standards are generally organized and disseminated by senior leadership at an organization, and by task owners.

Exam Probability: **Low**

12. Answer choices:

(see index for correct answer)

- a. Energy management software
- b. Task-oriented and relationship-oriented leadership
- c. Project team builder
- d. Performance management

Guidance: level 1

:: Asset ::

In financial accounting, an _____ is any resource owned by the business. Anything tangible or intangible that can be owned or controlled to produce value and that is held by a company to produce positive economic value is an _____ . Simply stated, _____ s represent value of ownership that can be converted into cash . The balance sheet of a firm records the monetary value of the _____ s owned by that firm. It covers money and other valuables belonging to an individual or to a business.

Exam Probability: **Medium**

13. Answer choices:

(see index for correct answer)

- a. Current asset
- b. Asset

Guidance: level 1

:: ::

_____ refers to the confirmation of certain characteristics of an object, person, or organization. This confirmation is often, but not always, provided by some form of external review, education, assessment, or audit. Accreditation is a specific organization's process of _____. According to the National Council on Measurement in Education, a _____ test is a credentialing test used to determine whether individuals are knowledgeable enough in a given occupational area to be labeled "competent to practice" in that area.

Exam Probability: **High**

14. *Answer choices:*

(see index for correct answer)

- a. Certification
- b. hierarchical perspective
- c. information systems assessment
- d. surface-level diversity

Guidance: level 1

:: ::

_____ is the amount of time someone works beyond normal working hours. The term is also used for the pay received for this time. Normal hours may be determined in several ways.

Exam Probability: **Medium**

15. *Answer choices:*

(see index for correct answer)

- a. levels of analysis
- b. deep-level diversity
- c. Overtime
- d. empathy

Guidance: level 1

:: Power (social and political) ::

_____ is a form of reverence gained by a leader who has strong interpersonal relationship skills. _____, as an aspect of personal power, becomes particularly important as organizational leadership becomes increasingly about collaboration and influence, rather than command and control.

Exam Probability: **Medium**

16. *Answer choices:*

(see index for correct answer)

- a. Referent power
- b. Expert power
- c. need for power

Guidance: level 1

:: Business models ::

A _____ is "an autonomous association of persons united voluntarily to meet their common economic, social, and cultural needs and aspirations through a jointly-owned and democratically-controlled enterprise". _____ s may include.

Exam Probability: **Low**

17. *Answer choices:*
(see index for correct answer)

- a. Subscription business model
- b. Small business
- c. Cooperative
- d. The Community Company

Guidance: level 1

:: Industrial relations ::

_____ or employee satisfaction is a measure of workers' contentedness with their job, whether or not they like the job or individual aspects or facets of jobs, such as nature of work or supervision. _____ can be measured in cognitive, affective, and behavioral components. Researchers have also noted that _____ measures vary in the extent to which they measure feelings about the job, or cognitions about the job.

Exam Probability: **High**

18. *Answer choices:*

(see index for correct answer)

- a. Workforce Investment Board
- b. Industrial violence
- c. European Journal of Industrial Relations
- d. Injury prevention

Guidance: level 1

:: Poker strategy ::

_____ is any measure taken to guard a thing against damage caused by outside forces. _____ can be provided to physical objects, including organisms, to systems, and to intangible things like civil and political rights. Although the mechanisms for providing _____ vary widely, the basic meaning of the term remains the same. This is illustrated by an explanation found in a manual on electrical wiring.

Exam Probability: **High**

19. *Answer choices:*

(see index for correct answer)

- a. Slow play
- b. Fundamental theorem of poker
- c. Q-ratio
- d. Protection

Guidance: level 1

:: Economic globalization ::

_____ is an agreement in which one company hires another company to be responsible for a planned or existing activity that is or could be done internally,and sometimes involves transferring employees and assets from one firm to another.

Exam Probability: **High**

20. *Answer choices:*

(see index for correct answer)

- a. global financial
- b. reshoring

Guidance: level 1

:: Evaluation ::

_____ is a way of preventing mistakes and defects in manufactured products and avoiding problems when delivering products or services to customers; which ISO 9000 defines as "part of quality management focused on providing confidence that quality requirements will be fulfilled". This defect prevention in _____ differs subtly from defect detection and rejection in quality control and has been referred to as a shift left since it focuses on quality earlier in the process.

Exam Probability: **Low**

21. *Answer choices:*

(see index for correct answer)

- a. Common Criteria Testing Laboratory
- b. Academic equivalency evaluation
- c. Scale of one to ten
- d. Defence Evaluation and Research Agency

Guidance: level 1

:: Employment ::

The _____ is an individual's metaphorical "journey" through learning, work and other aspects of life. There are a number of ways to define _____ and the term is used in a variety of ways.

Exam Probability: **High**

22. *Answer choices:*

(see index for correct answer)

- a. Career
- b. Ethical job
- c. Encore career
- d. Gofer

Guidance: level 1

:: Survey methodology ::

An _____ is a conversation where questions are asked and answers are given. In common parlance, the word "_____" refers to a one-on-one conversation between an _____ er and an _____ ee. The _____ er asks questions to which the _____ ee responds, usually so information may be transferred from _____ ee to _____ er. Sometimes, information can be transferred in both directions. It is a communication, unlike a speech, which produces a one-way flow of information.

Exam Probability: **High**

23. *Answer choices:*

(see index for correct answer)

- a. Public opinion
- b. Interview
- c. Inverse probability weighting
- d. American Association for Public Opinion Research

Guidance: level 1

:: International relations ::

A _____ is any event that is going to lead to an unstable and dangerous situation affecting an individual, group, community, or whole society. Crises are deemed to be negative changes in the security, economic, political, societal, or environmental affairs, especially when they occur abruptly, with little or no warning. More loosely, it is a term meaning "a testing time" or an "emergency event".

Exam Probability: **Medium**

24. *Answer choices:*

(see index for correct answer)

- a. Crisis
- b. Foreign agent
- c. Peaceful War
- d. Russian and Eurasian Security Network

Guidance: level 1

:: Business ::

_____ is a trade policy that does not restrict imports or exports; it can also be understood as the free market idea applied to international trade. In government, _____ is predominantly advocated by political parties that hold liberal economic positions while economically left-wing and nationalist political parties generally support protectionism, the opposite of _____ .

Exam Probability: **High**

25. *Answer choices:*

(see index for correct answer)

- a. Street marketing
- b. Professional conference organiser

- c. Open-book contract
- d. Free trade

Guidance: level 1

:: ::

_____ is the assignment of any responsibility or authority to another person to carry out specific activities. It is one of the core concepts of management leadership. However, the person who delegated the work remains accountable for the outcome of the delegated work. _____ empowers a subordinate to make decisions, i.e. it is a shifting of decision-making authority from one organizational level to a lower one. _____ , if properly done, is not fabrication. The opposite of effective _____ is micromanagement, where a manager provides too much input, direction, and review of delegated work. In general, _____ is good and can save money and time, help in building skills, and motivate people. On the other hand, poor _____ might cause frustration and confusion to all the involved parties. Some agents, however, do not favour a _____ and consider the power of making a decision rather burdensome.

Exam Probability: **High**

26. *Answer choices:*

(see index for correct answer)

- a. hierarchical
- b. empathy
- c. Delegation
- d. interpersonal communication

Guidance: level 1

:: Critical thinking ::

In psychology, _____ is regarded as the cognitive process resulting in the selection of a belief or a course of action among several alternative possibilities. Every _____ process produces a final choice, which may or may not prompt action.

Exam Probability: **Low**

27. *Answer choices:*

(see index for correct answer)

- a. Intellectual responsibility
- b. Precision questioning
- c. TregoED
- d. Decision-making

Guidance: level 1

:: Business models ::

A _____, _____ company or daughter company is a company that is owned or controlled by another company, which is called the parent company, parent, or holding company. The _____ can be a company, corporation, or limited liability company. In some cases it is a government or state-owned enterprise. In some cases, particularly in the music and book publishing industries, subsidiaries are referred to as imprints.

Exam Probability: **High**

28. *Answer choices:*

(see index for correct answer)

- a. Pay to play
- b. Professional open source
- c. Market game
- d. Strategy map

Guidance: level 1

:: Project management ::

In economics, _____ is the assignment of available resources to various uses. In the context of an entire economy, resources can be allocated by various means, such as markets or central planning.

Exam Probability: **Medium**

29. *Answer choices:*

(see index for correct answer)

- a. Extreme project management
- b. Resource allocation
- c. Cone of Uncertainty
- d. Stages of project finance

Guidance: level 1

:: Budgets ::

A _____ is a financial plan for a defined period, often one year. It may also include planned sales volumes and revenues, resource quantities, costs and expenses, assets, liabilities and cash flows. Companies, governments, families and other organizations use it to express strategic plans of activities or events in measurable terms.

Exam Probability: **High**

30. *Answer choices:*

(see index for correct answer)

- a. Envelope system
- b. Public budgeting
- c. Budget
- d. Black budget

Guidance: level 1

:: Evaluation methods ::

In social psychology, _____ is the process of looking at oneself in order to assess aspects that are important to one's identity. It is one of the motives that drive self-evaluation, along with self-verification and self-enhancement. Sedikides suggests that the _____ motive will prompt people to seek information to confirm their uncertain self-concept rather than their certain self-concept and at the same time people use _____ to enhance their certainty of their own self-knowledge. However, the _____ motive could be seen as quite different from the other two self-evaluation motives. Unlike the other two motives through _____ people are interested in the accuracy of their current self view, rather than improving their self-view. This makes _____ the only self-evaluative motive that may cause a person's self-esteem to be damaged.

Exam Probability: **Medium**

31. *Answer choices:*

(see index for correct answer)

- a. Business excellence
- b. Self-assessment
- c. Program process monitoring
- d. SAT Subject Tests

Guidance: level 1

:: Evaluation ::

A _____ is an evaluation of a publication, service, or company such as a movie, video game, musical composition, book; a piece of hardware like a car, home appliance, or computer; or an event or performance, such as a live music concert, play, musical theater show, dance show, or art exhibition. In addition to a critical evaluation, the _____'s author may assign the work a rating to indicate its relative merit. More loosely, an author may _____ current events, trends, or items in the news. A compilation of _____s may itself be called a _____. The New York _____ of Books, for instance, is a collection of essays on literature, culture, and current affairs. National _____, founded by William F. Buckley, Jr., is an influential conservative magazine, and Monthly _____ is a long-running socialist periodical.

Exam Probability: **High**

32. *Answer choices:*

(see index for correct answer)

- a. CESG Claims Tested Mark
- b. Career portfolio
- c. Impact assessment
- d. Educational assessment

Guidance: level 1

:: Human resource management ::

_____ is a family of procedures to identify the content of a job in terms of activities involved and attributes or job requirements needed to perform the activities. _____ provides information of organizations which helps to determine which employees are best fit for specific jobs. Through _____, the analyst needs to understand what the important tasks of the job are, how they are carried out, and the necessary human qualities needed to complete the job successfully.

Exam Probability: **Low**

33. *Answer choices:*

(see index for correct answer)

- a. Job enlargement
- b. Up or out
- c. Employee retention
- d. Talent management

Guidance: level 1

:: Business ethics ::

_____ is a type of harassment technique that relates to a sexual nature and the unwelcome or inappropriate promise of rewards in exchange for sexual favors. _____ includes a range of actions from mild transgressions to sexual abuse or assault. Harassment can occur in many different social settings such as the workplace, the home, school, churches, etc. Harassers or victims may be of any gender.

Exam Probability: **Low**

34. *Answer choices:*

(see index for correct answer)

- a. Altruistic corporate social responsibility
- b. Sustainability Accounting Standards Board
- c. Resource Conservation and Recovery Act
- d. Anti-consumerism

Guidance: level 1

:: ::

> Business is the activity of making one's living or making money by producing or buying and selling products. Simply put, it is "any activity or enterprise entered into for profit. It does not mean it is a company, a corporation, partnership, or have any such formal organization, but it can range from a street peddler to General Motors."

Exam Probability: **High**

35. *Answer choices:*

(see index for correct answer)

- a. empathy
- b. surface-level diversity

- c. Firm
- d. hierarchical perspective

Guidance: level 1

:: ::

A _____ is an approximate imitation of the operation of a process or system; the act of simulating first requires a model is developed. This model is a well-defined description of the simulated subject, and represents its key characteristics, such as its behaviour, functions and abstract or physical properties. The model represents the system itself, whereas the _____ represents its operation over time.

Exam Probability: **Low**

36. *Answer choices:*

(see index for correct answer)

- a. corporate values
- b. interpersonal communication
- c. process perspective
- d. empathy

Guidance: level 1

:: Organizational theory ::

Decentralisation is the process by which the activities of an organization, particularly those regarding planning and decision making, are distributed or delegated away from a central, authoritative location or group. Concepts of _____ have been applied to group dynamics and management science in private businesses and organizations, political science, law and public administration, economics, money and technology.

Exam Probability: **High**

37. *Answer choices:*

(see index for correct answer)

- a. Decentralization
- b. Contingency theory
- c. Formal consensus
- d. Smart city

Guidance: level 1

:: Meetings ::

A _____ is a body of one or more persons that is subordinate to a deliberative assembly. Usually, the assembly sends matters into a _____ as a way to explore them more fully than would be possible if the assembly itself were considering them. _____ s may have different functions and their type of work differ depending on the type of the organization and its needs.

Exam Probability: **Medium**

38. *Answer choices:*

(see index for correct answer)

- a. Annual Georgia European Union Summit
- b. Congress
- c. Stand-up meeting
- d. Committee

Guidance: level 1

:: ::

_____ is a kind of action that occur as two or more objects have an effect upon one another. The idea of a two-way effect is essential in the concept of _____ , as opposed to a one-way causal effect. A closely related term is interconnectivity, which deals with the _____ s of _____ s within systems: combinations of many simple _____ s can lead to surprising emergent phenomena. _____ has different tailored meanings in various sciences. Changes can also involve _____ .

Exam Probability: **High**

39. *Answer choices:*

(see index for correct answer)

- a. Interaction

- b. Sarbanes-Oxley act of 2002
- c. surface-level diversity
- d. Character

Guidance: level 1

:: ::

_____ is both a research area and a practical skill encompassing the ability of an individual or organization to "lead" or guide other individuals, teams, or entire organizations. Specialist literature debates various viewpoints, contrasting Eastern and Western approaches to _____, and also United States versus European approaches. U.S. academic environments define _____ as "a process of social influence in which a person can enlist the aid and support of others in the accomplishment of a common task".

Exam Probability: **Medium**

40. *Answer choices:*

(see index for correct answer)

- a. Leadership
- b. imperative
- c. empathy
- d. open system

Guidance: level 1

:: Management ::

The _____ is a strategy performance management tool – a semi-standard structured report, that can be used by managers to keep track of the execution of activities by the staff within their control and to monitor the consequences arising from these actions.

Exam Probability: **High**

41. *Answer choices:*

(see index for correct answer)

- a. Shrinkage
- b. Supply chain optimization
- c. PhD in management
- d. Balanced scorecard

Guidance: level 1

:: Labor ::

The workforce or labour force is the labour pool in employment. It is generally used to describe those working for a single company or industry, but can also apply to a geographic region like a city, state, or country. Within a company, its value can be labelled as its "Workforce in Place". The workforce of a country includes both the employed and the unemployed. The labour force participation rate, LFPR, is the ratio between the labour force and the overall size of their cohort. The term generally excludes the employers or management, and can imply those involved in manual labour. It may also mean all those who are available for work.

Exam Probability: **Low**

42. *Answer choices:*

(see index for correct answer)

- a. Anti-capitalism
- b. Indivisibility of labor
- c. Labor force
- d. Eurosclerosis

Guidance: level 1

:: Marketing ::

_____ comes from the Latin neg and otsia referring to businessmen who, unlike the patricians, had no leisure time in their industriousness; it held the meaning of business until the 17th century when it took on the diplomatic connotation as a dialogue between two or more people or parties intended to reach a beneficial outcome over one or more issues where a conflict exists with respect to at least one of these issues. Thus, _____ is a process of combining divergent positions into a joint agreement under a decision rule of unanimity.

Exam Probability: **Low**

43. *Answer choices:*

(see index for correct answer)

- a. Leverage
- b. Negotiation
- c. Marketing Week
- d. Performance-based advertising

Guidance: level 1

:: ::

An _____ in international trade is a good or service produced in one country that is bought by someone in another country. The seller of such goods and services is an _____ er; the foreign buyer is an importer.

Exam Probability: **Low**

44. Answer choices:

(see index for correct answer)

- a. surface-level diversity
- b. Export
- c. deep-level diversity
- d. interpersonal communication

Guidance: level 1

:: Production and manufacturing ::

> _____ is a set of techniques and tools for process improvement. Though as a shortened form it may be found written as 6S, it should not be confused with the methodology known as 6S .

Exam Probability: **High**

45. Answer choices:

(see index for correct answer)

- a. Transfer cars
- b. Countercurrent exchange
- c. Six Sigma
- d. Time to market

Guidance: level 1

:: Classification systems ::

_____ is the practice of comparing business processes and performance metrics to industry bests and best practices from other companies. Dimensions typically measured are quality, time and cost.

Exam Probability: **Low**

46. *Answer choices:*
(see index for correct answer)

- a. Celestial Emporium of Benevolent Knowledge
- b. Global Medical Device Nomenclature
- c. Benchmarking
- d. Bliss bibliographic classification

Guidance: level 1

:: Problem solving ::

In other words, _____ is a situation where a group of people meet to generate new ideas and solutions around a specific domain of interest by removing inhibitions. People are able to think more freely and they suggest as many spontaneous new ideas as possible. All the ideas are noted down and those ideas are not criticized and after _____ session the ideas are evaluated. The term was popularized by Alex Faickney Osborn in the 1953 book Applied Imagination.

Exam Probability: **Low**

47. *Answer choices:*

(see index for correct answer)

- a. Thinking outside the box
- b. Brainstorming
- c. Encyclopedia of World Problems and Human Potential
- d. Project Euler

Guidance: level 1

:: Business law ::

A _____ is a group of people who jointly supervise the activities of an organization, which can be either a for-profit business, nonprofit organization, or a government agency. Such a board's powers, duties, and responsibilities are determined by government regulations and the organization's own constitution and bylaws. These authorities may specify the number of members of the board, how they are to be chosen, and how often they are to meet.

Exam Probability: **High**

48. *Answer choices:*

(see index for correct answer)

- a. Official Assignee
- b. Board of directors
- c. Ease of doing business index
- d. Limited liability

Guidance: level 1

:: Workplace ::

A _____ , also referred to as a performance review, performance evaluation, development discussion, or employee appraisal is a method by which the job performance of an employee is documented and evaluated. _____ s are a part of career development and consist of regular reviews of employee performance within organizations.

Exam Probability: **Low**

49. *Answer choices:*

(see index for correct answer)

- a. Workplace relationships
- b. Performance appraisal

- c. Rat race
- d. 360-degree feedback

Guidance: level 1

:: Strategic management ::

_____ is a strategic planning technique used to help a person or organization identify strengths, weaknesses, opportunities, and threats related to business competition or project planning. It is intended to specify the objectives of the business venture or project and identify the internal and external factors that are favorable and unfavorable to achieving those objectives. Users of a _____ often ask and answer questions to generate meaningful information for each category to make the tool useful and identify their competitive advantage. SWOT has been described as the tried-and-true tool of strategic analysis.

Exam Probability: **High**

50. *Answer choices:*
(see index for correct answer)

- a. Nicolas De Santis
- b. SWOT analysis
- c. rank and yank
- d. Strategic control

Guidance: level 1

:: Behaviorism ::

In behavioral psychology, _____ is a consequence applied that will strengthen an organism's future behavior whenever that behavior is preceded by a specific antecedent stimulus. This strengthening effect may be measured as a higher frequency of behavior, longer duration, greater magnitude, or shorter latency. There are two types of _____, known as positive _____ and negative _____; positive is where by a reward is offered on expression of the wanted behaviour and negative is taking away an undesirable element in the persons environment whenever the desired behaviour is achieved.

Exam Probability: **High**

51. *Answer choices:*

(see index for correct answer)

- a. Reinforcement
- b. Systematic desensitization
- c. Programmed instruction
- d. Matching Law

Guidance: level 1

:: ::

A _____, or also known as foreman, overseer, facilitator, monitor, area coordinator, or sometimes gaffer, is the job title of a low level management position that is primarily based on authority over a worker or charge of a workplace. A _____ can also be one of the most senior in the staff at the place of work, such as a Professor who oversees a PhD dissertation. Supervision, on the other hand, can be performed by people without this formal title, for example by parents. The term _____ itself can be used to refer to any personnel who have this task as part of their job description.

Exam Probability: **High**

52. *Answer choices:*

(see index for correct answer)

- a. empathy
- b. similarity-attraction theory
- c. levels of analysis
- d. open system

Guidance: level 1

:: ::

In production, research, retail, and accounting, a _____ is the value of money that has been used up to produce something or deliver a service, and hence is not available for use anymore. In business, the _____ may be one of acquisition, in which case the amount of money expended to acquire it is counted as _____. In this case, money is the input that is gone in order to acquire the thing. This acquisition _____ may be the sum of the _____ of production as incurred by the original producer, and further _____ s of transaction as incurred by the acquirer over and above the price paid to the producer. Usually, the price also includes a mark-up for profit over the _____ of production.

Exam Probability: **High**

53. *Answer choices:*

(see index for correct answer)

- a. similarity-attraction theory
- b. Sarbanes-Oxley act of 2002
- c. co-culture
- d. Cost

Guidance: level 1

:: International trade ::

_____ or globalisation is the process of interaction and integration among people, companies, and governments worldwide. As a complex and multifaceted phenomenon, _____ is considered by some as a form of capitalist expansion which entails the integration of local and national economies into a global, unregulated market economy. _____ has grown due to advances in transportation and communication technology. With the increased global interactions comes the growth of international trade, ideas, and culture. _____ is primarily an economic process of interaction and integration that's associated with social and cultural aspects. However, conflicts and diplomacy are also large parts of the history of _____ , and modern _____ .

Exam Probability: **High**

54. *Answer choices:*

(see index for correct answer)

- a. Certificate of origin
- b. Cross-border cooperation
- c. Orderly marketing arrangement
- d. Globalization

Guidance: level 1

:: Information technology management ::

_____ is a collective term for all approaches to prepare, support and help individuals, teams, and organizations in making organizational change. The most common change drivers include: technological evolution, process reviews, crisis, and consumer habit changes; pressure from new business entrants, acquisitions, mergers, and organizational restructuring. It includes methods that redirect or redefine the use of resources, business process, budget allocations, or other modes of operation that significantly change a company or organization. Organizational _____ considers the full organization and what needs to change, while _____ may be used solely to refer to how people and teams are affected by such organizational transition. It deals with many different disciplines, from behavioral and social sciences to information technology and business solutions.

Exam Probability: **Low**

55. *Answer choices:*

(see index for correct answer)

- a. Soluto
- b. Change management
- c. Iteraplan
- d. CatDV

Guidance: level 1

:: Generally Accepted Accounting Principles ::

In accounting, _____ is the income that a business have from its normal business activities, usually from the sale of goods and services to customers. _____ is also referred to as sales or turnover. Some companies receive _____ from interest, royalties, or other fees. _____ may refer to business income in general, or it may refer to the amount, in a monetary unit, earned during a period of time, as in "Last year, Company X had _____ of $42 million". Profits or net income generally imply total _____ minus total expenses in a given period. In accounting, in the balance statement it is a subsection of the Equity section and _____ increases equity, it is often referred to as the "top line" due to its position on the income statement at the very top. This is to be contrasted with the "bottom line" which denotes net income .

Exam Probability: **Low**

56. *Answer choices:*

(see index for correct answer)

- a. Liability
- b. Cost principle
- c. Revenue
- d. Indian Accounting Standards

Guidance: level 1

:: ::

_____ is the means to see, hear, or become aware of something or someone through our fundamental senses. The term _____ derives from the Latin word perceptio, and is the organization, identification, and interpretation of sensory information in order to represent and understand the presented information, or the environment.

Exam Probability: **High**

57. *Answer choices:*

(see index for correct answer)

- a. Perception
- b. levels of analysis
- c. surface-level diversity
- d. imperative

Guidance: level 1

:: Information science ::

_____ is the resolution of uncertainty; it is that which answers the question of "what an entity is" and thus defines both its essence and nature of its characteristics. _____ relates to both data and knowledge, as data is meaningful _____ representing values attributed to parameters, and knowledge signifies understanding of a concept. _____ is uncoupled from an observer, which is an entity that can access _____ and thus discern what it specifies; _____ exists beyond an event horizon for example. In the case of knowledge, the _____ itself requires a cognitive observer to be obtained.

Exam Probability: **Low**

58. *Answer choices:*

(see index for correct answer)

- a. Information
- b. Informative modelling
- c. Source criticism
- d. Back-of-the-book index

Guidance: level 1

:: Statistical terminology ::

> _____ es can be learned implicitly within cultural contexts. People may develop _____ es toward or against an individual, an ethnic group, a sexual or gender identity, a nation, a religion, a social class, a political party, theoretical paradigms and ideologies within academic domains, or a species. _____ ed means one-sided, lacking a neutral viewpoint, or not having an open mind. _____ can come in many forms and is related to prejudice and intuition.

Exam Probability: **High**

59. *Answer choices:*

(see index for correct answer)

- a. Completeness

- b. Epps effect
- c. Invariant estimator
- d. Bias

Guidance: level 1

Business law

Corporate law (also known as business law) is the body of law governing the rights, relations, and conduct of persons, companies, organizations and businesses. It refers to the legal practice relating to, or the theory of corporations. Corporate law often describes the law relating to matters which derive directly from the life-cycle of a corporation. It thus encompasses the formation, funding, governance, and death of a corporation.

:: ::

At common law, _____ are a remedy in the form of a monetary award to be paid to a claimant as compensation for loss or injury. To warrant the award, the claimant must show that a breach of duty has caused foreseeable loss. To be recognised at law, the loss must involve damage to property, or mental or physical injury; pure economic loss is rarely recognised for the award of _____ .

Exam Probability: **Low**

1. *Answer choices:*

(see index for correct answer)

- a. Damages
- b. hierarchical
- c. surface-level diversity
- d. information systems assessment

Guidance: level 1

:: Legal terms ::

_____ , a form of alternative dispute resolution , is a way to resolve disputes outside the courts. The dispute will be decided by one or more persons , which renders the " _____ award". An _____ award is legally binding on both sides and enforceable in the courts.

Exam Probability: **High**

2. *Answer choices:*

(see index for correct answer)

- a. Perjury
- b. Law French
- c. Culprit
- d. Age of candidacy

Guidance: level 1

:: United States federal public corruption crime ::

Mail fraud and _____ are federal crimes in the United States that involve mailing or electronically transmitting something associated with fraud. Jurisdiction is claimed by the federal government if the illegal activity crosses interstate or international borders.

Exam Probability: **Medium**

3. *Answer choices:*

(see index for correct answer)

- a. Wire fraud
- b. RICO Act

Guidance: level 1

:: Legal doctrines and principles ::

In some common law jurisdictions, _____ is a defense to a tort claim based on negligence. If it is available, the defense completely bars plaintiffs from any recovery if they contribute to their own injury through their own negligence.

Exam Probability: **Low**

4. *Answer choices:*

(see index for correct answer)

- a. Attractive nuisance doctrine
- b. Parol evidence
- c. Contributory negligence
- d. Unilateral mistake

Guidance: level 1

:: Manufactured goods ::

> A _____ or final good is any commodity that is produced or consumed by the consumer to satisfy current wants or needs. _____ s are ultimately consumed, rather than used in the production of another good. For example, a microwave oven or a bicycle that is sold to a consumer is a final good or _____ , but the components that are sold to be used in those goods are intermediate goods. For example, textiles or transistors can be used to make some further goods.

Exam Probability: **High**

5. *Answer choices:*

(see index for correct answer)

- a. Bespoke

- b. Tarpaulin
- c. Product ecosystem theory
- d. Consumer Good

Guidance: level 1

:: Trade secrets ::

The _____ of 1996 was a 6 title Act of Congress dealing with a wide range of issues, including not only industrial espionage, but the insanity defense, matters regarding the Boys & Girls Clubs of America, requirements for presentence investigation reports, and the United States Sentencing Commission reports regarding encryption or scrambling technology, and other technical and minor amendments.

Exam Probability: **High**

6. *Answer choices:*

(see index for correct answer)

- a. WD-40
- b. Economic Espionage Act
- c. Inevitable disclosure
- d. Kayfabe

Guidance: level 1

:: Project management ::

_____ is the right to exercise power, which can be formalized by a state and exercised by way of judges, appointed executives of government, or the ecclesiastical or priestly appointed representatives of a God or other deities.

Exam Probability: **High**

7. *Answer choices:*

(see index for correct answer)

- a. Akihabara syndrome
- b. Cost-benefit
- c. Structured data analysis
- d. Authority

Guidance: level 1

:: ::

_____ is the consumption and saving opportunity gained by an entity within a specified timeframe, which is generally expressed in monetary terms. For households and individuals, "_____ is the sum of all the wages, salaries, profits, interest payments, rents, and other forms of earnings received in a given period of time."

Exam Probability: **High**

8. *Answer choices:*

(see index for correct answer)

- a. personal values
- b. Income
- c. Character
- d. corporate values

Guidance: level 1

:: Advertising ::

In law, _____ is speech or writing on behalf of a business with the intent of earning revenue or a profit. It is economic in nature and usually attempts to persuade consumers to purchase the business's product or service. The Supreme Court of the United States defines _____ as speech that "proposes a commercial transaction".

Exam Probability: **Medium**

9. *Answer choices:*

(see index for correct answer)

- a. Direct Agency / Rep Electronic Connection
- b. Commercial speech

- c. Video advertising
- d. 140 Proof

Guidance: level 1

:: ::

_____, also referred to as orthostasis, is a human position in which the body is held in an upright position and supported only by the feet.

Exam Probability: **Medium**

10. *Answer choices:*

(see index for correct answer)

- a. cultural
- b. Sarbanes-Oxley act of 2002
- c. hierarchical
- d. empathy

Guidance: level 1

:: Monopoly (economics) ::

A _____ is a form of intellectual property that gives its owner the legal right to exclude others from making, using, selling, and importing an invention for a limited period of years, in exchange for publishing an enabling public disclosure of the invention. In most countries _____ rights fall under civil law and the _____ holder needs to sue someone infringing the _____ in order to enforce his or her rights. In some industries _____ s are an essential form of competitive advantage; in others they are irrelevant.

Exam Probability: **High**

11. *Answer choices:*

(see index for correct answer)

- a. Special 301 Report
- b. Government monopoly
- c. Practice of law
- d. Patent

Guidance: level 1

:: Legal terms ::

_____ s may be governments, corporations or investment trusts. _____ s are legally responsible for the obligations of the issue and for reporting financial conditions, material developments and any other operational activities as required by the regulations of their jurisdictions.

Exam Probability: **Medium**

12. *Answer choices:*

(see index for correct answer)

- a. Medical advice
- b. Hereditament
- c. Officer of the court
- d. Issuer

Guidance: level 1

:: Sureties ::

In finance, a _____ , _____ bond or guaranty involves a promise by one party to assume responsibility for the debt obligation of a borrower if that borrower defaults. The person or company providing the promise is also known as a " _____ " or as a "guarantor".

Exam Probability: **High**

13. *Answer choices:*

(see index for correct answer)

- a. Parole bond
- b. Payment bond
- c. Surety

- d. Supersedeas bond

Guidance: level 1

:: ::

The Sherman Antitrust Act of 1890 was a United States antitrust law that regulates competition among enterprises, which was passed by Congress under the presidency of Benjamin Harrison.

Exam Probability: **Low**

14. *Answer choices:*

(see index for correct answer)

- a. Sherman Act
- b. hierarchical perspective
- c. similarity-attraction theory
- d. surface-level diversity

Guidance: level 1

:: Ethically disputed business practices ::

_____ is the trading of a public company's stock or other securities by individuals with access to nonpublic information about the company. In various countries, some kinds of trading based on insider information is illegal. This is because it is seen as unfair to other investors who do not have access to the information, as the investor with insider information could potentially make larger profits than a typical investor could make. The rules governing _____ are complex and vary significantly from country to country. The extent of enforcement also varies from one country to another. The definition of insider in one jurisdiction can be broad, and may cover not only insiders themselves but also any persons related to them, such as brokers, associates and even family members. A person who becomes aware of non-public information and trades on that basis may be guilty of a crime.

Exam Probability: **Medium**

15. *Answer choices:*

(see index for correct answer)

- a. Patent privateer
- b. Insider trading
- c. Suicide bidding
- d. Two sets of books

Guidance: level 1

:: ::

In legal terminology, a _____ is any formal legal document that sets out the facts and legal reasons that the filing party or parties believes are sufficient to support a claim against the party or parties against whom the claim is brought that entitles the plaintiff to a remedy. For example, the Federal Rules of Civil Procedure that govern civil litigation in United States courts provide that a civil action is commenced with the filing or service of a pleading called a _____. Civil court rules in states that have incorporated the Federal Rules of Civil Procedure use the same term for the same pleading.

Exam Probability: **Low**

16. *Answer choices:*

(see index for correct answer)

- a. deep-level diversity
- b. Complaint
- c. hierarchical
- d. cultural

Guidance: level 1

:: Promotion and marketing communications ::

In everyday language, _____ refers to exaggerated or false praise. In law, _____ is a promotional statement or claim that expresses subjective rather than objective views, which no "reasonable person" would take literally. _____ serves to "puff up" an exaggerated image of what is being described and is especially featured in testimonials.

Exam Probability: **Low**

17. *Answer choices:*

(see index for correct answer)

- a. Promotion
- b. London International Awards
- c. direct-mail
- d. Puffery

Guidance: level 1

:: Contract Clause case law ::

> The _____ appears in the United States Constitution, Article I, section 10, clause 1. The clause prohibits a State from passing any law that "impairs the obligation of contracts" or "makes any thing but gold and silver coin a tender in payment of debts". It states.

Exam Probability: **Low**

18. *Answer choices:*

(see index for correct answer)

- a. Smyth v. Ames
- b. Charles River Bridge v. Warren Bridge
- c. Contract Clause

Guidance: level 1

:: Anti-competitive behaviour ::

Restraints of trade is a common law doctrine relating to the enforceability of contractual restrictions on freedom to conduct business. It is a precursor of modern competition law. In an old leading case of Mitchel v Reynolds Lord Smith LC said,

Exam Probability: **High**

19. *Answer choices:*

(see index for correct answer)

- a. Bathtub Trust
- b. Tying
- c. Bid rigging
- d. Strategic entry deterrence

Guidance: level 1

:: Intention ::

_____ is the mental element of a person's intention to commit a crime; or knowledge that one's action or lack of action would cause a crime to be committed. It is a necessary element of many crimes.

Exam Probability: **Low**

20. *Answer choices:*

(see index for correct answer)

- a. Mens rea
- b. Letter of Intent

Guidance: level 1

:: Legal terms ::

A _____ is any "lesser" criminal act in some common law legal systems. _____ s are generally punished less severely than felonies, but theoretically more so than administrative infractions and regulatory offences. Many _____ s are punished with monetary fines.

Exam Probability: **High**

21. *Answer choices:*

(see index for correct answer)

- a. Misdemeanor

- b. Concurring opinion
- c. Agreement in principle
- d. Under seal

Guidance: level 1

:: Commercial crimes ::

_____ is the act of withholding assets for the purpose of conversion of such assets, by one or more persons to whom the assets were entrusted, either to be held or to be used for specific purposes. _____ is a type of financial fraud. For example, a lawyer might embezzle funds from the trust accounts of their clients; a financial advisor might embezzle the funds of investors; and a husband or a wife might embezzle funds from a bank account jointly held with the spouse.

Exam Probability: **Low**

22. *Answer choices:*

(see index for correct answer)

- a. Late trading
- b. Clearstream
- c. Gold laundering
- d. Embezzlement

Guidance: level 1

:: Mortgage ::

_____ is a legal process in which a lender attempts to recover the balance of a loan from a borrower who has stopped making payments to the lender by forcing the sale of the asset used as the collateral for the loan.

Exam Probability: **High**

23. *Answer choices:*

(see index for correct answer)

- a. Shared appreciation mortgage
- b. Foreclosure
- c. Commercial mortgage
- d. Mortgage analytics

Guidance: level 1

:: Working time ::

Labour law is the area of law most commonly relating to the relationship between trade unions, employers and the government.

Exam Probability: **High**

24. *Answer choices:*

(see index for correct answer)

- a. Shift plan
- b. Gallagher v. Crown Kosher Super Market of Massachusetts, Inc.
- c. Superwoman
- d. Money-rich, time-poor

Guidance: level 1

:: Marketing ::

> _____ comes from the Latin neg and otsia referring to businessmen who, unlike the patricians, had no leisure time in their industriousness; it held the meaning of business until the 17th century when it took on the diplomatic connotation as a dialogue between two or more people or parties intended to reach a beneficial outcome over one or more issues where a conflict exists with respect to at least one of these issues. Thus, _____ is a process of combining divergent positions into a joint agreement under a decision rule of unanimity.

Exam Probability: **High**

25. *Answer choices:*

(see index for correct answer)

- a. Leverage
- b. societal marketing
- c. Premium pricing

- d. Gold party

Guidance: level 1

:: Debt ::

A _____ is a party that has a claim on the services of a second party. It is a person or institution to whom money is owed. The first party, in general, has provided some property or service to the second party under the assumption that the second party will return an equivalent property and service. The second party is frequently called a debtor or borrower. The first party is called the _____ , which is the lender of property, service, or money.

Exam Probability: **Low**

26. *Answer choices:*
(see index for correct answer)

- a. Debt compliance
- b. Creditor
- c. Vulture fund
- d. Debtors Anonymous

Guidance: level 1

:: Legal terms ::

_____ is the set of laws that governs how members of a society are to behave. It is contrasted with procedural law, which is the set of procedures for making, administering, and enforcing _____. _____ defines rights and responsibilities in civil law, and crimes and punishments in criminal law. It may be codified in statutes or exist through precedent in common law.

Exam Probability: **Medium**

27. *Answer choices:*

(see index for correct answer)

- a. Community standards
- b. Cure or quit
- c. Jointure
- d. Prejudice

Guidance: level 1

:: Industrial agreements ::

_____ is a process of negotiation between employers and a group of employees aimed at agreements to regulate working salaries, working conditions, benefits, and other aspects of workers' compensation and rights for workers. The interests of the employees are commonly presented by representatives of a trade union to which the employees belong. The collective agreements reached by these negotiations usually set out wage scales, working hours, training, health and safety, overtime, grievance mechanisms, and rights to participate in workplace or company affairs.

Exam Probability: **High**

28. *Answer choices:*

(see index for correct answer)

- a. Court of Arbitration
- b. Collective bargaining
- c. Pattern bargaining
- d. In Place of Strife

Guidance: level 1

:: Insolvency ::

_____ is the process in accounting by which a company is brought to an end in the United Kingdom, Republic of Ireland and United States. The assets and property of the company are redistributed. _____ is also sometimes referred to as winding-up or dissolution, although dissolution technically refers to the last stage of _____ . The process of _____ also arises when customs, an authority or agency in a country responsible for collecting and safeguarding customs duties, determines the final computation or ascertainment of the duties or drawback accruing on an entry.

Exam Probability: **High**

29. *Answer choices:*

(see index for correct answer)

- a. Debt consolidation
- b. Insolvency
- c. Financial distress
- d. Preferential creditor

Guidance: level 1

:: ::

_____ is the practice of protecting the natural environment by individuals, organizations and governments. Its objectives are to conserve natural resources and the existing natural environment and, where possible, to repair damage and reverse trends.

Exam Probability: **High**

30. *Answer choices:*

(see index for correct answer)

- a. functional perspective
- b. Environmental Protection
- c. hierarchical perspective
- d. surface-level diversity

Guidance: level 1

:: Notes (finance) ::

> A _____ , sometimes referred to as a note payable, is a legal instrument , in which one party promises in writing to pay a determinate sum of money to the other , either at a fixed or determinable future time or on demand of the payee, under specific terms.

Exam Probability: **Medium**

31. *Answer choices:*

(see index for correct answer)

- a. note payable
- b. Surplus note
- c. Promissory note
- d. Equity-linked note

Guidance: level 1

:: ::

An _____ is an area of the production, distribution, or trade, and consumption of goods and services by different agents. Understood in its broadest sense, 'The _____ is defined as a social domain that emphasize the practices, discourses, and material expressions associated with the production, use, and management of resources'. Economic agents can be individuals, businesses, organizations, or governments. Economic transactions occur when two parties agree to the value or price of the transacted good or service, commonly expressed in a certain currency. However, monetary transactions only account for a small part of the economic domain.

Exam Probability: **Low**

32. *Answer choices:*

(see index for correct answer)

- a. open system
- b. personal values
- c. Economy
- d. similarity-attraction theory

Guidance: level 1

:: Contract law ::

_____ is a legal process for collecting a monetary judgment on behalf of a plaintiff from a defendant. _____ allows the plaintiff to take the money or property of the debtor from the person or institution that holds that property. A similar legal mechanism called execution allows the seizure of money or property held directly by the debtor.

Exam Probability: **High**

33. *Answer choices:*

(see index for correct answer)

- a. Per minas
- b. Executory contract
- c. Contract lifecycle management
- d. Garnishment

Guidance: level 1

:: International relations ::

_____ is double mindedness or double heartedness in duplicity, fraud, or deception. It may involve intentional deceit of others, or self-deception.

Exam Probability: **High**

34. *Answer choices:*

(see index for correct answer)

- a. Liberal international economic order
- b. Tranquillitas Ordinis
- c. Bad faith
- d. Epistemic community

Guidance: level 1

:: ::

_____ is property that is movable. In common law systems, _____ may also be called chattels or personalty. In civil law systems, _____ is often called movable property or movables – any property that can be moved from one location to another.

Exam Probability: **Low**

35. *Answer choices:*

(see index for correct answer)

- a. personal values
- b. Sarbanes-Oxley act of 2002
- c. process perspective
- d. similarity-attraction theory

Guidance: level 1

:: Insurance terms ::

A _____ in the broadest sense is a natural person or other legal entity who receives money or other benefits from a benefactor. For example, the _____ of a life insurance policy is the person who receives the payment of the amount of insurance after the death of the insured.

Exam Probability: **Low**

36. *Answer choices:*

(see index for correct answer)

- a. Mid-term adjustment
- b. Pro rata
- c. Beneficiary
- d. surrender value

Guidance: level 1

:: Manufacturing ::

A _____ is a building for storing goods. _____ s are used by manufacturers, importers, exporters, wholesalers, transport businesses, customs, etc. They are usually large plain buildings in industrial parks on the outskirts of cities, towns or villages.

Exam Probability: **Low**

37. *Answer choices:*

(see index for correct answer)

- a. Guitar manufacturing
- b. Manufacturing resource planning
- c. Taguchi methods
- d. Finished good

Guidance: level 1

:: ::

_____ is a type of government support for the citizens of that society. _____ may be provided to people of any income level, as with social security, but it is usually intended to ensure that the poor can meet their basic human needs such as food and shelter. _____ attempts to provide poor people with a minimal level of well-being, usually either a free- or a subsidized-supply of certain goods and social services, such as healthcare, education, and vocational training.

Exam Probability: **Medium**

38. *Answer choices:*

(see index for correct answer)

- a. Welfare
- b. empathy
- c. personal values
- d. functional perspective

Guidance: level 1

:: Stock market ::

[blank] is freedom from, or resilience against, potential harm caused by others. Beneficiaries of [blank] may be of persons and social groups, objects and institutions, ecosystems or any other entity or phenomenon vulnerable to unwanted change by its environment.

Exam Probability: **Low**

39. *Answer choices:*

(see index for correct answer)

- a. H share
- b. Wash sale
- c. Monthly income preferred stock
- d. End of day

Guidance: level 1

:: Sexual harassment in the United States ::

In law, a _____ , reasonable man, or the man on the Clapham omnibus is a hypothetical person of legal fiction crafted by the courts and communicated through case law and jury instructions.

Exam Probability: **Medium**

40. *Answer choices:*

(see index for correct answer)

- a. Reasonable person
- b. Charol Shakeshaft
- c. Puerto Rican Day Parade attacks
- d. Blakey v. Continental Airlines

Guidance: level 1

:: ::

_____ Motor Company is an American multinational automaker that has its main headquarter in Dearborn, Michigan, a suburb of Detroit. It was founded by Henry _____ and incorporated on June 16, 1903. The company sells automobiles and commercial vehicles under the _____ brand and most luxury cars under the Lincoln brand. _____ also owns Brazilian SUV manufacturer Troller, an 8% stake in Aston Martin of the United Kingdom and a 32% stake in Jiangling Motors. It also has joint-ventures in China , Taiwan , Thailand , Turkey , and Russia . The company is listed on the New York Stock Exchange and is controlled by the _____ family; they have minority ownership but the majority of the voting power.

Exam Probability: **Low**

41. *Answer choices:*

(see index for correct answer)

- a. process perspective
- b. Character
- c. levels of analysis
- d. empathy

Guidance: level 1

:: Contract law ::

> An _____ —or acceleration covenant— in the law of contracts, is a term that fully matures the performance due from a party upon a breach of the contract. Such clauses are most prevalent in mortgages and similar contracts to purchase real estate in installments.

Exam Probability: **Medium**

42. *Answer choices:*

(see index for correct answer)

- a. Undue influence
- b. Unsolicited goods
- c. Acceleration clause

- d. Drop dead date

Guidance: level 1

:: Debt ::

_____ , in finance and economics, is payment from a borrower or deposit-taking financial institution to a lender or depositor of an amount above repayment of the principal sum , at a particular rate. It is distinct from a fee which the borrower may pay the lender or some third party. It is also distinct from dividend which is paid by a company to its shareholders from its profit or reserve, but not at a particular rate decided beforehand, rather on a pro rata basis as a share in the reward gained by risk taking entrepreneurs when the revenue earned exceeds the total costs.

Exam Probability: **High**

43. *Answer choices:*

(see index for correct answer)

- a. Legal liability
- b. Debt crisis
- c. Phantom debt
- d. Interest

Guidance: level 1

:: Real property law ::

A _____ is any legal instrument in writing which passes, affirms or confirms an interest, right, or property and that is signed, attested, delivered, and in some jurisdictions, sealed. It is commonly associated with transferring title to property. The _____ has a greater presumption of validity and is less rebuttable than an instrument signed by the party to the _____. A _____ can be unilateral or bilateral. _____s include conveyances, commissions, licenses, patents, diplomas, and conditionally powers of attorney if executed as _____s. The _____ is the modern descendant of the medieval charter, and delivery is thought to symbolically replace the ancient ceremony of livery of seisin.

Exam Probability: **Medium**

44. *Answer choices:*

(see index for correct answer)

- a. Retaliatory eviction
- b. Deed
- c. Structural encroachment
- d. Council for Licensed Conveyancers

Guidance: level 1

:: ::

In contract law, rescission is an equitable remedy which allows a contractual party to cancel the contract. Parties may _____ if they are the victims of a vitiating factor, such as misrepresentation, mistake, duress, or undue influence. Rescission is the unwinding of a transaction. This is done to bring the parties, as far as possible, back to the position in which they were before they entered into a contract .

Exam Probability: **Medium**

45. *Answer choices:*

(see index for correct answer)

- a. empathy
- b. information systems assessment
- c. deep-level diversity
- d. Rescind

Guidance: level 1

:: ::

_____ is the study and management of exchange relationships. _____ is the business process of creating relationships with and satisfying customers. With its focus on the customer, _____ is one of the premier components of business management.

Exam Probability: **Low**

46. *Answer choices:*

(see index for correct answer)

- a. empathy
- b. interpersonal communication
- c. Marketing
- d. Character

Guidance: level 1

:: Contract law ::

_____ is a doctrine in contract law that describes terms that are so extremely unjust, or overwhelmingly one-sided in favor of the party who has the superior bargaining power, that they are contrary to good conscience. Typically, an unconscionable contract is held to be unenforceable because no reasonable or informed person would otherwise agree to it. The perpetrator of the conduct is not allowed to benefit, because the consideration offered is lacking, or is so obviously inadequate, that to enforce the contract would be unfair to the party seeking to escape the contract.

Exam Probability: **High**

47. *Answer choices:*

(see index for correct answer)

- a. Unconscionability
- b. Acceleration clause

- c. Posting rule
- d. Terms of service

Guidance: level 1

:: Law ::

_____ is a body of law which defines the role, powers, and structure of different entities within a state, namely, the executive, the parliament or legislature, and the judiciary; as well as the basic rights of citizens and, in federal countries such as the United States and Canada, the relationship between the central government and state, provincial, or territorial governments.

Exam Probability: **Medium**

48. *Answer choices:*

(see index for correct answer)

- a. Constitutional law
- b. Comparative law

Guidance: level 1

:: ::

The words "_____" and "testify" both derive from the Latin word testis, referring to the notion of a disinterested third-party witness.

Exam Probability: **Medium**

49. *Answer choices:*

(see index for correct answer)

- a. Character
- b. imperative
- c. functional perspective
- d. Testimony

Guidance: level 1

:: Insurance terms ::

_____ is the assumption by a third party of another party's legal right to collect a debt or damages. It is a legal doctrine whereby one person is entitled to enforce the subsisting or revived rights of another for one's own benefit. A right of _____ typically arises by operation of law, but can also arise by statute or by agreement. _____ is an equitable remedy, having first developed in the English Court of Chancery. It is a familiar feature of common law systems. Analogous doctrines exist in civil law jurisdictions.

Exam Probability: **Medium**

50. *Answer choices:*

(see index for correct answer)

- a. Subrogation
- b. Insurance broker
- c. Actual cash value
- d. Additional insured

Guidance: level 1

:: Utilitarianism ::

_____ is a family of consequentialist ethical theories that promotes actions that maximize happiness and well-being for the majority of a population. Although different varieties of _____ admit different characterizations, the basic idea behind all of them is to in some sense maximize utility, which is often defined in terms of well-being or related concepts. For instance, Jeremy Bentham, the founder of _____ , described utility as

Exam Probability: **High**

51. *Answer choices:*

(see index for correct answer)

- a. Utilitarianism
- b. Average and total utilitarianism
- c. Utility monster

- d. The Theory of Good and Evil

Guidance: level 1

:: Legal procedure ::

An _____ is generally the first occasion that the trier of fact has to hear from a lawyer in a trial, aside possibly from questioning during voir dire. The _____ is generally constructed to serve as a "road map" for the fact-finder. This is especially essential, in many jury trials, since jurors know nothing at all about the case before the trial, . Though such statements may be dramatic and vivid, they must be limited to the evidence reasonably expected to be presented during the trial. Attorneys generally conclude _____ s with a reminder that at the conclusion of evidence, the attorney will return to ask the fact-finder to find in his or her client's favor.

Exam Probability: **High**

52. *Answer choices:*

(see index for correct answer)

- a. Opening statement
- b. civil procedure
- c. Closing argument
- d. appellate

Guidance: level 1

:: Contract law ::

A _____, unlike a void contract, is a valid contract which may be either affirmed or rejected at the option of one of the parties. At most, one party to the contract is bound. The unbound party may repudiate the contract, at which time the contract becomes void.

Exam Probability: **Low**

53. *Answer choices:*
(see index for correct answer)

- a. Offer and acceptance
- b. Fixed-price contract
- c. Community Benefits Agreement
- d. Broad Agency Announcement

Guidance: level 1

:: ::

The U.S. _____ is an independent agency of the United States federal government. The SEC holds primary responsibility for enforcing the federal securities laws, proposing securities rules, and regulating the securities industry, the nation's stock and options exchanges, and other activities and organizations, including the electronic securities markets in the United States.

Exam Probability: **High**

54. *Answer choices:*

(see index for correct answer)

- a. open system
- b. Securities and Exchange Commission
- c. process perspective
- d. Character

Guidance: level 1

:: Real property law ::

_____, sometimes colloquially described as 'squatter's rights', is a legal principle under which a person who does not have legal title to a piece of property—usually land—acquires legal ownership based on continuous possession or occupation of the land without the permission of its legal owner.

Exam Probability: **Low**

55. *Answer choices:*

(see index for correct answer)

- a. Land Registry
- b. 72-hour clause
- c. Conveyancing

- d. Adverse possession

Guidance: level 1

:: Business ::

_____ is a trade policy that does not restrict imports or exports; it can also be understood as the free market idea applied to international trade. In government, _____ is predominantly advocated by political parties that hold liberal economic positions while economically left-wing and nationalist political parties generally support protectionism, the opposite of _____.

Exam Probability: **Medium**

56. *Answer choices:*
(see index for correct answer)

- a. Cost externalizing
- b. Free trade
- c. Counter trade
- d. Employee experience management

Guidance: level 1

:: Contract law ::

In jurisprudence, _____ is an equitable doctrine that involves one person taking advantage of a position of power over another person. This inequity in power between the parties can vitiate one party's consent as they are unable to freely exercise their independent will.

Exam Probability: **Low**

57. *Answer choices:*

(see index for correct answer)

- a. Undue influence
- b. Partial integration
- c. Oral contract
- d. Cover

Guidance: level 1

:: Corporate finance ::

_____ is a contract law concept about the purchase of the release from a debt obligation. It is one of the methods by which parties to a contract may terminate their agreement. The release is completed by the transfer of valuable consideration that must not be the actual performance of the obligation itself. The accord is the agreement to discharge the obligation and the satisfaction is the legal "consideration" which binds the parties to the agreement. A valid accord does not discharge the prior contract; instead it suspends the right to enforce it in accordance with the terms of the accord contract, in which satisfaction, or performance of the contract will discharge both contracts. If the creditor breaches the accord, then the debtor will be able to bring up the existence of the accord in order to enjoin any action against him.

Exam Probability: **High**

58. *Answer choices:*

(see index for correct answer)

- a. Equity issuance
- b. Corporate spin-off
- c. Corporate finance
- d. Accord and satisfaction

Guidance: level 1

:: Data management ::

_____ is a form of intellectual property that grants the creator of an original creative work an exclusive legal right to determine whether and under what conditions this original work may be copied and used by others, usually for a limited term of years. The exclusive rights are not absolute but limited by limitations and exceptions to _____ law, including fair use. A major limitation on _____ on ideas is that _____ protects only the original expression of ideas, and not the underlying ideas themselves.

Exam Probability: **Low**

59. *Answer choices:*

(see index for correct answer)

- a. Data binding
- b. SQL programming tool
- c. Copyright
- d. Chunked transfer encoding

Guidance: level 1

Finance

Finance is a field that is concerned with the allocation (investment) of assets and liabilities over space and time, often under conditions of risk or uncertainty. Finance can also be defined as the science of money management. Participants in the market aim to price assets based on their risk level, fundamental value, and their expected rate of return. Finance can be split into three sub-categories: public finance, corporate finance and personal finance.

:: Business ::

The seller, or the provider of the goods or services, completes a sale in response to an acquisition, appropriation, requisition or a direct interaction with the buyer at the point of sale. There is a passing of title of the item, and the settlement of a price, in which agreement is reached on a price for which transfer of ownership of the item will occur. The seller, not the purchaser typically executes the sale and it may be completed prior to the obligation of payment. In the case of indirect interaction, a person who sells goods or service on behalf of the owner is known as a salesman or saleswoman or salesperson, but this often refers to someone _____ goods in a store/shop, in which case other terms are also common, including salesclerk, shop assistant, and retail clerk.

Exam Probability: **Low**

1. *Answer choices:*

(see index for correct answer)

- a. Business interaction networks
- b. Closure
- c. Intangible asset finance
- d. Selling

Guidance: level 1

:: ::

An _____ is a comprehensive report on a company's activities throughout the preceding year. _____ s are intended to give shareholders and other interested people information about the company's activities and financial performance. They may be considered as grey literature. Most jurisdictions require companies to prepare and disclose _____ s, and many require the _____ to be filed at the company's registry. Companies listed on a stock exchange are also required to report at more frequent intervals.

Exam Probability: **High**

2. *Answer choices:*

(see index for correct answer)

- a. Annual report
- b. Character
- c. personal values
- d. surface-level diversity

Guidance: level 1

:: Accounting terminology ::

In accounting/accountancy, _____ are journal entries usually made at the end of an accounting period to allocate income and expenditure to the period in which they actually occurred. The revenue recognition principle is the basis of making _____ that pertain to unearned and accrued revenues under accrual-basis accounting. They are sometimes called Balance Day adjustments because they are made on balance day.

Exam Probability: **Low**

3. *Answer choices:*

(see index for correct answer)

- a. Adjusting entries
- b. Accounts payable
- c. Impairment cost
- d. Record to report

Guidance: level 1

:: Investment ::

> The _____ is a measure of an investment's rate of return. The term internal refers to the fact that the calculation excludes external factors, such as the risk-free rate, inflation, the cost of capital, or various financial risks.

Exam Probability: **Low**

4. *Answer choices:*

(see index for correct answer)

- a. Price return
- b. Internal rate of return
- c. Traditional investments

- d. Spell Capital Partners

Guidance: level 1

:: Stock market ::

A _____ or stock divide increases the number of shares in a company. The price is adjusted such that the before and after market capitalization of the company remains the same and dilution does not occur. Options and warrants are included.

Exam Probability: **Low**

5. *Answer choices:*

(see index for correct answer)

- a. Order book
- b. Bombay Stock Exchange
- c. Piqqem
- d. Stock split

Guidance: level 1

:: Bonds (finance) ::

An _____ is a legal contract that reflects or covers a debt or purchase obligation. It specifically refers to two types of practices: in historical usage, an _____ d servant status, and in modern usage, it is an instrument used for commercial debt or real estate transaction.

Exam Probability: **Low**

6. *Answer choices:*

(see index for correct answer)

- a. Bearer bond
- b. Callable bond
- c. Industrial revenue bond
- d. Indenture

Guidance: level 1

:: Generally Accepted Accounting Principles ::

An _____ or profit and loss account is one of the financial statements of a company and shows the company's revenues and expenses during a particular period.

Exam Probability: **High**

7. *Answer choices:*

(see index for correct answer)

- a. Construction in progress
- b. Income statement
- c. Insurance asset management
- d. Earnings before interest, taxes and depreciation

Guidance: level 1

:: Management accounting ::

_____, or dollar contribution per unit, is the selling price per unit minus the variable cost per unit. "Contribution" represents the portion of sales revenue that is not consumed by variable costs and so contributes to the coverage of fixed costs. This concept is one of the key building blocks of break-even analysis.

Exam Probability: **Low**

8. *Answer choices:*

(see index for correct answer)

- a. Net present value
- b. Contribution margin
- c. Institute of Certified Management Accountants
- d. Certified Management Accountants of Canada

Guidance: level 1

:: Real estate ::

Amortisation is paying off an amount owed over time by making planned, incremental payments of principal and interest. To amortise a loan means "to kill it off". In accounting, amortisation refers to charging or writing off an intangible asset's cost as an operational expense over its estimated useful life to reduce a company's taxable income.

Exam Probability: **Medium**

9. *Answer choices:*

(see index for correct answer)

- a. Boundary
- b. Open-Realty
- c. Association law
- d. Rent control in the United States

Guidance: level 1

:: ::

An _____ is an area of the production, distribution, or trade, and consumption of goods and services by different agents. Understood in its broadest sense, 'The _____ is defined as a social domain that emphasize the practices, discourses, and material expressions associated with the production, use, and management of resources'. Economic agents can be individuals, businesses, organizations, or governments. Economic transactions occur when two parties agree to the value or price of the transacted good or service, commonly expressed in a certain currency. However, monetary transactions only account for a small part of the economic domain.

Exam Probability: **Medium**

10. *Answer choices:*

(see index for correct answer)

- a. personal values
- b. Economy
- c. empathy
- d. co-culture

Guidance: level 1

:: Debt ::

_____, in finance and economics, is payment from a borrower or deposit-taking financial institution to a lender or depositor of an amount above repayment of the principal sum, at a particular rate. It is distinct from a fee which the borrower may pay the lender or some third party. It is also distinct from dividend which is paid by a company to its shareholders from its profit or reserve, but not at a particular rate decided beforehand, rather on a pro rata basis as a share in the reward gained by risk taking entrepreneurs when the revenue earned exceeds the total costs.

Exam Probability: **Low**

11. *Answer choices:*

(see index for correct answer)

- a. Teacher Loan Forgiveness
- b. Default
- c. Interest
- d. Museum of Foreign Debt

Guidance: level 1

:: Generally Accepted Accounting Principles ::

A _____ is a reduction of the recognized value of something. In accounting, this is a recognition of the reduced or zero value of an asset. In income tax statements, this is a reduction of taxable income, as a recognition of certain expenses required to produce the income.

Exam Probability: **High**

12. *Answer choices:*

(see index for correct answer)

- a. Access to finance
- b. Financial position of the United States
- c. Generally accepted accounting principles
- d. Vendor-specific objective evidence

Guidance: level 1

:: Manufacturing ::

_____ costs are all manufacturing costs that are related to the cost object but cannot be traced to that cost object in an economically feasible way.

Exam Probability: **Medium**

13. *Answer choices:*

(see index for correct answer)

- a. Quick response
- b. Distributed manufacturing
- c. Discrete manufacturing
- d. Manufacturing overhead

Guidance: level 1

:: ::

> _____ is an eight-block-long street running roughly northwest to southeast from Broadway to South Street, at the East River, in the Financial District of Lower Manhattan in New York City. Over time, the term has become a metonym for the financial markets of the United States as a whole, the American financial services industry, or New York–based financial interests.

Exam Probability: **Low**

14. *Answer choices:*

(see index for correct answer)

- a. cultural
- b. Wall Street
- c. imperative
- d. information systems assessment

Guidance: level 1

:: ::

A _____ is an individual or institution that legally owns one or more shares of stock in a public or private corporation. _____ s may be referred to as members of a corporation. Legally, a person is not a _____ in a corporation until their name and other details are entered in the corporation's register of _____ s or members.

Exam Probability: **Low**

15. *Answer choices:*

(see index for correct answer)

- a. interpersonal communication
- b. hierarchical
- c. co-culture
- d. Shareholder

Guidance: level 1

:: Debt ::

_____ is the trust which allows one party to provide money or resources to another party wherein the second party does not reimburse the first party immediately, but promises either to repay or return those resources at a later date. In other words, _____ is a method of making reciprocity formal, legally enforceable, and extensible to a large group of unrelated people.

Exam Probability: **Low**

16. *Answer choices:*

(see index for correct answer)

- a. Compulsive buying disorder
- b. Credit
- c. Debit note
- d. Perpetual subordinated debt

Guidance: level 1

:: Generally Accepted Accounting Principles ::

> In accrual accounting, the revenue recognition principle states that expenses should be recorded during the period in which they are incurred, regardless of when the transfer of cash occurs. Conversely, cash basis accounting calls for the recognition of an expense when the cash is paid, regardless of when the expense was actually incurred.

Exam Probability: **Medium**

17. *Answer choices:*

(see index for correct answer)

- a. Insurance asset management
- b. Engagement letter
- c. Net income
- d. Matching principle

Guidance: level 1

:: Finance ::

A _____ , publicly-traded company, publicly-held company, publicly-listed company, or public limited company is a corporation whose ownership is dispersed among the general public in many shares of stock which are freely traded on a stock exchange or in over-the-counter markets. In some jurisdictions, public companies over a certain size must be listed on an exchange. A _____ can be listed or unlisted.

Exam Probability: **Low**

18. *Answer choices:*

(see index for correct answer)

- a. AzeriCard
- b. Public company
- c. Ultra high-net-worth individual
- d. Shadow banking system

Guidance: level 1

:: Financial ratios ::

A _____ or accounting ratio is a relative magnitude of two selected numerical values taken from an enterprise's financial statements. Often used in accounting, there are many standard ratios used to try to evaluate the overall financial condition of a corporation or other organization. _____s may be used by managers within a firm, by current and potential shareholders of a firm, and by a firm's creditors. Financial analysts use _____s to compare the strengths and weaknesses in various companies. If shares in a company are traded in a financial market, the market price of the shares is used in certain _____s.

Exam Probability: **Low**

19. *Answer choices:*

(see index for correct answer)

- a. Total expense ratio
- b. Dividend yield
- c. Days sales outstanding
- d. Treynor ratio

Guidance: level 1

:: Valuation (finance) ::

_____ refers to an assessment of the viability, stability, and profitability of a business, sub-business or project.

Exam Probability: **Medium**

20. *Answer choices:*

(see index for correct answer)

- a. Financial analysis
- b. Diminution in value
- c. International Valuation Standards Council
- d. Graham number

Guidance: level 1

:: Business law ::

A _____ is a group of people who jointly supervise the activities of an organization, which can be either a for-profit business, nonprofit organization, or a government agency. Such a board's powers, duties, and responsibilities are determined by government regulations and the organization's own constitution and bylaws. These authorities may specify the number of members of the board, how they are to be chosen, and how often they are to meet.

Exam Probability: **Medium**

21. *Answer choices:*

(see index for correct answer)

- a. Personal Property Security Act
- b. Board of directors
- c. Bulk transfer

- d. Oppression remedy

Guidance: level 1

:: Accounting journals and ledgers ::

_____ is a daybook or journal which is used to record transactions relating to adjustment entries, opening stock, accounting errors etc. The source documents of this prime entry book are journal voucher, copy of management reports and invoices.

Exam Probability: **Low**

22. *Answer choices:*
(see index for correct answer)

- a. Subsidiary ledger
- b. General journal
- c. Check register
- d. Journal entry

Guidance: level 1

:: ::

The _____ is a private, non-profit organization standard-setting body whose primary purpose is to establish and improve Generally Accepted Accounting Principles within the United States in the public's interest. The Securities and Exchange Commission designated the FASB as the organization responsible for setting accounting standards for public companies in the US. The FASB replaced the American Institute of Certified Public Accountants' Accounting Principles Board on July 1, 1973.

Exam Probability: **High**

23. *Answer choices:*

(see index for correct answer)

- a. empathy
- b. hierarchical perspective
- c. open system
- d. Financial Accounting Standards Board

Guidance: level 1

:: Markets (customer bases) ::

In economics, _____ is the economic price for which a good or service is offered in the marketplace. It is of interest mainly in the study of microeconomics. Market value and _____ are equal only under conditions of market efficiency, equilibrium, and rational expectations.

Exam Probability: **Low**

24. *Answer choices:*

(see index for correct answer)

- a. Parity product
- b. Market system
- c. Market price
- d. Horizontal market

Guidance: level 1

:: International taxation ::

_____ is the levying of tax by two or more jurisdictions on the same declared income, asset, or financial transaction. Double liability is mitigated in a number of ways, for example.

Exam Probability: **High**

25. *Answer choices:*

(see index for correct answer)

- a. Controlled foreign corporation
- b. Double taxation
- c. Expatriation tax
- d. Foreign personal holding company

Guidance: level 1

:: Financial risk ::

_____ is the risk that arises for bond owners from fluctuating interest rates. How much _____ a bond has depends on how sensitive its price is to interest rate changes in the market. The sensitivity depends on two things, the bond's time to maturity, and the coupon rate of the bond.

Exam Probability: **Low**

26. *Answer choices:*

(see index for correct answer)

- a. ORRF Risk Research Forum
- b. Liquidity risk
- c. Interest rate risk
- d. Systematic risk

Guidance: level 1

:: Management ::

The _____ is a strategy performance management tool – a semi-standard structured report, that can be used by managers to keep track of the execution of activities by the staff within their control and to monitor the consequences arising from these actions.

Exam Probability: **Medium**

27. *Answer choices:*

(see index for correct answer)

- a. Innovation management
- b. Design leadership
- c. Production flow analysis
- d. Balanced scorecard

Guidance: level 1

:: Project management ::

Some scenarios associate "this kind of planning" with learning "life skills". _____s are necessary, or at least useful, in situations where individuals need to know what time they must be at a specific location to receive a specific service, and where people need to accomplish a set of goals within a set time period.

Exam Probability: **High**

28. *Answer choices:*

(see index for correct answer)

- a. Schedule
- b. Gregory T. Haugan

- c. Participatory impact pathways analysis
- d. Schedule chicken

Guidance: level 1

:: Accounting terminology ::

Total _____ is a method of Accounting cost which entails the full cost of manufacturing or providing a service. TAC includes not just the costs of materials and labour, but also of all manufacturing overheads. The cost of each cost center can be direct or indirect. The direct cost can be easily identified with individual cost centers. Whereas indirect cost cannot be easily identified with the cost center. The distribution of overhead among the departments is called apportionment.

Exam Probability: **Low**

29. *Answer choices:*

(see index for correct answer)

- a. Capital surplus
- b. Total absorption costing
- c. Absorption costing
- d. profit and loss statement

Guidance: level 1

:: Separation of investment and commercial banking ::

A _____ is a type of bank that provides services such as accepting deposits, making business loans, and offering basic investment products that is operated as a business for profit.

Exam Probability: **High**

30. *Answer choices:*

(see index for correct answer)

- a. Bank holding company
- b. Bank Holding Company Act
- c. Commercial bank
- d. investment bank

Guidance: level 1

:: Financial risk ::

_____ is any of various types of risk associated with financing, including financial transactions that include company loans in risk of default. Often it is understood to include only downside risk, meaning the potential for financial loss and uncertainty about its extent.

Exam Probability: **High**

31. *Answer choices:*

(see index for correct answer)

- a. Bielard, Biehl and Kaiser five-way model
- b. Financial risk
- c. Market portfolio
- d. Active risk

Guidance: level 1

:: ::

_____ is a political and social philosophy promoting traditional social institutions in the context of culture and civilization. The central tenets of _____ include tradition, human imperfection, organic society, hierarchy, authority, and property rights. Conservatives seek to preserve a range of institutions such as religion, parliamentary government, and property rights, with the aim of emphasizing social stability and continuity. The more traditional elements—reactionaries—oppose modernism and seek a return to "the way things were".

Exam Probability: **Low**

32. *Answer choices:*

(see index for correct answer)

- a. Conservatism
- b. Sarbanes-Oxley act of 2002

- c. cultural
- d. hierarchical perspective

Guidance: level 1

:: Commerce ::

A _____ , is a document acknowledging that a person has received money or property in payment following a sale or other transfer of goods or provision of a service. All _____ s must have the date of purchase on them. If the recipient of the payment is legally required to collect sales tax or VAT from the customer, the amount would be added to the _____ and the collection would be deemed to have been on behalf of the relevant tax authority. In many countries, a retailer is required to include the sales tax or VAT in the displayed price of goods sold, from which the tax amount would be calculated at point of sale and remitted to the tax authorities in due course. Similarly, amounts may be deducted from amounts payable, as in the case of wage withholding taxes. On the other hand, tips or other gratuities given by a customer, for example in a restaurant, would not form part of the payment amount or appear on the _____ .

Exam Probability: **Low**

33. *Answer choices:*

(see index for correct answer)

- a. Acquiring bank
- b. Haul video
- c. Receipt
- d. Mail order

Guidance: level 1

:: ::

A tax is a compulsory financial charge or some other type of levy imposed upon a taxpayer by a governmental organization in order to fund various public expenditures. A failure to pay, along with evasion of or resistance to _____ , is punishable by law. Taxes consist of direct or indirect taxes and may be paid in money or as its labour equivalent.

Exam Probability: **Low**

34. *Answer choices:*

(see index for correct answer)

- a. Taxation
- b. functional perspective
- c. personal values
- d. levels of analysis

Guidance: level 1

:: ::

In accounting, the _____ is a measure of the number of times inventory is sold or used in a time period such as a year. It is calculated to see if a business has an excessive inventory in comparison to its sales level. The equation for _____ equals the cost of goods sold divided by the average inventory. _____ is also known as inventory turns, merchandise turnover, stockturn, stock turns, turns, and stock turnover.

Exam Probability: **High**

35. *Answer choices:*

(see index for correct answer)

- a. Sarbanes-Oxley act of 2002
- b. deep-level diversity
- c. co-culture
- d. Inventory turnover

Guidance: level 1

:: E-commerce ::

A _____ is a plastic payment card that can be used instead of cash when making purchases. It is similar to a credit card, but unlike a credit card, the money is immediately transferred directly from the cardholder's bank account when performing a transaction.

Exam Probability: **Medium**

36. *Answer choices:*

(see index for correct answer)

- a. E-commerce
- b. Debit card
- c. Paid content
- d. GamersGate

Guidance: level 1

:: Finance ::

_____ is a field that is concerned with the allocation of assets and liabilities over space and time, often under conditions of risk or uncertainty. _____ can also be defined as the art of money management. Participants in the market aim to price assets based on their risk level, fundamental value, and their expected rate of return. _____ can be split into three sub-categories: public _____ , corporate _____ and personal _____ .

Exam Probability: **Low**

37. *Answer choices:*

(see index for correct answer)

- a. Convention of conservatism
- b. Offset loan
- c. Finance

- d. Negative gearing

Guidance: level 1

:: Options (finance) ::

In finance, a put or _____ is a stock market device which gives the owner the right, but not the obligation, to sell an asset, at a specified price, by a predetermined date to a given party. The purchase of a _____ is interpreted as a negative sentiment about the future value of theunderlying stock. The term "put" comes from the fact that the owner has the right to "put up for sale" the stock or index.

Exam Probability: **High**

38. *Answer choices:*

(see index for correct answer)

- a. Put option
- b. Options writing
- c. Stock option return
- d. Cash or share option

Guidance: level 1

:: ::

_____ is the collection of mechanisms, processes and relations by which corporations are controlled and operated. Governance structures and principles identify the distribution of rights and responsibilities among different participants in the corporation and include the rules and procedures for making decisions in corporate affairs. _____ is necessary because of the possibility of conflicts of interests between stakeholders, primarily between shareholders and upper management or among shareholders.

Exam Probability: **High**

39. *Answer choices:*

(see index for correct answer)

- a. Corporate governance
- b. personal values
- c. corporate values
- d. Sarbanes-Oxley act of 2002

Guidance: level 1

:: Competition (economics) ::

_____ arises whenever at least two parties strive for a goal which cannot be shared: where one's gain is the other's loss.

Exam Probability: **Low**

40. *Answer choices:*

(see index for correct answer)

- a. Leapfrogging
- b. Category killer
- c. Competition
- d. Transfer pricing

Guidance: level 1

:: ::

_____ is a marketing communication that employs an openly sponsored, non-personal message to promote or sell a product, service or idea. Sponsors of _____ are typically businesses wishing to promote their products or services. _____ is differentiated from public relations in that an advertiser pays for and has control over the message. It differs from personal selling in that the message is non-personal, i.e., not directed to a particular individual. _____ is communicated through various mass media, including traditional media such as newspapers, magazines, television, radio, outdoor _____ or direct mail; and new media such as search results, blogs, social media, websites or text messages. The actual presentation of the message in a medium is referred to as an advertisement, or "ad" or advert for short.

Exam Probability: **Low**

41. *Answer choices:*

(see index for correct answer)

- a. Advertising
- b. functional perspective
- c. personal values
- d. deep-level diversity

Guidance: level 1

:: Business economics ::

A _____ is a term used primarily in cost accounting to describe something to which costs are assigned. Common examples of _____ s are: product lines, geographic territories, customers, departments or anything else for which management would like to quantify cost.

Exam Probability: **Low**

42. *Answer choices:*

(see index for correct answer)

- a. Cost object
- b. Inclusive business finance
- c. Risk financing
- d. Tradespace

Guidance: level 1

:: Actuarial science ::

The _____ is the greater benefit of receiving money now rather than an identical sum later. It is founded on time preference.

Exam Probability: **Medium**

43. *Answer choices:*
(see index for correct answer)

- a. Economic capital
- b. Reinsurance
- c. Embedded value
- d. Time value of money

Guidance: level 1

:: ::

In finance, return is a profit on an investment. It comprises any change in value of the investment, and/or cash flows which the investor receives from the investment, such as interest payments or dividends. It may be measured either in absolute terms or as a percentage of the amount invested. The latter is also called the holding period return.

Exam Probability: **High**

44. Answer choices:

(see index for correct answer)

- a. cultural
- b. Rate of return
- c. interpersonal communication
- d. deep-level diversity

Guidance: level 1

:: Accounting ::

_____ is a process of providing relief to shared service organization's cost centers that provide a product or service. In turn, the associated expense is assigned to internal clients' cost centers that consume the products and services. For example, the CIO may provide all IT services within the company and assign the costs back to the business units that consume each offering.

Exam Probability: **High**

45. Answer choices:

(see index for correct answer)

- a. Cost allocation
- b. KashFlow
- c. Trading statement
- d. Russian GAAP

Guidance: level 1

:: Business ::

The seller, or the provider of the goods or services, completes a sale in response to an acquisition, appropriation, requisition or a direct interaction with the buyer at the point of sale. There is a passing of title of the item, and the settlement of a price, in which agreement is reached on a price for which transfer of ownership of the item will occur. The seller, not the purchaser typically executes the sale and it may be completed prior to the obligation of payment. In the case of indirect interaction, a person who sells goods or service on behalf of the owner is known as a _____ man or _____ woman or _____ person, but this often refers to someone selling goods in a store/shop, in which case other terms are also common, including _____ clerk, shop assistant, and retail clerk.

Exam Probability: **Medium**

46. *Answer choices:*
(see index for correct answer)

- a. OrderUp
- b. Sales
- c. SONGZIO
- d. Demand chain

Guidance: level 1

:: Management accounting ::

_____ is a managerial accounting cost concept. Under this method, manufacturing overhead is incurred in the period that a product is produced. This addresses the issue of absorption costing that allows income to rise as production rises. Under an absorption cost method, management can push forward costs to the next period when products are sold. This artificially inflates profits in the period of production by incurring less cost than would be incurred under a _____ system. _____ is generally not used for external reporting purposes. Under the Tax Reform Act of 1986, income statements must use absorption costing to comply with GAAP.

Exam Probability: **High**

47. *Answer choices:*

(see index for correct answer)

- a. Accounting management
- b. Variable Costing
- c. Environmental full-cost accounting
- d. Owner earnings

Guidance: level 1

:: Debt ::

A _____ is a party that has a claim on the services of a second party. It is a person or institution to whom money is owed. The first party, in general, has provided some property or service to the second party under the assumption that the second party will return an equivalent property and service. The second party is frequently called a debtor or borrower. The first party is called the _____ , which is the lender of property, service, or money.

Exam Probability: **High**

48. *Answer choices:*

(see index for correct answer)

- a. Sum certain
- b. Creditor
- c. Exchangeable bond
- d. Teacher Loan Forgiveness

Guidance: level 1

:: Leasing ::

A finance lease is a type of lease in which a finance company is typically the legal owner of the asset for the duration of the lease, while the lessee not only has operating control over the asset, but also has a some share of the economic risks and returns from the change in the valuation of the underlying asset.

Exam Probability: **High**

49. *Answer choices:*

(see index for correct answer)

- a. Farmout agreement
- b. Synthetic lease

Guidance: level 1

:: ::

An _____ is a contingent motivator. Traditional _____ s are extrinsic motivators which reward actions to yield a desired outcome. The effectiveness of traditional _____ s has changed as the needs of Western society have evolved. While the traditional _____ model is effective when there is a defined procedure and goal for a task, Western society started to require a higher volume of critical thinkers, so the traditional model became less effective. Institutions are now following a trend in implementing strategies that rely on intrinsic motivations rather than the extrinsic motivations that the traditional _____ s foster.

Exam Probability: **Low**

50. *Answer choices:*

(see index for correct answer)

- a. open system
- b. information systems assessment

- c. Incentive
- d. interpersonal communication

Guidance: level 1

:: Cash flow ::

In corporate finance, _____ or _____ to firm is a way of looking at a business's cash flow to see what is available for distribution among all the securities holders of a corporate entity. This may be useful to parties such as equity holders, debt holders, preferred stock holders, and convertible security holders when they want to see how much cash can be extracted from a company without causing issues to its operations.

Exam Probability: **High**

51. *Answer choices:*

(see index for correct answer)

- a. Valuation using discounted cash flows
- b. Invoice discounting
- c. Propequity
- d. Cash flow statement

Guidance: level 1

:: Financial markets ::

The _____ is the part of the capital market that deals with the issuance and sale of equity-backed securities to investors directly by the issuer. Investor buy securities that were never traded before. _____ s create long term instruments through which corporate entities raise funds from the capital market. It is also known as the New Issue Market.

Exam Probability: **High**

52. *Answer choices:*

(see index for correct answer)

- a. Primary market
- b. Global Financial Centres Index
- c. Limits to arbitrage
- d. Market impact cost

Guidance: level 1

:: Loans ::

In corporate finance, a _____ is a medium- to long-term debt instrument used by large companies to borrow money, at a fixed rate of interest. The legal term "_____" originally referred to a document that either creates a debt or acknowledges it, but in some countries the term is now used interchangeably with bond, loan stock or note. A _____ is thus like a certificate of loan or a loan bond evidencing the fact that the company is liable to pay a specified amount with interest and although the money raised by the _____ s becomes a part of the company's capital structure, it does not become share capital. Senior _____ s get paid before subordinate _____ s, and there are varying rates of risk and payoff for these categories.

Exam Probability: **High**

53. *Answer choices:*

(see index for correct answer)

- a. Expected loss
- b. Debenture
- c. Graduated payment mortgage
- d. Participation loan

Guidance: level 1

:: Financial statements ::

In financial accounting, a _____ or statement of financial position or statement of financial condition is a summary of the financial balances of an individual or organization, whether it be a sole proprietorship, a business partnership, a corporation, private limited company or other organization such as Government or not-for-profit entity. Assets, liabilities and ownership equity are listed as of a specific date, such as the end of its financial year. A _____ is often described as a "snapshot of a company's financial condition". Of the four basic financial statements, the _____ is the only statement which applies to a single point in time of a business' calendar year.

Exam Probability: **High**

54. *Answer choices:*

(see index for correct answer)

- a. Government financial statements
- b. Clean surplus accounting
- c. PnL Explained
- d. Balance sheet

Guidance: level 1

:: ::

An _____ is a person that allocates capital with the expectation of a future financial return. Types of investments include: equity, debt securities, real estate, currency, commodity, token, derivatives such as put and call options, futures, forwards, etc. This definition makes no distinction between the _____ s in the primary and secondary markets. That is, someone who provides a business with capital and someone who buys a stock are both _____ s. An _____ who owns a stock is a shareholder.

Exam Probability: **Medium**

55. *Answer choices:*

(see index for correct answer)

- a. open system
- b. similarity-attraction theory
- c. cultural
- d. levels of analysis

Guidance: level 1

:: ::

_____ is the consumption and saving opportunity gained by an entity within a specified timeframe, which is generally expressed in monetary terms. For households and individuals, " _____ is the sum of all the wages, salaries, profits, interest payments, rents, and other forms of earnings received in a given period of time."

Exam Probability: **Low**

56. *Answer choices:*

(see index for correct answer)

- a. similarity-attraction theory
- b. imperative
- c. deep-level diversity
- d. corporate values

Guidance: level 1

:: Financial markets ::

A _____ is a market in which people trade financial securities and derivatives such as futures and options at low transaction costs. Securities include stocks and bonds, and precious metals.

Exam Probability: **High**

57. *Answer choices:*

(see index for correct answer)

- a. Stock correlation network
- b. Reset
- c. Financial market
- d. Convergence trade

Guidance: level 1

:: Real estate valuation ::

_____ or OMV is the price at which an asset would trade in a competitive auction setting. _____ is often used interchangeably with open _____, fair value or fair _____, although these terms have distinct definitions in different standards, and may or may not differ in some circumstances.

Exam Probability: **High**

58. *Answer choices:*

(see index for correct answer)

- a. Broker%27s Price Opinion
- b. Market value
- c. Hedonic regression
- d. International Right of Way Association

Guidance: level 1

:: Management accounting ::

_____ are costs that are not directly accountable to a cost object. _____ may be either fixed or variable. _____ include administration, personnel and security costs. These are those costs which are not directly related to production. Some _____ may be overhead. But some overhead costs can be directly attributed to a project and are direct costs.

Exam Probability: **Low**

59. *Answer choices:*

(see index for correct answer)

- a. Indirect costs
- b. Invested capital
- c. Construction accounting
- d. Variance

Guidance: level 1

Human resource management

Human resource (HR) management is the strategic approach to the effective management of organization workers so that they help the business gain a competitive advantage. It is designed to maximize employee performance in service of an employer's strategic objectives. HR is primarily concerned with the management of people within organizations, focusing on policies and on systems. HR departments are responsible for overseeing employee-benefits design, employee recruitment, training and development, performance appraisal, and rewarding (e.g., managing pay and benefit systems). HR also concerns itself with organizational change and industrial relations, that is, the balancing of organizational practices with requirements arising from collective bargaining and from governmental laws.

:: Unemployment in the United States ::

The _____ is a unit of the United States Department of Labor. It is the principal fact-finding agency for the U.S. government in the broad field of labor economics and statistics and serves as a principal agency of the U.S. Federal Statistical System. The BLS is a governmental statistical agency that collects, processes, analyzes, and disseminates essential statistical data to the American public, the U.S. Congress, other Federal agencies, State and local governments, business, and labor representatives. The BLS also serves as a statistical resource to the United States Department of Labor, and conducts research into how much families need to earn to be able to enjoy a decent standard of living.

Exam Probability: **High**

1. *Answer choices:*

(see index for correct answer)

- a. Ticket to Work
- b. Underearners Anonymous
- c. Bureau of Labor Statistics
- d. Current Population Survey

Guidance: level 1

:: ::

_____ is a method for employees to organize into a labor union in which a majority of employees in a bargaining unit sign authorization forms, or "cards", stating they wish to be represented by the union. Since the National Labor Relations Act became law in 1935, _____ has been an alternative to the National Labor Relations Board's election process. _____ and election are both overseen by the National Labor Relations Board. The difference is that with card sign-up, employees sign authorization cards stating they want a union, the cards are submitted to the NLRB and if more than 50% of the employees submitted cards, the NLRB requires the employer to recognize the union. The NLRA election process is an additional step with the NLRB conducting a secret ballot election after authorization cards are submitted. In both cases the employer never sees the authorization cards or any information that would disclose how individual employees voted.

Exam Probability: **High**

2. *Answer choices:*

(see index for correct answer)

- a. co-culture
- b. empathy
- c. process perspective
- d. personal values

Guidance: level 1

:: Employee relations ::

_____ are tools used by organizational leadership to gain feedback on and measure employee engagement, employee morale, and performance. Usually answered anonymously, surveys are also used to gain a holistic picture of employees' feelings on such areas as working conditions, supervisory impact, and motivation that regular channels of communication may not. Surveys are considered effective in this regard provided they are well-designed, effectively administered, have validity, and evoke changes and improvements.

Exam Probability: **High**

3. *Answer choices:*

(see index for correct answer)

- a. Employee handbook
- b. Employee surveys
- c. Employee morale
- d. Employee motivation

Guidance: level 1

:: Industrial relations ::

_____ or employee satisfaction is a measure of workers' contentedness with their job, whether or not they like the job or individual aspects or facets of jobs, such as nature of work or supervision. _____ can be measured in cognitive, affective, and behavioral components. Researchers have also noted that _____ measures vary in the extent to which they measure feelings about the job, or cognitions about the job.

Exam Probability: **Medium**

4. *Answer choices:*

(see index for correct answer)

- a. Industrial violence
- b. European Journal of Industrial Relations
- c. Workforce Investment Board
- d. Job satisfaction

Guidance: level 1

:: Supply chain management terms ::

In business and finance, _____ is a system of organizations, people, activities, information, and resources involved in moving a product or service from supplier to customer. _____ activities involve the transformation of natural resources, raw materials, and components into a finished product that is delivered to the end customer. In sophisticated _____ systems, used products may re-enter the _____ at any point where residual value is recyclable. _____ s link value chains.

Exam Probability: **High**

5. *Answer choices:*

(see index for correct answer)

- a. Cool Chain Quality Indicator

- b. Supply chain
- c. Stockout
- d. Consumable

Guidance: level 1

:: Organizational behavior ::

Greenberg introduced the concept of _____ with regard to how an employee judges the behaviour of the organization and the employee's resulting attitude and behaviour..

Exam Probability: **High**

6. *Answer choices:*

(see index for correct answer)

- a. Achievement Motivation Inventory
- b. Organizational citizenship behavior
- c. Organizational justice
- d. Counterproductive norms

Guidance: level 1

:: Employment ::

_____ is measuring the output of a particular business process or procedure, then modifying the process or procedure to increase the output, increase efficiency, or increase the effectiveness of the process or procedure. _____ can be applied to either individual performance such as an athlete or organizational performance such as a racing team or a commercial business.

Exam Probability: **High**

7. *Answer choices:*

(see index for correct answer)

- a. Attendance allowance
- b. Liza Wright
- c. Gofer
- d. Performance improvement

Guidance: level 1

:: Employment compensation ::

A _____ is an agreement between a company and an employee specifying that the employee will receive certain significant benefits if employment is terminated. Most definitions specify the employment termination is as a result of a merger or takeover, also known as "Change-in-control benefits", but more recently the term has been used to describe perceived excessive CEO severance packages unrelated to change in ownership. The benefits may include severance pay, cash bonuses, stock options, or other benefits.

Exam Probability: **Low**

8. *Answer choices:*

(see index for correct answer)

- a. Golden parachute
- b. Law Enforcement Availability Pay
- c. IDS Pay Report
- d. Basic Income Earth Network

Guidance: level 1

:: ::

An _____ is a process where candidates are examined to determine their suitability for specific types of employment, especially management or military command. The candidates' personality and aptitudes are determined by techniques including interviews, group exercises, presentations, examinations and psychometric testing.

Exam Probability: **High**

9. *Answer choices:*

(see index for correct answer)

- a. hierarchical
- b. Assessment center

- c. open system
- d. similarity-attraction theory

Guidance: level 1

:: Survey methodology ::

A _____ is the procedure of systematically acquiring and recording information about the members of a given population. The term is used mostly in connection with national population and housing _____ es; other common _____ es include agriculture, business, and traffic _____ es. The United Nations defines the essential features of population and housing _____ es as "individual enumeration, universality within a defined territory, simultaneity and defined periodicity", and recommends that population _____ es be taken at least every 10 years. United Nations recommendations also cover _____ topics to be collected, official definitions, classifications and other useful information to co-ordinate international practice.

Exam Probability: **Medium**

10. *Answer choices:*

(see index for correct answer)

- a. Self-report study
- b. Scale analysis
- c. Census
- d. Computer-assisted survey information collection

Guidance: level 1

:: Occupational safety and health ::

A safety data sheet, _____, or product safety data sheet is a document that lists information relating to occupational safety and health for the use of various substances and products. SDSs are a widely used system for cataloging information on chemicals, chemical compounds, and chemical mixtures. SDS information may include instructions for the safe use and potential hazards associated with a particular material or product, along with spill-handling procedures. SDS formats can vary from source to source within a country depending on national requirements.

Exam Probability: **High**

11. *Answer choices:*

(see index for correct answer)

- a. Threshold limit value
- b. Material safety data sheet
- c. Radiation dose reconstruction
- d. Job safety analysis

Guidance: level 1

:: International trade ::

_____ or globalisation is the process of interaction and integration among people, companies, and governments worldwide. As a complex and multifaceted phenomenon, _____ is considered by some as a form of capitalist expansion which entails the integration of local and national economies into a global, unregulated market economy. _____ has grown due to advances in transportation and communication technology. With the increased global interactions comes the growth of international trade, ideas, and culture. _____ is primarily an economic process of interaction and integration that's associated with social and cultural aspects. However, conflicts and diplomacy are also large parts of the history of _____, and modern _____.

Exam Probability: **Medium**

12. *Answer choices:*

(see index for correct answer)

- a. Absolute advantage
- b. Portuguese India Armadas
- c. Uppsala model
- d. Globalization

Guidance: level 1

:: Income ::

In business and accounting, net income is an entity's income minus cost of goods sold, expenses and taxes for an accounting period. It is computed as the residual of all revenues and gains over all expenses and losses for the period, and has also been defined as the net increase in shareholders' equity that results from a company's operations. In the context of the presentation of financial statements, the IFRS Foundation defines net income as synonymous with profit and loss. The difference between revenue and the cost of making a product or providing a service, before deducting overheads, payroll, taxation, and interest payments. This is different from operating income .

Exam Probability: **High**

13. *Answer choices:*

(see index for correct answer)

- a. Windfall gain
- b. Bottom line
- c. Independent income
- d. Real estate investing

Guidance: level 1

:: Labour relations ::

_____ is a form of protest in which people congregate outside a place of work or location where an event is taking place. Often, this is done in an attempt to dissuade others from going in, but it can also be done to draw public attention to a cause. Picketers normally endeavor to be non-violent. It can have a number of aims, but is generally to put pressure on the party targeted to meet particular demands or cease operations. This pressure is achieved by harming the business through loss of customers and negative publicity, or by discouraging or preventing workers or customers from entering the site and thereby preventing the business from operating normally.

Exam Probability: **Medium**

14. *Answer choices:*

(see index for correct answer)

- a. Inflatable rat
- b. Boulwarism
- c. Social dialogue
- d. Union shop

Guidance: level 1

:: Business law ::

An _____ is a natural person, business, or corporation that provides goods or services to another entity under terms specified in a contract or within a verbal agreement. Unlike an employee, an _____ does not work regularly for an employer but works as and when required, during which time they may be subject to law of agency. _____ s are usually paid on a freelance basis. Contractors often work through a limited company or franchise, which they themselves own, or may work through an umbrella company.

Exam Probability: **High**

15. *Answer choices:*

(see index for correct answer)

- a. Limited liability
- b. Independent contractor
- c. Unfair business practices
- d. Extraordinary resolution

Guidance: level 1

:: Employment compensation ::

_____ is time off from work that workers can use to stay home to address their health and safety needs without losing pay. Paid _____ is a statutory requirement in many nations. Most European, many Latin American, a few African and a few Asian countries have legal requirements for paid _____.

16. *Answer choices:*

(see index for correct answer)

- a. Thirteenth salary
- b. Golden parachute
- c. Streamlining Claims Processing for Federal Contractor Employees Act
- d. Sick leave

Guidance: level 1

:: Sociological terminology ::

In moral and political philosophy, the _____ is a theory or model that originated during the Age of Enlightenment and usually concerns the legitimacy of the authority of the state over the individual. _____ arguments typically posit that individuals have consented, either explicitly or tacitly, to surrender some of their freedoms and submit to the authority in exchange for protection of their remaining rights or maintenance of the social order. The relation between natural and legal rights is often a topic of _____ theory. The term takes its name from The _____ , a 1762 book by Jean-Jacques Rousseau that discussed this concept. Although the antecedents of _____ theory are found in antiquity, in Greek and Stoic philosophy and Roman and Canon Law, the heyday of the _____ was the mid-17th to early 19th centuries, when it emerged as the leading doctrine of political legitimacy.

17. *Answer choices:*

(see index for correct answer)

- a. Anticipatory socialization
- b. latent function
- c. Third place
- d. Social contract

Guidance: level 1

:: Recruitment ::

_____ is a specialized recruitment service which organizations pay to seek out and recruit highly qualified candidates for senior-level and executive jobs. Headhunters may also seek out and recruit other highly specialized and/or skilled positions in organizations for which there is strong competition in the job market for the top talent, such as senior data analysts or computer programmers. The method usually involves commissioning a third-party organization, typically an _____ firm, but possibly a standalone consultant or consulting firm, to research the availability of suitable qualified candidates working for competitors or related businesses or organizations. Having identified a shortlist of qualified candidates who match the client's requirements, the _____ firm may act as an intermediary to contact the individual and see if they might be interested in moving to a new employer. The _____ firm may also carry out initial screening of the candidate, negotiations on remuneration and benefits, and preparing the employment contract. In some markets there has been a move towards using _____ for lower positions driven by the fact that there are less candidates for some positions even on lower levels than executive.

Exam Probability: **Medium**

18. *Answer choices:*

(see index for correct answer)

- a. E-recruitment
- b. Vetting
- c. Association of Graduate Recruiters
- d. Europass

Guidance: level 1

:: Unemployment ::

In economics, a _____ is a business cycle contraction when there is a general decline in economic activity. Macroeconomic indicators such as GDP, investment spending, capacity utilization, household income, business profits, and inflation fall, while bankruptcies and the unemployment rate rise. In the United Kingdom, it is defined as a negative economic growth for two consecutive quarters.

Exam Probability: **Low**

19. *Answer choices:*

(see index for correct answer)

- a. Phillips curve
- b. Misery index
- c. Recession
- d. Employment-to-population ratio

Guidance: level 1

:: ::

In production, research, retail, and accounting, a _____ is the value of money that has been used up to produce something or deliver a service, and hence is not available for use anymore. In business, the _____ may be one of acquisition, in which case the amount of money expended to acquire it is counted as _____ . In this case, money is the input that is gone in order to acquire the thing. This acquisition _____ may be the sum of the _____ of production as incurred by the original producer, and further _____ s of transaction as incurred by the acquirer over and above the price paid to the producer. Usually, the price also includes a mark-up for profit over the _____ of production.

Exam Probability: **Medium**

20. *Answer choices:*

(see index for correct answer)

- a. hierarchical perspective
- b. corporate values
- c. open system
- d. deep-level diversity

Guidance: level 1

:: Human resource management ::

An _____ is a diagram that shows the structure of an organization and the relationships and relative ranks of its parts and positions/jobs. The term is also used for similar diagrams, for example ones showing the different elements of a field of knowledge or a group of languages.

Exam Probability: **Medium**

21. *Answer choices:*

(see index for correct answer)

- a. Organizational chart
- b. Job sharing
- c. Bradford Factor
- d. Cultural capital

Guidance: level 1

:: United States employment discrimination case law ::

_____ , 641 F.2d 934 , was a D.C. Circuit opinion, written by Judge Skelly Wright, that held that workplace sexual harassment could constitute employment discrimination under the Civil Rights Act of 1964.

Exam Probability: **High**

22. *Answer choices:*

(see index for correct answer)

- a. New York City Transit Authority v. Beazer
- b. Reeves v. Sanderson Plumbing Products, Inc.
- c. Bundy v. Jackson
- d. Faragher v. City of Boca Raton

Guidance: level 1

:: Stress ::

_____ means beneficial stress—either psychological, physical, or biochemical/radiological.

Exam Probability: **Low**

23. *Answer choices:*
(see index for correct answer)

- a. Avoidance coping
- b. Biotic stress
- c. Prenatal stress
- d. Eustress

Guidance: level 1

:: Majority–minority relations ::

_____, also known as reservation in India and Nepal, positive discrimination / action in the United Kingdom, and employment equity in Canada and South Africa, is the policy of promoting the education and employment of members of groups that are known to have previously suffered from discrimination. Historically and internationally, support for _____ has sought to achieve goals such as bridging inequalities in employment and pay, increasing access to education, promoting diversity, and redressing apparent past wrongs, harms, or hindrances.

Exam Probability: **High**

24. *Answer choices:*
(see index for correct answer)

- a. positive discrimination
- b. cultural dissonance
- c. cultural Relativism

Guidance: level 1

:: Leadership ::

_____ is a theory of leadership where a leader works with teams to identify needed change, creating a vision to guide the change through inspiration, and executing the change in tandem with committed members of a group; it is an integral part of the Full Range Leadership Model. _____ serves to enhance the motivation, morale, and job performance of followers through a variety of mechanisms; these include connecting the follower's sense of identity and self to a project and to the collective identity of the organization; being a role model for followers in order to inspire them and to raise their interest in the project; challenging followers to take greater ownership for their work, and understanding the strengths and weaknesses of followers, allowing the leader to align followers with tasks that enhance their performance.

Exam Probability: **Low**

25. *Answer choices:*

(see index for correct answer)

- a. European Center for Leadership Development
- b. Spirit of Enniskillen Trust
- c. Servant leadership
- d. Transformational leadership

Guidance: level 1

:: Ethically disputed business practices ::

An _____ in US labor law refers to certain actions taken by employers or unions that violate the National Labor Relations Act of 1935 29 U.S.C. § 151–169 and other legislation. Such acts are investigated by the National Labor Relations Board.

Exam Probability: **Medium**

26. *Answer choices:*

(see index for correct answer)

- a. Bill and hold
- b. Off-label use
- c. Unfair labor practice
- d. Two sets of books

Guidance: level 1

:: Employment ::

A flat organization has an organizational structure with few or no levels of middle management between staff and executives. An organization's structure refers to the nature of the distribution of the units and positions within it, also to the nature of the relationships among those units and positions. Tall and flat organizations differ based on how many levels of management are present in the organization, and how much control managers are endowed with.

Exam Probability: **Low**

27. *Answer choices:*

(see index for correct answer)

- a. Work experience
- b. Delayering
- c. Work sharing
- d. In-basket test

Guidance: level 1

:: Validity (statistics) ::

In psychometrics, _____ refers to the extent to which a measure represents all facets of a given construct. For example, a depression scale may lack _____ if it only assesses the affective dimension of depression but fails to take into account the behavioral dimension. An element of subjectivity exists in relation to determining _____ , which requires a degree of agreement about what a particular personality trait such as extraversion represents. A disagreement about a personality trait will prevent the gain of a high _____ .

Exam Probability: **Medium**

28. *Answer choices:*

(see index for correct answer)

- a. Content validity
- b. Concurrent validity

- c. Construct validity
- d. Validation

Guidance: level 1

:: ::

> _____ is the process of collecting, analyzing and/or reporting information regarding the performance of an individual, group, organization, system or component. _____ is not a new concept, some of the earliest records of human activity relate to the counting or recording of activities.

Exam Probability: **Medium**

29. *Answer choices:*

(see index for correct answer)

- a. co-culture
- b. Performance measurement
- c. Sarbanes-Oxley act of 2002
- d. similarity-attraction theory

Guidance: level 1

:: Training ::

_____ is the process of ensuring compliance with laws, regulations, rules, standards, or social norms. By enforcing laws and regulations, governments attempt to effectuate successful implementation of policies.

Exam Probability: **High**

30. *Answer choices:*

(see index for correct answer)

- a. Safety Services Company
- b. Confidence-based learning
- c. Youth Training Scheme
- d. Enforcement

Guidance: level 1

:: Trade unions ::

A _____ is an association of workers forming a legal unit or legal personhood, usually called a "bargaining unit", which acts as bargaining agent and legal representative for a unit of employees in all matters of law or right arising from or in the administration of a collective agreement. Labour unions typically fund the formal organisation, head office, and legal team functions of the labour union through regular fees or union dues. The delegate staff of the labour union representation in the workforce are made up of workplace volunteers who are appointed by members in democratic elections.

Exam Probability: **Medium**

31. *Answer choices:*

(see index for correct answer)

- a. Trade union
- b. Bump
- c. Opposition to trade unions
- d. Independent union

Guidance: level 1

:: Organizational theory ::

> Decentralisation is the process by which the activities of an organization, particularly those regarding planning and decision making, are distributed or delegated away from a central, authoritative location or group. Concepts of _____ have been applied to group dynamics and management science in private businesses and organizations, political science, law and public administration, economics, money and technology.

Exam Probability: **High**

32. *Answer choices:*

(see index for correct answer)

- a. Participatory management
- b. Organisational semiotics
- c. Decentralization
- d. Sociogram

Guidance: level 1

:: Management ::

In organizational studies, _____ is the efficient and effective development of an organization's resources when they are needed. Such resources may include financial resources, inventory, human skills, production resources, or information technology and natural resources.

Exam Probability: **Low**

33. *Answer choices:*
(see index for correct answer)

- a. Project management
- b. Authoritarian leadership style
- c. Public sector consulting
- d. Clean-sheet review

Guidance: level 1

:: Business process ::

Outsourcing is an agreement in which one company hires another company to be responsible for a planned or existing activity that is or could be done internally,and sometimes involves transferring employees and assets from one firm to another.

Exam Probability: **Medium**

34. *Answer choices:*
(see index for correct answer)

- a. Business process outsourcing
- b. Signavio
- c. Process capital
- d. Process mining

Guidance: level 1

:: Corporate governance ::

An _____ is generally a person responsible for running an organization, although the exact nature of the role varies depending on the organization. In many militaries, an _____ , or "XO," is the second-in-command, reporting to the commanding officer. The XO is typically responsible for the management of day-to-day activities, freeing the commander to concentrate on strategy and planning the unit's next move.

Exam Probability: **High**

35. *Answer choices:*

(see index for correct answer)

- a. Chief governing officer
- b. Chief administrative officer
- c. Model Audit Rule 205
- d. Chief content officer

Guidance: level 1

:: Employment ::

_____ is a relationship between two parties, usually based on a contract where work is paid for, where one party, which may be a corporation, for profit, not-for-profit organization, co-operative or other entity is the employer and the other is the employee. Employees work in return for payment, which may be in the form of an hourly wage, by piecework or an annual salary, depending on the type of work an employee does or which sector she or he is working in. Employees in some fields or sectors may receive gratuities, bonus payment or stock options. In some types of _____, employees may receive benefits in addition to payment. Benefits can include health insurance, housing, disability insurance or use of a gym. _____ is typically governed by _____ laws, regulations or legal contracts.

Exam Probability: **Low**

36. *Answer choices:*

(see index for correct answer)

- a. Vanpool
- b. Blacklist
- c. The Kingdom of Could Be You
- d. Employment

Guidance: level 1

:: Human resource management ::

> _____ is the corporate management term for the act of reorganizing the legal, ownership, operational, or other structures of a company for the purpose of making it more profitable, or better organized for its present needs. Other reasons for _____ include a change of ownership or ownership structure, demerger, or a response to a crisis or major change in the business such as bankruptcy, repositioning, or buyout. _____ may also be described as corporate _____ , debt _____ and financial _____ .

Exam Probability: **Medium**

37. *Answer choices:*

(see index for correct answer)

- a. Job performance
- b. Restructuring
- c. Professional employer organization
- d. Vendor management system

Guidance: level 1

:: Self ::

_____ is a term that has been used in various psychology theories, often in different ways. The term was originally introduced by the organismic theorist Kurt Goldstein for the motive to realize one's full potential. In Goldstein's view, it is the organism's master motive, the only real motive: "the tendency to actualize itself as fully as possible is the basic drive ... the drive of _____ ." Carl Rogers similarly wrote of "the curative force in psychotherapy man's tendency to actualize himself, to become his potentialities ... to express and activate all the capacities of the organism." The concept was brought most fully to prominence in Abraham Maslow's hierarchy of needs theory as the final level of psychological development that can be achieved when all basic and mental needs are essentially fulfilled and the "actualization" of the full personal potential takes place, although he adapted this viewpoint later on in life to be more flexible.

Exam Probability: **High**

38. *Answer choices:*

(see index for correct answer)

- a. Narcissism
- b. Egocentrism
- c. Self-actualization
- d. Generalized other

Guidance: level 1

:: Employment compensation ::

An _____ is an employee benefit program that assists employees with personal problems and/or work-related problems that may impact their job performance, health, mental and emotional well-being. EAPs generally offer free and confidential assessments, short-term counseling, referrals, and follow-up services for employees and their household members. EAP counselors also work in a consultative role with managers and supervisors to address employee and organizational challenges and needs. Many corporations, academic institution and/or government agencies are active in helping organizations prevent and cope with workplace violence, trauma, and other emergency response situations. There is a variety of support programs offered for employees. Even though EAPs are mainly aimed at work-related problems, there are a variety of programs that can assist with problems outside of the workplace. EAPs have grown over the years, and are more desirable economically and socially.

Exam Probability: **Medium**

39. *Answer choices:*

(see index for correct answer)

- a. Employee assistance program
- b. Wage payment systems
- c. Sick leave
- d. My Family Care

Guidance: level 1

:: Business ::

_____ is a trade policy that does not restrict imports or exports; it can also be understood as the free market idea applied to international trade. In government, _____ is predominantly advocated by political parties that hold liberal economic positions while economically left-wing and nationalist political parties generally support protectionism, the opposite of _____ .

Exam Probability: **Low**

40. *Answer choices:*

(see index for correct answer)

- a. Free Trade
- b. Customer experience
- c. Policy capturing
- d. Business interoperability interface

Guidance: level 1

:: Office work ::

The _____ is a concept in management developed by Laurence J. Peter, which observes that people in a hierarchy tend to rise to their "level of incompetence". In other words, an employee is promoted based on their success in previous jobs until they reach a level at which they are no longer competent, as skills in one job do not necessarily translate to another. The concept was elucidated in the 1969 book The _____ by Peter and Raymond Hull.

Exam Probability: **Low**

41. *Answer choices:*

(see index for correct answer)

- a. Salaryman
- b. Workplace politics
- c. Service bureau
- d. Office of the future

Guidance: level 1

:: Human resource management ::

An _____ is a software application that enables the electronic handling of recruitment needs. An ATS can be implemented or accessed online on an enterprise or small business level, depending on the needs of the company and there is also free and open source ATS software available. An ATS is very similar to customer relationship management systems, but are designed for recruitment tracking purposes. In many cases they filter applications automatically based on given criteria such as keywords, skills, former employers, years of experience and schools attended. This has caused many to adapt resume optimization techniques similar to those used in search engine optimization when creating and formatting their résumé.

Exam Probability: **High**

42. *Answer choices:*

(see index for correct answer)

- a. Applicant tracking system
- b. Workforce planning
- c. Induction training
- d. Job analysis

Guidance: level 1

:: Behavioral and social facets of systemic risk ::

_____ is the difficulty in understanding an issue and effectively making decisions when one has too much information about that issue. Generally, the term is associated with the excessive quantity of daily information. _____ most likely originated from information theory, which are studies in the storage, preservation, communication, compression, and extraction of information. The term, _____, was first used in Bertram Gross' 1964 book, The Managing of Organizations, and it was further popularized by Alvin Toffler in his bestselling 1970 book Future Shock. Speier et al. stated.

Exam Probability: **Low**

43. *Answer choices:*

(see index for correct answer)

- a. Behavioral Finance
- b. Emotional contagion
- c. Information overload
- d. Collective intelligence

Guidance: level 1

:: Human resource management ::

_____ , also known as management by results, was first popularized by Peter Drucker in his 1954 book The Practice of Management. _____ is the process of defining specific objectives within an organization that management can convey to organization members, then deciding on how to achieve each objective in sequence. This process allows managers to take work that needs to be done one step at a time to allow for a calm, yet productive work environment. This process also helps organization members to see their accomplishments as they achieve each objective, which reinforces a positive work environment and a sense of achievement. An important part of MBO is the measurement and comparison of an employee's actual performance with the standards set. Ideally, when employees themselves have been involved with the goal-setting and choosing the course of action to be followed by them, they are more likely to fulfill their responsibilities.According to George S. Odiorne, the system of _____ can be described as a process whereby the superior and subordinate jointly identify common goals, define each individual's major areas of responsibility in terms of the results expected of him or her, and use these measures as guides for operating the unit and assessing the contribution of each of its members.

Exam Probability: **Medium**

44. *Answer choices:*

(see index for correct answer)

- a. Inclusion
- b. human resource
- c. Open plan

- d. Health human resources

Guidance: level 1

:: Grounds for termination of employment ::

> _____ is a habitual pattern of absence from a duty or obligation without good reason. Generally, _____ is unplanned absences. _____ has been viewed as an indicator of poor individual performance, as well as a breach of an implicit contract between employee and employer. It is seen as a management problem, and framed in economic or quasi-economic terms. More recent scholarship seeks to understand _____ as an indicator of psychological, medical, or social adjustment to work.

Exam Probability: **High**

45. *Answer choices:*
(see index for correct answer)

- a. Defense Intelligence Community Whistleblower Protection
- b. Department of Defense Whistleblower Program
- c. Absenteeism
- d. Presidential Policy Directive 19

Guidance: level 1

:: ::

An _____ is a period of work experience offered by an organization for a limited period of time. Once confined to medical graduates, the term is now used for a wide range of placements in businesses, non-profit organizations and government agencies. They are typically undertaken by students and graduates looking to gain relevant skills and experience in a particular field. Employers benefit from these placements because they often recruit employees from their best interns, who have known capabilities, thus saving time and money in the long run. _____ s are usually arranged by third-party organizations which recruit interns on behalf of industry groups. Rules vary from country to country about when interns should be regarded as employees. The system can be open to exploitation by unscrupulous employers.

Exam Probability: **Low**

46. *Answer choices:*

(see index for correct answer)

- a. similarity-attraction theory
- b. personal values
- c. process perspective
- d. information systems assessment

Guidance: level 1

:: Asset ::

In financial accounting, an _____ is any resource owned by the business. Anything tangible or intangible that can be owned or controlled to produce value and that is held by a company to produce positive economic value is an _____. Simply stated, _____s represent value of ownership that can be converted into cash. The balance sheet of a firm records the monetary value of the _____s owned by that firm. It covers money and other valuables belonging to an individual or to a business.

Exam Probability: **Low**

47. *Answer choices:*

(see index for correct answer)

- a. Fixed asset
- b. Asset

Guidance: level 1

:: Personal finance ::

_____ is an arrangement in which a portion of an employee's income is paid out at a later date after which the income was earned. Examples of _____ include pensions, retirement plans, and employee stock options. The primary benefit of most _____ is the deferral of tax to the date at which the employee receives the income.

Exam Probability: **High**

48. *Answer choices:*

(see index for correct answer)

- a. Deferred compensation
- b. Likelemba
- c. Repossession
- d. Courtesy signing

Guidance: level 1

:: Occupational safety and health organizations ::

The _____ is the United States federal agency responsible for conducting research and making recommendations for the prevention of work-related injury and illness. NIOSH is part of the Centers for Disease Control and Prevention within the U.S. Department of Health and Human Services.

Exam Probability: **Low**

49. *Answer choices:*

(see index for correct answer)

- a. American Conference of Governmental Industrial Hygienists
- b. National Institute for Occupational Safety and Health
- c. Health and Safety Executive for Northern Ireland
- d. Canadian Centre for Occupational Health and Safety

Guidance: level 1

:: Labour law ::

A _____ is a legal contract that is meant to limit the liability of an employer whose employees are romantically involved. An employer may choose to require a _____ when a romantic relationship within the company becomes known, in order to indemnify the company in case the employees' romantic relationship fails, primarily so that one party can't bring a sexual harassment lawsuit against the company. To that end, the _____ states that the relationship is consensual, and both parties of the relationship must sign it. The _____ may also stipulate rules for acceptable romantic behavior in the workplace.

Exam Probability: **Medium**

50. *Answer choices:*

(see index for correct answer)

- a. Maximum medical improvement
- b. Agency worker law
- c. Involvement and Participation Association
- d. Transfers of Undertakings Directive

Guidance: level 1

:: Recruitment ::

The _____ is an American nonprofit professional association established in 1956 in Bethlehem, Pennsylvania, for college career services, recruiting practitioners, and others who wish to hire the college educated.

Exam Probability: **High**

51. *Answer choices:*

(see index for correct answer)

- a. National Association of Colleges and Employers
- b. Blue Octopus Recruitment Ltd
- c. Multiple mini interview
- d. Probation

Guidance: level 1

:: Validity (statistics) ::

In psychometrics, _____ is the extent to which a score on a scale or test predicts scores on some criterion measure.

Exam Probability: **Medium**

52. *Answer choices:*

(see index for correct answer)

- a. Concurrent validity
- b. Internal validity
- c. Verification and validation
- d. Predictive validity

Guidance: level 1

:: Financial terminology ::

_____ is the cost of maintaining a certain standard of living. Changes in the _____ over time are often operationalized in a cost-of-living index. _____ calculations are also used to compare the cost of maintaining a certain standard of living in different geographic areas. Differences in _____ between locations can also be measured in terms of purchasing power parity rates.

Exam Probability: **Medium**

53. *Answer choices:*

(see index for correct answer)

- a. Nancy Reagan defense
- b. Earnings test
- c. Bulge bracket
- d. Free float

Guidance: level 1

:: ::

A _____ service is an online platform which people use to build social networks or social relationship with other people who share similar personal or career interests, activities, backgrounds or real-life connections.

Exam Probability: **Medium**

54. *Answer choices:*

(see index for correct answer)

- a. interpersonal communication
- b. co-culture
- c. levels of analysis
- d. open system

Guidance: level 1

:: ::

_____ involves the development of an action plan designed to motivate and guide a person or group toward a goal. _____ can be guided by goal-setting criteria such as SMART criteria. _____ is a major component of personal-development and management literature.

Exam Probability: **Low**

55. *Answer choices:*

(see index for correct answer)

- a. Character
- b. information systems assessment
- c. corporate values
- d. Goal setting

Guidance: level 1

:: Cognitive biases ::

The _____ is a type of immediate judgement discrepancy, or cognitive bias, where a person making an initial assessment of another person, place, or thing will assume ambiguous information based upon concrete information. A simplified example of the _____ is when an individual noticing that the person in the photograph is attractive, well groomed, and properly attired, assumes, using a mental heuristic, that the person in the photograph is a good person based upon the rules of that individual's social concept. This constant error in judgment is reflective of the individual's preferences, prejudices, ideology, aspirations, and social perception. The _____ is an evaluation by an individual and can affect the perception of a decision, action, idea, business, person, group, entity, or other whenever concrete data is generalized or influences ambiguous information.

Exam Probability: **Medium**

56. *Answer choices:*

(see index for correct answer)

- a. Fundamental attribution error
- b. End-of-history illusion
- c. Halo effect
- d. Scope neglect

Guidance: level 1

:: ::

A _____ is a research instrument consisting of a series of questions for the purpose of gathering information from respondents. The _____ was invented by the Statistical Society of London in 1838.

Exam Probability: **Medium**

57. *Answer choices:*

(see index for correct answer)

- a. deep-level diversity
- b. information systems assessment
- c. surface-level diversity
- d. Questionnaire

Guidance: level 1

:: Personnel economics ::

In labor economics, the _____ hypothesis argues that wages, at least in some markets, form in a way that is not market-clearing. Specifically, it points to the incentive for managers to pay their employees more than the market-clearing wage in order to increase their productivity or efficiency, or reduce costs associated with turnover, in industries where the costs of replacing labor are high. This increased labor productivity and/or decreased costs pay for the higher wages.

Exam Probability: **Low**

58. *Answer choices:*

(see index for correct answer)

- a. Efficiency wage
- b. Personnel economics
- c. Work self-efficacy

Guidance: level 1

:: Employment of foreign-born ::

_____ refers to the international labor pool of workers, including those employed by multinational companies and connected through a global system of networking and production, immigrant workers, transient migrant workers, telecommuting workers, those in export-oriented employment, contingent work or other precarious employment. As of 2012, the global labor pool consisted of approximately 3 billion workers, around 200 million unemployed.

Exam Probability: **High**

59. *Answer choices:*

(see index for correct answer)

- a. Foreign born
- b. Optional Practical Training
- c. Global workforce
- d. H-2B visa

Guidance: level 1

Information systems

Information systems (IS) are formal, sociotechnical, organizational systems designed to collect, process, store, and distribute information. In a sociotechnical perspective Information Systems are composed by four components: technology, process, people and organizational structure.

:: Intrusion detection systems ::

An _____ is a device or software application that monitors a network or systems for malicious activity or policy violations. Any malicious activity or violation is typically reported either to an administrator or collected centrally using a security information and event management system. A SIEM system combines outputs from multiple sources, and uses alarm filtering techniques to distinguish malicious activity from false alarms.

Exam Probability: **High**

1. *Answer choices:*

(see index for correct answer)

- a. Intrusion detection system
- b. Bro
- c. Application protocol-based intrusion detection system
- d. Network intrusion detection system

Guidance: level 1

:: Marketing by medium ::

_____ or viral advertising is a business strategy that uses existing social networks to promote a product. Its name refers to how consumers spread information about a product with other people in their social networks, much in the same way that a virus spreads from one person to another. It can be delivered by word of mouth or enhanced by the network effects of the Internet and mobile networks.

Exam Probability: **Low**

2. *Answer choices:*

(see index for correct answer)

- a. Online advertising
- b. Social intelligence architect

- c. Social video marketing
- d. Viral marketing

Guidance: level 1

:: Survey methodology ::

A _____ is the procedure of systematically acquiring and recording information about the members of a given population. The term is used mostly in connection with national population and housing _____ es; other common _____ es include agriculture, business, and traffic _____ es. The United Nations defines the essential features of population and housing _____ es as "individual enumeration, universality within a defined territory, simultaneity and defined periodicity", and recommends that population _____ es be taken at least every 10 years. United Nations recommendations also cover _____ topics to be collected, official definitions, classifications and other useful information to co-ordinate international practice.

Exam Probability: **Medium**

3. *Answer choices:*

(see index for correct answer)

- a. Enterprise feedback management
- b. Self-report study
- c. Scale analysis
- d. Census

Guidance: level 1

:: E-commerce ::

> _____, cybersecurity or information technology security is the protection of computer systems from theft or damage to their hardware, software or electronic data, as well as from disruption or misdirection of the services they provide.

Exam Probability: **Low**

4. *Answer choices:*

(see index for correct answer)

- a. Freelance marketplace
- b. Online shopping
- c. Computer security
- d. Mobilpenge

Guidance: level 1

:: Payment systems ::

_____s are part of a payment system issued by financial institutions, such as a bank, to a customer that enables its owner to access the funds in the customer's designated bank accounts, or through a credit account and make payments by electronic funds transfer and access automated teller machines. Such cards are known by a variety of names including bank cards, ATM cards, MAC, client cards, key cards or cash cards.

Exam Probability: **High**

5. *Answer choices:*

(see index for correct answer)

- a. Ready Financial
- b. Official Payments Corporation
- c. Payment card
- d. Bad check restitution program

Guidance: level 1

:: Computer memory ::

_____ is a type of non-volatile memory used in computers and other electronic devices. Data stored in ROM can only be modified slowly, with difficulty, or not at all, so it is mainly used to store firmware or application software in plug-in cartridges.

Exam Probability: **Low**

6. Answer choices:

(see index for correct answer)

- a. Phison
- b. Read-only memory
- c. IBM 2361 Large Capacity Storage
- d. Far pointer

Guidance: level 1

:: Management ::

In business, a _____ is the attribute that allows an organization to outperform its competitors. A _____ may include access to natural resources, such as high-grade ores or a low-cost power source, highly skilled labor, geographic location, high entry barriers, and access to new technology.

Exam Probability: **Low**

7. Answer choices:

(see index for correct answer)

- a. Task-oriented and relationship-oriented leadership
- b. Intelligent customer
- c. Formula for change
- d. Knowledge ecosystem

Guidance: level 1

:: ::

Within the Internet, _____ s are formed by the rules and procedures of the _____ System. Any name registered in the DNS is a _____. _____ s are used in various networking contexts and for application-specific naming and addressing purposes. In general, a _____ represents an Internet Protocol resource, such as a personal computer used to access the Internet, a server computer hosting a web site, or the web site itself or any other service communicated via the Internet. In 2017, 330.6 million _____ s had been registered.

Exam Probability: **High**

8. *Answer choices:*

(see index for correct answer)

- a. interpersonal communication
- b. co-culture
- c. Character
- d. similarity-attraction theory

Guidance: level 1

:: E-commerce ::

A _____ is a plastic payment card that can be used instead of cash when making purchases. It is similar to a credit card, but unlike a credit card, the money is immediately transferred directly from the cardholder's bank account when performing a transaction.

Exam Probability: **Medium**

9. *Answer choices:*

(see index for correct answer)

- a. Net settlement
- b. ISO 8583
- c. Point of sale
- d. Storenvy

Guidance: level 1

:: Advertising techniques ::

The _____ is a story from the Trojan War about the subterfuge that the Greeks used to enter the independent city of Troy and win the war. In the canonical version, after a fruitless 10-year siege, the Greeks constructed a huge wooden horse, and hid a select force of men inside including Odysseus. The Greeks pretended to sail away, and the Trojans pulled the horse into their city as a victory trophy. That night the Greek force crept out of the horse and opened the gates for the rest of the Greek army, which had sailed back under cover of night. The Greeks entered and destroyed the city of Troy, ending the war.

Exam Probability: **Medium**

10. *Answer choices:*

(see index for correct answer)

- a. Trojan horse
- b. Testimonial
- c. Roll-in
- d. Unipole sign

Guidance: level 1

:: Costs ::

In economics, _____ is the total economic cost of production and is made up of variable cost, which varies according to the quantity of a good produced and includes inputs such as labour and raw materials, plus fixed cost, which is independent of the quantity of a good produced and includes inputs that cannot be varied in the short term: fixed costs such as buildings and machinery, including sunk costs if any. Since cost is measured per unit of time, it is a flow variable.

Exam Probability: **High**

11. *Answer choices:*

(see index for correct answer)

- a. Opportunity cost of capital

- b. Prospective costs
- c. Further processing cost
- d. Total cost

Guidance: level 1

:: IT risk management ::

_____ involves a set of policies, tools and procedures to enable the recovery or continuation of vital technology infrastructure and systems following a natural or human-induced disaster. _____ focuses on the IT or technology systems supporting critical business functions, as opposed to business continuity, which involves keeping all essential aspects of a business functioning despite significant disruptive events. _____ can therefore be considered as a subset of business continuity.

Exam Probability: **Medium**

12. *Answer choices:*
(see index for correct answer)

- a. Disaster recovery
- b. Business continuity
- c. Information assurance

Guidance: level 1

:: Management ::

_____ is the kind of knowledge that is difficult to transfer to another person by means of writing it down or verbalizing it. For example, that London is in the United Kingdom is a piece of explicit knowledge that can be written down, transmitted, and understood by a recipient. However, the ability to speak a language, ride a bicycle, knead dough, play a musical instrument, or design and use complex equipment requires all sorts of knowledge that is not always known explicitly, even by expert practitioners, and which is difficult or impossible to explicitly transfer to other people.

Exam Probability: **Low**

13. *Answer choices:*

(see index for correct answer)

- a. Value migration
- b. Personal offshoring
- c. Director
- d. Resource breakdown structure

Guidance: level 1

:: Reputation management ::

_____ refers to the influencing and controlling of an individual's or group's reputation. Originally a public relations term, the growth of the internet and social media, along with _____ companies, have made search results a core part of an individual's or group's reputation. Online _____, sometimes abbreviated as ORM, focuses on the management of product and service search website results. Ethical grey areas include mug shot removal sites, astroturfing customer review sites, censoring negative complaints, and using search engine optimization tactics to influence results.

Exam Probability: **Low**

14. *Answer choices:*

(see index for correct answer)

- a. Whuffie
- b. Meta-moderation system
- c. Yasni
- d. Hilltop algorithm

Guidance: level 1

:: Management ::

_____ is the identification of an organization's assets, followed by the development, documentation, and implementation of policies and procedures for protecting these assets.

Exam Probability: **High**

15. *Answer choices:*

(see index for correct answer)

- a. Cross ownership
- b. Security management
- c. Total security management
- d. Design leadership

Guidance: level 1

:: User interfaces ::

_____, keystroke biometrics, typing dynamics and lately typing biometrics, is the detailed timing information which describes exactly when each key was pressed and when it was released as a person is typing at a computer keyboard.

Exam Probability: **Low**

16. *Answer choices:*

(see index for correct answer)

- a. Keystroke dynamics
- b. Plesk
- c. Virtual console
- d. SDL Passolo

Guidance: level 1

:: Network management ::

_____ is the process of administering and managing computer networks. Services provided by this discipline include fault analysis, performance management, provisioning of networks and maintaining the quality of service. Software that enables network administrators to perform their functions is called _____ software.

Exam Probability: **High**

17. *Answer choices:*

(see index for correct answer)

- a. Joint Inter-Domain Management
- b. Network management
- c. Op5 Monitor
- d. Out-of-band infrastructure

Guidance: level 1

:: Data management ::

An _____ is any kind of information system which improves the functions of enterprise business processes by integration. This means typically offering high quality of service, dealing with large volumes of data and capable of supporting some large and possibly complex organization or enterprise. An EIS must be able to be used by all parts and all levels of an enterprise.

Exam Probability: **Low**

18. *Answer choices:*

(see index for correct answer)

- a. Information integration
- b. Uniform data access
- c. Enterprise information system
- d. PL/Perl

Guidance: level 1

:: Teams ::

A _____ usually refers to a group of individuals who work together from different geographic locations and rely on communication technology such as email, FAX, and video or voice conferencing services in order to collaborate. The term can also refer to groups or teams that work together asynchronously or across organizational levels. Powell, Piccoli and Ives define _____ s as "groups of geographically, organizationally and/or time dispersed workers brought together by information and telecommunication technologies to accomplish one or more organizational tasks." According to Ale Ebrahim et. al., _____ s can also be defined as "small temporary groups of geographically, organizationally and/or time dispersed knowledge workers who coordinate their work predominantly with electronic information and communication technologies in order to accomplish one or more organization tasks."

Exam Probability: **Low**

19. *Answer choices:*

(see index for correct answer)

- a. team composition
- b. Virtual team

Guidance: level 1

:: Information systems ::

_____s are information systems that are developed in response to corporate business initiative. They are intended to give competitive advantage to the organization. They may deliver a product or service that is at a lower cost, that is differentiated, that focuses on a particular market segment, or is innovative.

Exam Probability: **High**

20. *Answer choices:*

(see index for correct answer)

- a. Laws of information systems
- b. SAP Information Interchange OnDemand
- c. System of record
- d. Strategic information system

Guidance: level 1

:: Data management ::

Given organizations' increasing dependency on information technology to run their operations, Business continuity planning covers the entire organization, and Disaster recovery focuses on IT.

Exam Probability: **Low**

21. *Answer choices:*

(see index for correct answer)

- a. Disaster recovery plan
- b. Data conditioning
- c. Online analytical processing
- d. ROOT

Guidance: level 1

:: ::

A _____ is a knowledge base website on which users collaboratively modify content and structure directly from the web browser. In a typical _____, text is written using a simplified markup language and often edited with the help of a rich-text editor.

Exam Probability: **Medium**

22. *Answer choices:*

(see index for correct answer)

- a. functional perspective
- b. Wiki
- c. imperative
- d. surface-level diversity

Guidance: level 1

:: Information technology organisations ::

The Internet Corporation for Assigned Names and Numbers is a nonprofit organization responsible for coordinating the maintenance and procedures of several databases related to the namespaces and numerical spaces of the Internet, ensuring the network's stable and secure operation. _____ performs the actual technical maintenance work of the Central Internet Address pools and DNS root zone registries pursuant to the Internet Assigned Numbers Authority function contract. The contract regarding the IANA stewardship functions between _____ and the National Telecommunications and Information Administration of the United States Department of Commerce ended on October 1, 2016, formally transitioning the functions to the global multistakeholder community.

Exam Probability: **Medium**

23. *Answer choices:*

(see index for correct answer)

- a. ICANN
- b. ArabDev
- c. ITCRA
- d. Girl Geek Dinners

Guidance: level 1

:: Google services ::

_____ is a web mapping service developed by Google. It offers satellite imagery, aerial photography, street maps, 360° panoramic views of streets, real-time traffic conditions, and route planning for traveling by foot, car, bicycle and air, or public transportation.

Exam Probability: **Low**

24. *Answer choices:*

(see index for correct answer)

- a. Google Maps
- b. Google Videos
- c. Google Ngram Viewer
- d. Chrome Web Store

Guidance: level 1

:: Computer access control ::

_____ is the act of confirming the truth of an attribute of a single piece of data claimed true by an entity. In contrast with identification, which refers to the act of stating or otherwise indicating a claim purportedly attesting to a person or thing's identity, _____ is the process of actually confirming that identity. It might involve confirming the identity of a person by validating their identity documents, verifying the authenticity of a website with a digital certificate, determining the age of an artifact by carbon dating, or ensuring that a product is what its packaging and labeling claim to be. In other words, _____ often involves verifying the validity of at least one form of identification.

Exam Probability: **Medium**

25. *Answer choices:*

(see index for correct answer)

- a. Internet Authentication Service
- b. WS-Trust
- c. Authentication
- d. Software token

Guidance: level 1

:: Information systems ::

_____ is the process of creating, sharing, using and managing the knowledge and information of an organisation. It refers to a multidisciplinary approach to achieving organisational objectives by making the best use of knowledge.

Exam Probability: **High**

26. *Answer choices:*

(see index for correct answer)

- a. Notify NYC
- b. Self-service software
- c. Management information system

- d. Knowledge management

Guidance: level 1

:: Satellite navigation systems ::

> _____ Galilei was an Italian astronomer, physicist and engineer, sometimes described as a polymath. _____ has been called the "father of observational astronomy", the "father of modern physics", the "father of the scientific method", and the "father of modern science".

Exam Probability: **Low**

27. *Answer choices:*
(see index for correct answer)

- a. GPS Block IIF
- b. Virtual Reference Station
- c. Galileo
- d. Multi-functional Satellite Augmentation System

Guidance: level 1

:: Finance ::

_____ is a financial estimate intended to help buyers and owners determine the direct and indirect costs of a product or system. It is a management accounting concept that can be used in full cost accounting or even ecological economics where it includes social costs.

Exam Probability: **Medium**

28. *Answer choices:*

(see index for correct answer)

- a. Minimum acceptable rate of return
- b. Tear sheet
- c. Cell Captive
- d. Quantitative easing

Guidance: level 1

:: Strategic management ::

In marketing strategy, first-mover advantage is the advantage gained by the initial significant occupant of a market segment. First-mover advantage may be gained by technological leadership, or early purchase of resources.

Exam Probability: **Medium**

29. *Answer choices:*

(see index for correct answer)

- a. First mover advantage
- b. business unit
- c. Journal of Contingencies and Crisis Management
- d. BSC SWOT

Guidance: level 1

:: Web security exploits ::

> A _____ is a baked or cooked food that is small, flat and sweet. It usually contains flour, sugar and some type of oil or fat. It may include other ingredients such as raisins, oats, chocolate chips, nuts, etc.

Exam Probability: **High**

30. *Answer choices:*

(see index for correct answer)

- a. Evil twin
- b. PLA Unit 61398
- c. Cross-site tracing
- d. Browser security

Guidance: level 1

:: Business planning ::

> _____ is an organization's process of defining its strategy, or direction, and making decisions on allocating its resources to pursue this strategy. It may also extend to control mechanisms for guiding the implementation of the strategy. _____ became prominent in corporations during the 1960s and remains an important aspect of strategic management. It is executed by strategic planners or strategists, who involve many parties and research sources in their analysis of the organization and its relationship to the environment in which it competes.

Exam Probability: **Low**

31. *Answer choices:*

(see index for correct answer)

- a. Open Options Corporation
- b. Community Futures
- c. Gap analysis
- d. Strategic planning

Guidance: level 1

:: Google services ::

_____ is a discontinued image organizer and image viewer for organizing and editing digital photos, plus an integrated photo-sharing website, originally created by a company named Lifescape in 2002. In July 2004, Google acquired _____ from Lifescape and began offering it as freeware. "_____" is a blend of the name of Spanish painter Pablo Picasso, the phrase mi casa and "pic" for pictures.

Exam Probability: **Medium**

32. *Answer choices:*

(see index for correct answer)

- a. Google Contacts
- b. Picasa
- c. Google Search
- d. Zygote Body

Guidance: level 1

:: Payment systems ::

_____ is a mobile phone-based money transfer, financing and microfinancing service, launched in 2007 by Vodafone for Safaricom and Vodacom, the largest mobile network operators in Kenya and Tanzania. It has since expanded to Afghanistan, South Africa, India and in 2014 to Romania and in 2015 to Albania. _____ allows users to deposit, withdraw, transfer money and pay for goods and services easily with a mobile device.

Exam Probability: **Low**

33. *Answer choices:*

(see index for correct answer)

- a. Payment service provider
- b. Mobile purchasing
- c. M-Pesa
- d. MoneyGram

Guidance: level 1

:: Production economics ::

_____ is a way of producing goods and services that relies on self-organizing communities of individuals. In such communities, the labor of a large number of people is coordinated towards a shared outcome.

Exam Probability: **Medium**

34. *Answer choices:*

(see index for correct answer)

- a. Economic batch quantity
- b. Peer production
- c. Production theory
- d. Economies of scale

Guidance: level 1

:: Information and communication technologies for development ::

_____ is a non-profit initiative established with the goal of transforming education for children around the world; this goal was to be achieved by creating and distributing educational devices for the developing world, and by creating software and content for those devices.

Exam Probability: **High**

35. *Answer choices:*

(see index for correct answer)

- a. One Laptop per Child
- b. United Nations Information and Communication Technologies Task Force
- c. Web 2.0 for development
- d. WomensHub

Guidance: level 1

:: Financial markets ::

The _____ business model is a business model in which a customer must pay a recurring price at regular intervals for access to a product or service. The model was pioneered by publishers of books and periodicals in the 17th century, and is now used by many businesses and websites.

Exam Probability: **High**

36. *Answer choices:*

(see index for correct answer)

- a. Round lot
- b. TradersStudio
- c. Capital market
- d. Subscription

Guidance: level 1

:: Management ::

The _____ is a strategy performance management tool – a semi-standard structured report, that can be used by managers to keep track of the execution of activities by the staff within their control and to monitor the consequences arising from these actions.

Exam Probability: **Low**

37. *Answer choices:*

(see index for correct answer)

- a. Process management
- b. Balanced scorecard
- c. Corporate recovery
- d. Stovepipe

Guidance: level 1

:: Infographics ::

A _____ is a graphical representation of data, in which "the data is represented by symbols, such as bars in a bar _____ , lines in a line _____ , or slices in a pie _____ ". A _____ can represent tabular numeric data, functions or some kinds of qualitative structure and provides different info.

Exam Probability: **Low**

38. *Answer choices:*

(see index for correct answer)

- a. DataViva
- b. Chart
- c. Patent visualisation
- d. Staircase model

Guidance: level 1

:: Metadata ::

_____ s usage can be discovered by inspection of software applications or application data files through a process of manual or automated Application Discovery and Understanding. Once _____ s are discovered they can be registered in a metadata registry.

Exam Probability: **High**

39. *Answer choices:*

(see index for correct answer)

- a. Exchangeable image file format
- b. International Standard Bibliographic Description
- c. Metadata Working Group
- d. CcREL

Guidance: level 1

:: Statistical laws ::

In statistics and business, a _____ of some distributions of numbers is the portion of the distribution having a large number of occurrences far from the "head" or central part of the distribution. The distribution could involve popularities, random numbers of occurrences of events with various probabilities, etc. The term is often used loosely, with no definition or arbitrary definition, but precise definitions are possible.

Exam Probability: **High**

40. *Answer choices:*

(see index for correct answer)

- a. Long tail
- b. Law of total cumulance
- c. Safety in numbers
- d. Law of the unconscious statistician

Guidance: level 1

:: Data transmission ::

In telecommunication a _____ is the means of connecting one location to another for the purpose of transmitting and receiving digital information. It can also refer to a set of electronics assemblies, consisting of a transmitter and a receiver and the interconnecting data telecommunication circuit. These are governed by a link protocol enabling digital data to be transferred from a data source to a data sink.

Exam Probability: **High**

41. *Answer choices:*

(see index for correct answer)

- a. Data link
- b. Degree of start-stop distortion
- c. Information-transfer transaction
- d. Store-and-forward switching center

Guidance: level 1

:: Supply chain management terms ::

In business and finance, _____ is a system of organizations, people, activities, information, and resources involved in moving a product or service from supplier to customer. _____ activities involve the transformation of natural resources, raw materials, and components into a finished product that is delivered to the end customer. In sophisticated _____ systems, used products may re-enter the _____ at any point where residual value is recyclable. _____ s link value chains.

Exam Probability: **Medium**

42. *Answer choices:*

(see index for correct answer)

- a. Most valuable customers

- b. Final assembly schedule
- c. Consumables
- d. Supply chain

Guidance: level 1

:: Data management ::

_____ is "data [information] that provides information about other data". Many distinct types of _____ exist, among these descriptive _____, structural _____, administrative _____, reference _____ and statistical _____.

Exam Probability: **High**

43. *Answer choices:*
(see index for correct answer)

- a. Linear medium
- b. Metadata
- c. Savepoint
- d. Automatic data processing equipment

Guidance: level 1

:: Contract law ::

_____ refers to a situation where a statement's author cannot successfully dispute its authorship or the validity of an associated contract. The term is often seen in a legal setting when the authenticity of a signature is being challenged. In such an instance, the authenticity is being "repudiated".

Exam Probability: **Medium**

44. *Answer choices:*

(see index for correct answer)

- a. Escalator clause
- b. Cohabitation agreement
- c. Meeting of the minds
- d. Seaworthiness

Guidance: level 1

:: Data quality ::

_____ or data cleaning is the process of detecting and correcting corrupt or inaccurate records from a record set, table, or database and refers to identifying incomplete, incorrect, inaccurate or irrelevant parts of the data and then replacing, modifying, or deleting the dirty or coarse data. _____ may be performed interactively with data wrangling tools, or as batch processing through scripting.

Exam Probability: **High**

45. Answer choices:

(see index for correct answer)

- a. Data cleansing
- b. Data Quality Campaign
- c. Data corruption
- d. Data quality assessment

Guidance: level 1

:: ::

A _____ is server software, or hardware dedicated to running said software, that can satisfy World Wide Web client requests. A _____ can, in general, contain one or more websites. A _____ processes incoming network requests over HTTP and several other related protocols.

Exam Probability: **Low**

46. Answer choices:

(see index for correct answer)

- a. Sarbanes-Oxley act of 2002
- b. personal values
- c. Web server
- d. surface-level diversity

Guidance: level 1

:: Information systems ::

A _____ is an information system used for decision-making, and for the coordination, control, analysis, and visualization of information in an organization; especially in a company.

Exam Probability: **High**

47. *Answer choices:*

(see index for correct answer)

- a. Management information system
- b. Disparate system
- c. Digital firm
- d. Master of Business Informatics

Guidance: level 1

:: Network architecture ::

An _____ is a controlled private network that allows access to partners, vendors and suppliers or an authorized set of customers – normally to a subset of the information accessible from an organization's intranet. An _____ is similar to a DMZ in that it provides access to needed services for authorized parties, without granting access to an organization's entire network. An _____ is a private network organization.

Exam Probability: **High**

48. *Answer choices:*

(see index for correct answer)

- a. Internetworking
- b. client-server

Guidance: level 1

:: Web analytics ::

A click path or _____ is the sequence of hyperlinks one or more website visitors follows on a given site, presented in the order viewed. A visitor's click path may start within the website or at a separate 3rd party website, often a search engine results page, and it continues as a sequence of successive webpages visited by the user. Click paths take call data and can match it to ad sources, keywords, and/or referring domains, in order to capture data.

Exam Probability: **High**

49. *Answer choices:*

(see index for correct answer)

- a. Topsy
- b. Apptegic
- c. Intlock
- d. Telemetry

Guidance: level 1

:: Intelligence (information gathering) ::

_____ comprises the strategies and technologies used by enterprises for the data analysis of business information. BI technologies provide historical, current and predictive views of business operations. Common functions of _____ technologies include reporting, online analytical processing, analytics, data mining, process mining, complex event processing, business performance management, benchmarking, text mining, predictive analytics and prescriptive analytics. BI technologies can handle large amounts of structured and sometimes unstructured data to help identify, develop and otherwise create new strategic business opportunities. They aim to allow for the easy interpretation of these big data. Identifying new opportunities and implementing an effective strategy based on insights can provide businesses with a competitive market advantage and long-term stability.

Exam Probability: **High**

50. *Answer choices:*

(see index for correct answer)

- a. Business intelligence
- b. Village files
- c. Nuclear MASINT
- d. Eclipse Group

Guidance: level 1

:: Industrial design ::

Across the many fields concerned with _____, including information science, computer science, human-computer interaction, communication, and industrial design, there is little agreement over the meaning of the term "_____", although all are related to interaction with computers and other machines with a user interface.

Exam Probability: **High**

51. *Answer choices:*

(see index for correct answer)

- a. Interactivity
- b. Sustainable furniture design
- c. Design and Technology
- d. Bauhaus

Guidance: level 1

:: Computer security standards ::

The _____ for Information Technology Security Evaluation is an international standard for computer security certification. It is currently in version 3.1 revision 5.

Exam Probability: **Low**

52. *Answer choices:*

(see index for correct answer)

- a. IEEE 802.10
- b. BS 7799
- c. IEC 60870-6
- d. Common Criteria

Guidance: level 1

:: Production economics ::

In microeconomics, _____ are the cost advantages that enterprises obtain due to their scale of operation, with cost per unit of output decreasing with increasing scale.

Exam Probability: **High**

53. *Answer choices:*

(see index for correct answer)

- a. Economies of scale
- b. Fragmentation
- c. Marginal product
- d. Average fixed cost

Guidance: level 1

:: Computing output devices ::

An _____ is any piece of computer hardware equipment which converts information into human-readable form.

Exam Probability: **High**

54. *Answer choices:*

(see index for correct answer)

- a. GammaFax
- b. Flicker fixer
- c. Powerwall
- d. Output device

Guidance: level 1

:: ::

A _____ is a computer file which stores data to be used by a computer application or system, including input and output data. A _____ usually does not contain instructions or code to be executed.

Exam Probability: **Low**

55. *Answer choices:*

(see index for correct answer)

- a. co-culture
- b. process perspective
- c. interpersonal communication
- d. cultural

Guidance: level 1

:: Data management ::

Data aggregation is the compiling of information from databases with intent to prepare combined datasets for data processing.

Exam Probability: **High**

56. Answer choices:

(see index for correct answer)

- a. Super column
- b. Tagsistant
- c. Storage area network
- d. Data aggregator

Guidance: level 1

:: Enterprise architecture ::

Enterprise software, also known as _____ software, is computer software used to satisfy the needs of an organization rather than individual users. Such organizations include businesses, schools, interest-based user groups, clubs, charities, and governments. Enterprise software is an integral part of a information system.

Exam Probability: **Medium**

57. Answer choices:

(see index for correct answer)

- a. Association of Enterprise Architects
- b. Enterprise application
- c. Enterprise architecture management
- d. INgage Networks

Guidance: level 1

:: Market research ::

_____s are many different distantly related animals that typically have a long cylindrical tube-like body and no limbs. _____s vary in size from microscopic to over 1 metre in length for marine polychaete _____s , 6.7 metres for the African giant earth _____, Microchaetus rappi, and 58 metres for the marine nemertean _____, Lineus longissimus. Various types of _____ occupy a small variety of parasitic niches, living inside the bodies of other animals. Free-living _____ species do not live on land, but instead, live in marine or freshwater environments, or underground by burrowing. In biology, "_____" refers to an obsolete taxon, vermes, used by Carolus Linnaeus and Jean-Baptiste Lamarck for all non-arthropod invertebrate animals, now seen to be paraphyletic. The name stems from the Old English word wyrm. Most animals called "_____s" are invertebrates, but the term is also used for the amphibian caecilians and the slow _____ Anguis, a legless burrowing lizard. Invertebrate animals commonly called "_____s" include annelids, nematodes, platyhelminthes, marine nemertean _____s, marine Chaetognatha, priapulid _____s, and insect larvae such as grubs and maggots.

Exam Probability: **Medium**

58. *Answer choices:*

(see index for correct answer)

- a. CRISIL
- b. DIY research
- c. Worm
- d. Nielsen VideoScan

Guidance: level 1

:: ::

_____ is the function of specifying access rights/privileges to resources, which is related to information security and computer security in general and to access control in particular. More formally, "to authorize" is to define an access policy. For example, human resources staff are normally authorized to access employee records and this policy is usually formalized as access control rules in a computer system. During operation, the system uses the access control rules to decide whether access requests from consumers shall be approved or disapproved . Resources include individual files or an item's data, computer programs, computer devices and functionality provided by computer applications. Examples of consumers are computer users, computer Software and other Hardware on the computer.

Exam Probability: **Low**

59. *Answer choices:*

(see index for correct answer)

- a. cultural
- b. co-culture
- c. interpersonal communication
- d. Sarbanes-Oxley act of 2002

Guidance: level 1

Marketing

Marketing is the study and management of exchange relationships. Marketing is the business process of creating relationships with and satisfying customers. With its focus on the customer, marketing is one of the premier components of business management.

Marketing is defined by the American Marketing Association as "the activity, set of institutions, and processes for creating, communicating, delivering, and exchanging offerings that have value for customers, clients, partners, and society at large."

A _____ is an organization, usually a group of people or a company, authorized to act as a single entity and recognized as such in law. Early incorporated entities were established by charter. Most jurisdictions now allow the creation of new _____ s through registration.

Exam Probability: **Low**

1. *Answer choices:*

(see index for correct answer)

- a. cultural
- b. hierarchical perspective
- c. Corporation
- d. similarity-attraction theory

Guidance: level 1

:: Management ::

_____ is the process of thinking about the activities required to achieve a desired goal. It is the first and foremost activity to achieve desired results. It involves the creation and maintenance of a plan, such as psychological aspects that require conceptual skills. There are even a couple of tests to measure someone's capability of _____ well. As such, _____ is a fundamental property of intelligent behavior. An important further meaning, often just called " _____ " is the legal context of permitted building developments.

Exam Probability: **Medium**

2. *Answer choices:*

(see index for correct answer)

- a. Competitive heterogeneity
- b. Dynamic enterprise modeling
- c. Real property administrator
- d. Planning

Guidance: level 1

:: Marketing ::

_____, in marketing, manufacturing, call centres and management, is the use of flexible computer-aided manufacturing systems to produce custom output. Such systems combine the low unit costs of mass production processes with the flexibility of individual customization.

Exam Probability: **Low**

3. *Answer choices:*

(see index for correct answer)

- a. Mass customization
- b. Electronic money
- c. Pre-order

- d. Cultural consumer

Guidance: level 1

:: Reputation management ::

A _____ is an astronomical object consisting of a luminous spheroid of plasma held together by its own gravity. The nearest _____ to Earth is the Sun. Many other _____ s are visible to the naked eye from Earth during the night, appearing as a multitude of fixed luminous points in the sky due to their immense distance from Earth. Historically, the most prominent _____ s were grouped into constellations and asterisms, the brightest of which gained proper names. Astronomers have assembled _____ catalogues that identify the known _____ s and provide standardized stellar designations. However, most of the estimated 300 sextillion _____ s in the Universe are invisible to the naked eye from Earth, including all _____ s outside our galaxy, the Milky Way.

Exam Probability: **High**

4. *Answer choices:*

(see index for correct answer)

- a. BrandYourself
- b. EigenTrust
- c. Star
- d. personal brand

Guidance: level 1

:: Survey methodology ::

_____ is often used to assess thoughts, opinions, and feelings. Surveys can be specific and limited, or they can have more global, widespread goals. Psychologists and sociologists often use surveys to analyze behavior, while it is also used to meet the more pragmatic needs of the media, such as, in evaluating political candidates, public health officials, professional organizations, and advertising and marketing directors. A survey consists of a predetermined set of questions that is given to a sample. With a representative sample, that is, one that is representative of the larger population of interest, one can describe the attitudes of the population from which the sample was drawn. Further, one can compare the attitudes of different populations as well as look for changes in attitudes over time. A good sample selection is key as it allows one to generalize the findings from the sample to the population, which is the whole purpose of _____ .

Exam Probability: **Low**

5. *Answer choices:*
(see index for correct answer)

- a. Survey research
- b. American Association for Public Opinion Research
- c. Total survey error
- d. Public opinion

Guidance: level 1

:: Direct selling ::

_____ consists of two main business models: single-level marketing, in which a direct seller makes money by buying products from a parent organization and selling them directly to customers, and multi-level marketing, in which the direct seller may earn money from both direct sales to customers and by sponsoring new direct sellers and potentially earning a commission from their efforts.

Exam Probability: **Low**

6. *Answer choices:*

(see index for correct answer)

- a. CVSL
- b. Direct Selling News
- c. The Longaberger Company
- d. Direct selling

Guidance: level 1

:: Business planning ::

_____ is an organization's process of defining its strategy, or direction, and making decisions on allocating its resources to pursue this strategy. It may also extend to control mechanisms for guiding the implementation of the strategy. _____ became prominent in corporations during the 1960s and remains an important aspect of strategic management. It is executed by strategic planners or strategists, who involve many parties and research sources in their analysis of the organization and its relationship to the environment in which it competes.

Exam Probability: **Medium**

7. *Answer choices:*

(see index for correct answer)

- a. Business war games
- b. Customer Demand Planning
- c. Strategic planning
- d. Open Options Corporation

Guidance: level 1

:: ::

In marketing, a _____ is a ticket or document that can be redeemed for a financial discount or rebate when purchasing a product.

Exam Probability: **Medium**

8. *Answer choices:*

(see index for correct answer)

- a. cultural
- b. interpersonal communication
- c. open system
- d. corporate values

Guidance: level 1

:: Promotion and marketing communications ::

> A _____ is the intended audience or readership of a publication, advertisement, or other message. In marketing and advertising, it is a particular group of consumers within the predetermined target market, identified as the targets or recipients for a particular advertisement or message. Businesses that have a wide target market will focus on a specific _____ for certain messages to send, such as The Body Shops Mother's Day advertisements, which were aimed at the children and spouses of women, rather than the whole market which would have included the women themselves.

Exam Probability: **Low**

9. *Answer choices:*

(see index for correct answer)

- a. Target audience
- b. Nielsen Broadcast Data Systems
- c. Custom media
- d. Air Miles

Guidance: level 1

:: Contract law ::

A _____ is a legally-binding agreement which recognises and governs the rights and duties of the parties to the agreement. A _____ is legally enforceable because it meets the requirements and approval of the law. An agreement typically involves the exchange of goods, services, money, or promises of any of those. In the event of breach of _____ , the law awards the injured party access to legal remedies such as damages and cancellation.

Exam Probability: **Low**

10. *Answer choices:*

(see index for correct answer)

- a. Contract
- b. Mandatory rule
- c. Marriage privatization
- d. Estoppel by deed

Guidance: level 1

:: ::

A brand is an overall experience of a customer that distinguishes an organization or product from its rivals in the eyes of the customer. Brands are used in business, marketing, and advertising. Name brands are sometimes distinguished from generic or store brands.

Exam Probability: **High**

11. *Answer choices:*

(see index for correct answer)

- a. hierarchical
- b. deep-level diversity
- c. personal values
- d. Brand image

Guidance: level 1

:: National accounts ::

_____ is a monetary measure of the market value of all the final goods and services produced in a period of time, often annually. GDP per capita does not, however, reflect differences in the cost of living and the inflation rates of the countries; therefore using a basis of GDP per capita at purchasing power parity is arguably more useful when comparing differences in living standards between nations.

Exam Probability: **High**

12. *Answer choices:*

(see index for correct answer)

- a. capital formation
- b. Gross domestic product
- c. Fixed capital

Guidance: level 1

:: Decision theory ::

A _____ is a deliberate system of principles to guide decisions and achieve rational outcomes. A _____ is a statement of intent, and is implemented as a procedure or protocol. Policies are generally adopted by a governance body within an organization. Policies can assist in both subjective and objective decision making. Policies to assist in subjective decision making usually assist senior management with decisions that must be based on the relative merits of a number of factors, and as a result are often hard to test objectively, e.g. work-life balance _____ . In contrast policies to assist in objective decision making are usually operational in nature and can be objectively tested, e.g. password _____ .

Exam Probability: **Medium**

13. *Answer choices:*

(see index for correct answer)

- a. Rademacher complexity
- b. Social and Decision Sciences
- c. Decision field theory
- d. Policy

Guidance: level 1

:: Retailing ::

A _____ is a retail establishment offering a wide range of consumer goods in different product categories known as "departments". In modern major cities, the _____ made a dramatic appearance in the middle of the 19th century, and permanently reshaped shopping habits, and the definition of service and luxury. Similar developments were under way in London , in Paris and in New York .

Exam Probability: **Medium**

14. *Answer choices:*

(see index for correct answer)

- a. Department store
- b. Shelving engineering
- c. Store-within-a-store
- d. Tack shop

Guidance: level 1

:: Meetings ::

A _____ is a body of one or more persons that is subordinate to a deliberative assembly. Usually, the assembly sends matters into a _____ as a way to explore them more fully than would be possible if the assembly itself were considering them. _____ s may have different functions and their type of work differ depending on the type of the organization and its needs.

Exam Probability: **High**

15. *Answer choices:*

(see index for correct answer)

- a. Unconference
- b. Mighty Men Conference
- c. Official function
- d. Popular assembly

Guidance: level 1

:: Brand management ::

_____ is defined as positive feelings towards a brand and dedication to purchase the same product or service repeatedly now and in the future from the same brand, regardless of a competitor's actions or changes in the environment. It can also be demonstrated with other behaviors such as positive word-of-mouth advocacy. _____ is where an individual buys products from the same manufacturer repeatedly rather than from other suppliers. Businesses whose financial and ethical values, for example ESG responsibilities, rest in large part on their _____ are said to use the loyalty business model.

Exam Probability: **Low**

16. *Answer choices:*

(see index for correct answer)

- a. Brand networking
- b. Superbrands
- c. Brand loyalty
- d. Fictional brand

Guidance: level 1

:: Marketing ::

> A _____ is something that is necessary for an organism to live a healthy life. _____ s are distinguished from wants in that, in the case of a _____, a deficiency causes a clear adverse outcome: a dysfunction or death. In other words, a _____ is something required for a safe, stable and healthy life while a want is a desire, wish or aspiration. When _____ s or wants are backed by purchasing power, they have the potential to become economic demands.

Exam Probability: **Low**

17. *Answer choices:*

(see index for correct answer)

- a. Need
- b. Corporate capabilities package
- c. Net idol
- d. Market segmentation index

Guidance: level 1

:: Project management ::

_____ is the right to exercise power, which can be formalized by a state and exercised by way of judges, appointed executives of government, or the ecclesiastical or priestly appointed representatives of a God or other deities.

Exam Probability: **Low**

18. *Answer choices:*

(see index for correct answer)

- a. Gregory T. Haugan
- b. Authority
- c. Product flow diagram
- d. Resource allocation

Guidance: level 1

:: Consumer theory ::

A _____ is a technical term in psychology, economics and philosophy usually used in relation to choosing between alternatives. For example, someone prefers A over B if they would rather choose A than B.

Exam Probability: **Low**

19. *Answer choices:*

(see index for correct answer)

- a. Elasticity of substitution
- b. intertemporal substitution
- c. Slutsky equation
- d. Preference

Guidance: level 1

:: Monopoly (economics) ::

The _____ of 1890 was a United States antitrust law that regulates competition among enterprises, which was passed by Congress under the presidency of Benjamin Harrison.

Exam Probability: **Medium**

20. *Answer choices:*

(see index for correct answer)

- a. Herfindahl index
- b. Sherman Antitrust Act
- c. Monopoly
- d. State monopoly capitalism

Guidance: level 1

:: Retailing ::

_____ is the process of selling consumer goods or services to customers through multiple channels of distribution to earn a profit. _____ ers satisfy demand identified through a supply chain. The term "_____ er" is typically applied where a service provider fills the small orders of a large number of individuals, who are end-users, rather than large orders of a small number of wholesale, corporate or government clientele. Shopping generally refers to the act of buying products. Sometimes this is done to obtain final goods, including necessities such as food and clothing; sometimes it takes place as a recreational activity. Recreational shopping often involves window shopping and browsing: it does not always result in a purchase.

Exam Probability: **High**

21. *Answer choices:*

(see index for correct answer)

- a. Big-box store
- b. Retail
- c. Warehouse store
- d. Flea market

Guidance: level 1

:: Basic financial concepts ::

_____ is a sustained increase in the general price level of goods and services in an economy over a period of time. When the general price level rises, each unit of currency buys fewer goods and services; consequently, _____ reflects a reduction in the purchasing power per unit of money a loss of real value in the medium of exchange and unit of account within the economy. The measure of _____ is the _____ rate, the annualized percentage change in a general price index, usually the consumer price index, over time. The opposite of _____ is deflation.

Exam Probability: **Low**

22. *Answer choices:*

(see index for correct answer)

- a. Financial transaction
- b. Inflation
- c. Leverage cycle
- d. balloon payment

Guidance: level 1

:: Marketing by medium ::

_____ or viral advertising is a business strategy that uses existing social networks to promote a product. Its name refers to how consumers spread information about a product with other people in their social networks, much in the same way that a virus spreads from one person to another. It can be delivered by word of mouth or enhanced by the network effects of the Internet and mobile networks.

Exam Probability: **Medium**

23. *Answer choices:*

(see index for correct answer)

- a. Brand infiltration
- b. Viral marketing
- c. Growth hacking
- d. Social video marketing

Guidance: level 1

:: ::

_____ is the process whereby a business sets the price at which it will sell its products and services, and may be part of the business's marketing plan. In setting prices, the business will take into account the price at which it could acquire the goods, the manufacturing cost, the market place, competition, market condition, brand, and quality of product.

Exam Probability: **High**

24. *Answer choices:*

(see index for correct answer)

- a. Pricing
- b. corporate values

- c. hierarchical perspective
- d. information systems assessment

Guidance: level 1

:: Television terminology ::

A _____ organization, also known as a non-business entity, not-for-profit organization, or _____ institution, is dedicated to furthering a particular social cause or advocating for a shared point of view. In economic terms, it is an organization that uses its surplus of the revenues to further achieve its ultimate objective, rather than distributing its income to the organization's shareholders, leaders, or members. _____s are tax exempt or charitable, meaning they do not pay income tax on the money that they receive for their organization. They can operate in religious, scientific, research, or educational settings.

Exam Probability: **Low**

25. *Answer choices:*

(see index for correct answer)

- a. Satellite television
- b. multiplexing
- c. not-for-profit
- d. Nonprofit

Guidance: level 1

:: ::

In business and engineering, new _____ covers the complete process of bringing a new product to market. A central aspect of NPD is product design, along with various business considerations. New _____ is described broadly as the transformation of a market opportunity into a product available for sale. The product can be tangible or intangible, though sometimes services and other processes are distinguished from "products." NPD requires an understanding of customer needs and wants, the competitive environment, and the nature of the market. Cost, time and quality are the main variables that drive customer needs. Aiming at these three variables, innovative companies develop continuous practices and strategies to better satisfy customer requirements and to increase their own market share by a regular development of new products. There are many uncertainties and challenges which companies must face throughout the process. The use of best practices and the elimination of barriers to communication are the main concerns for the management of the NPD.

Exam Probability: **Low**

26. *Answer choices:*

(see index for correct answer)

- a. levels of analysis
- b. empathy
- c. Product development
- d. deep-level diversity

Guidance: level 1

:: Direct marketing ::

_____ is a form of direct marketing using databases of customers or potential customers to generate personalized communications in order to promote a product or service for marketing purposes. The method of communication can be any addressable medium, as in direct marketing.

Exam Probability: **High**

27. *Answer choices:*

(see index for correct answer)

- a. International Masters Publishers
- b. Robinson list
- c. Database marketing
- d. Synapse Group, Inc.

Guidance: level 1

:: ::

A _____ is a graphic mark, emblem, or symbol used to aid and promote public identification and recognition. It may be of an abstract or figurative design or include the text of the name it represents as in a wordmark.

Exam Probability: **High**

28. *Answer choices:*

(see index for correct answer)

- a. hierarchical
- b. interpersonal communication
- c. Logo
- d. similarity-attraction theory

Guidance: level 1

:: Product development ::

In business and engineering, _____ covers the complete process of bringing a new product to market. A central aspect of NPD is product design, along with various business considerations. _____ is described broadly as the transformation of a market opportunity into a product available for sale. The product can be tangible or intangible , though sometimes services and other processes are distinguished from "products." NPD requires an understanding of customer needs and wants, the competitive environment, and the nature of the market.Cost, time and quality are the main variables that drive customer needs. Aiming at these three variables, innovative companies develop continuous practices and strategies to better satisfy customer requirements and to increase their own market share by a regular development of new products. There are many uncertainties and challenges which companies must face throughout the process. The use of best practices and the elimination of barriers to communication are the main concerns for the management of the NPD .

Exam Probability: **Medium**

29. *Answer choices:*

(see index for correct answer)

- a. Specification tree
- b. Design for assembly
- c. New product development
- d. WhiteBoard Product Solutions

Guidance: level 1

:: ::

_____ is a means of protection from financial loss. It is a form of risk management, primarily used to hedge against the risk of a contingent or uncertain loss

Exam Probability: **High**

30. *Answer choices:*

(see index for correct answer)

- a. information systems assessment
- b. interpersonal communication
- c. levels of analysis
- d. co-culture

Guidance: level 1

:: Communication design ::

An _____ is a series of advertisement messages that share a single idea and theme which make up an integrated marketing communication. An IMC is a platform in which a group of people can group their ideas, beliefs, and concepts into one large media base. _____s utilize diverse media channels over a particular time frame and target identified audiences.

Exam Probability: **Medium**

31. *Answer choices:*

(see index for correct answer)

- a. Flat Eric
- b. Motion graphic design
- c. Advertising campaign
- d. Comprehensive layout

Guidance: level 1

:: ::

In international relations, _____ is – from the perspective of governments – a voluntary transfer of resources from one country to another.

Exam Probability: **Low**

32. Answer choices:

(see index for correct answer)

- a. similarity-attraction theory
- b. co-culture
- c. Aid
- d. information systems assessment

Guidance: level 1

:: ::

> A _____ is a professional who provides expert advice in a particular area such as security, management, education, accountancy, law, human resources, marketing, finance, engineering, science or any of many other specialized fields.

Exam Probability: **High**

33. Answer choices:

(see index for correct answer)

- a. Consultant
- b. functional perspective
- c. imperative
- d. interpersonal communication

Guidance: level 1

:: Income ::

In business and accounting, net income is an entity's income minus cost of goods sold, expenses and taxes for an accounting period. It is computed as the residual of all revenues and gains over all expenses and losses for the period, and has also been defined as the net increase in shareholders' equity that results from a company's operations. In the context of the presentation of financial statements, the IFRS Foundation defines net income as synonymous with profit and loss. The difference between revenue and the cost of making a product or providing a service, before deducting overheads, payroll, taxation, and interest payments. This is different from operating income.

Exam Probability: **High**

34. *Answer choices:*
(see index for correct answer)

- a. Family income
- b. Return on investment
- c. Per capita income
- d. Bottom line

Guidance: level 1

:: Marketing ::

_____ s are structured marketing strategies designed by merchants to encourage customers to continue to shop at or use the services of businesses associated with each program. These programs exist covering most types of commerce, each one having varying features and rewards-schemes.

Exam Probability: **Medium**

35. *Answer choices:*

(see index for correct answer)

- a. push and pull
- b. Contribution margin-based pricing
- c. Mass marketing
- d. Loyalty program

Guidance: level 1

:: Data analysis ::

_____ is a process of inspecting, cleansing, transforming, and modeling data with the goal of discovering useful information, informing conclusions, and supporting decision-making. _____ has multiple facets and approaches, encompassing diverse techniques under a variety of names, and is used in different business, science, and social science domains. In today's business world, _____ plays a role in making decisions more scientific and helping businesses operate more effectively.

Exam Probability: **Medium**

36. *Answer choices:*

(see index for correct answer)

- a. Exponential smoothing
- b. Test set
- c. Principal geodesic analysis
- d. Exploratory data analysis

Guidance: level 1

:: Supply chain management ::

The _____ is a barcode symbology that is widely used in the United States, Canada, United Kingdom, Australia, New Zealand, in Europe and other countries for tracking trade items in stores.

Exam Probability: **Low**

37. *Answer choices:*

(see index for correct answer)

- a. Mobile asset management
- b. Supply-chain operations reference
- c. Supply chain surplus
- d. Cross-border leasing

Guidance: level 1

:: ::

Retail is the process of selling consumer goods or services to customers through multiple channels of distribution to earn a profit. Retailers satisfy demand identified through a supply chain. The term "retailer" is typically applied where a service provider fills the small orders of a large number of individuals, who are end-users, rather than large orders of a small number of wholesale, corporate or government clientele. Shopping generally refers to the act of buying products. Sometimes this is done to obtain final goods, including necessities such as food and clothing; sometimes it takes place as a recreational activity. Recreational shopping often involves window shopping and browsing: it does not always result in a purchase.

Exam Probability: **Low**

38. *Answer choices:*

(see index for correct answer)

- a. interpersonal communication
- b. functional perspective
- c. similarity-attraction theory
- d. Sarbanes-Oxley act of 2002

Guidance: level 1

:: Competition regulators ::

The _____ is an independent agency of the United States government, established in 1914 by the _____ Act. Its principal mission is the promotion of consumer protection and the elimination and prevention of anticompetitive business practices, such as coercive monopoly. It is headquartered in the _____ Building in Washington, D.C.

Exam Probability: **Medium**

39. *Answer choices:*

(see index for correct answer)

- a. Superintendency of Industry and Commerce
- b. Federal Trade Commission
- c. Competition Commission of India
- d. Office of Fair Trading

Guidance: level 1

:: Product management ::

A _____, trade mark, or trade-mark is a recognizable sign, design, or expression which identifies products or services of a particular source from those of others, although _____ s used to identify services are usually called service marks. The _____ owner can be an individual, business organization, or any legal entity. A _____ may be located on a package, a label, a voucher, or on the product itself. For the sake of corporate identity, _____ s are often displayed on company buildings. It is legally recognized as a type of intellectual property.

Exam Probability: **High**

40. *Answer choices:*

(see index for correct answer)

- a. Service life
- b. Crossing the Chasm
- c. Trademark
- d. Whole product

Guidance: level 1

:: Evaluation methods ::

_____ is a scientific method of observation to gather non-numerical data. This type of research "refers to the meanings, concepts definitions, characteristics, metaphors, symbols, and description of things" and not to their "counts or measures." This research answers why and how a certain phenomenon may occur rather than how often. _____ approaches are employed across many academic disciplines, focusing particularly on the human elements of the social and natural sciences; in less academic contexts, areas of application include qualitative market research, business, service demonstrations by non-profits, and journalism.

Exam Probability: **Low**

41. *Answer choices:*

(see index for correct answer)

- a. Economic impact analysis
- b. Electronic patient-reported outcome
- c. Logic model
- d. Naturalistic observation

Guidance: level 1

:: Stochastic processes ::

_____ in its modern meaning is a "new idea, creative thoughts, new imaginations in form of device or method". _____ is often also viewed as the application of better solutions that meet new requirements, unarticulated needs, or existing market needs. Such _____ takes place through the provision of more-effective products, processes, services, technologies, or business models that are made available to markets, governments and society. An _____ is something original and more effective and, as a consequence, new, that "breaks into" the market or society. _____ is related to, but not the same as, invention, as _____ is more apt to involve the practical implementation of an invention to make a meaningful impact in the market or society, and not all _____ s require an invention. _____ often manifests itself via the engineering process, when the problem being solved is of a technical or scientific nature. The opposite of _____ is exnovation.

Exam Probability: **Medium**

42. *Answer choices:*

(see index for correct answer)

- a. Innovation
- b. BCMP network

- c. Finite-dimensional distribution
- d. Fractional Brownian motion

Guidance: level 1

:: E-commerce ::

_____ is the activity of buying or selling of products on online services or over the Internet. Electronic commerce draws on technologies such as mobile commerce, electronic funds transfer, supply chain management, Internet marketing, online transaction processing, electronic data interchange , inventory management systems, and automated data collection systems.

Exam Probability: **Medium**

43. *Answer choices:*

(see index for correct answer)

- a. Extended Validation Certificate
- b. Andy Dunn
- c. E-commerce
- d. Scriptlance

Guidance: level 1

:: Management accounting ::

In economics, _____ s, indirect costs or overheads are business expenses that are not dependent on the level of goods or services produced by the business. They tend to be time-related, such as interest or rents being paid per month, and are often referred to as overhead costs. This is in contrast to variable costs, which are volume-related and unknown at the beginning of the accounting year. For a simple example, such as a bakery, the monthly rent for the baking facilities, and the monthly payments for the security system and basic phone line are _____ s, as they do not change according to how much bread the bakery produces and sells. On the other hand, the wage costs of the bakery are variable, as the bakery will have to hire more workers if the production of bread increases. Economists reckon _____ as a entry barrier for new entrepreneurs.

Exam Probability: **Low**

44. *Answer choices:*
(see index for correct answer)

- a. Fixed cost
- b. Dual overhead rate
- c. Net present value
- d. Factory overhead

Guidance: level 1

:: ::

Management is the administration of an organization, whether it is a business, a not-for-profit organization, or government body. Management includes the activities of setting the strategy of an organization and coordinating the efforts of its employees to accomplish its objectives through the application of available resources, such as financial, natural, technological, and human resources. The term "management" may also refer to those people who manage an organization.

Exam Probability: **High**

45. *Answer choices:*

(see index for correct answer)

- a. process perspective
- b. cultural
- c. Manager
- d. Sarbanes-Oxley act of 2002

Guidance: level 1

:: Types of marketing ::

_____ was first defined as a form of marketing developed from direct response marketing campaigns which emphasizes customer retention and satisfaction, rather than a focus on sales transactions.

Exam Probability: **High**

46. Answer choices:

(see index for correct answer)

- a. Limited edition candy
- b. Consumer Generated Advertising
- c. Relationship marketing
- d. Account planning

Guidance: level 1

:: Management ::

In economics and marketing, _____ is the process of distinguishing a product or service from others, to make it more attractive to a particular target market. This involves differentiating it from competitors' products as well as a firm's own products. The concept was proposed by Edward Chamberlin in his 1933 The Theory of Monopolistic Competition.

Exam Probability: **Medium**

47. Answer choices:

(see index for correct answer)

- a. Product differentiation
- b. Earned schedule
- c. Information excellence
- d. Infrastructure asset management

Guidance: level 1

:: Marketing ::

A _____ is the quantity of payment or compensation given by one party to another in return for one unit of goods or services.. A _____ is influenced by both production costs and demand for the product. A _____ may be determined by a monopolist or may be imposed on the firm by market conditions.

Exam Probability: **Medium**

48. *Answer choices:*

(see index for correct answer)

- a. Customer acquisition management
- b. Price
- c. Discounting
- d. Icon brand

Guidance: level 1

:: Trade associations ::

A _____ , also known as an industry trade group, business association, sector association or industry body, is an organization founded and funded by businesses that operate in a specific industry. An industry _____ participates in public relations activities such as advertising, education, political donations, lobbying and publishing, but its focus is collaboration between companies. Associations may offer other services, such as producing conferences, networking or charitable events or offering classes or educational materials. Many associations are non-profit organizations governed by bylaws and directed by officers who are also members.

Exam Probability: **Medium**

49. *Answer choices:*

(see index for correct answer)

- a. National Association of Family Entertainment Centers
- b. Trade association
- c. ANDEBU
- d. European Rail Infrastructure Managers

Guidance: level 1

:: Business ::

The seller, or the provider of the goods or services, completes a sale in response to an acquisition, appropriation, requisition or a direct interaction with the buyer at the point of sale. There is a passing of title of the item, and the settlement of a price, in which agreement is reached on a price for which transfer of ownership of the item will occur. The seller, not the purchaser typically executes the sale and it may be completed prior to the obligation of payment. In the case of indirect interaction, a person who sells goods or service on behalf of the owner is known as a _____ man or _____ woman or _____ person, but this often refers to someone selling goods in a store/shop, in which case other terms are also common, including _____ clerk, shop assistant, and retail clerk.

Exam Probability: **Medium**

50. *Answer choices:*

(see index for correct answer)

- a. Sales
- b. Post-transaction marketing
- c. Countertrade
- d. Business partnering

Guidance: level 1

:: ::

Bloomberg Businessweek is an American weekly business magazine published since 2009 by Bloomberg L.P. Businessweek, founded in 1929, aimed to provide information and interpretation about events in the business world. The magazine is headquartered in New York City. Megan Murphy served as editor from November 2016; she stepped down from the role in January 2018 and Joel Weber was appointed in her place. The magazine is published 47 times a year.

Exam Probability: **Medium**

51. *Answer choices:*

(see index for correct answer)

- a. Character
- b. hierarchical
- c. levels of analysis
- d. functional perspective

Guidance: level 1

:: Materials ::

A _____, also known as a feedstock, unprocessed material, or primary commodity, is a basic material that is used to produce goods, finished products, energy, or intermediate materials which are feedstock for future finished products. As feedstock, the term connotes these materials are bottleneck assets and are highly important with regard to producing other products. An example of this is crude oil, which is a _____ and a feedstock used in the production of industrial chemicals, fuels, plastics, and pharmaceutical goods; lumber is a _____ used to produce a variety of products including all types of furniture. The term "_____" denotes materials in minimally processed or unprocessed in states; e.g., raw latex, crude oil, cotton, coal, raw biomass, iron ore, air, logs, or water i.e. "...any product of agriculture, forestry, fishing and any other mineral that is in its natural form or which has undergone the transformation required to prepare it for internationally marketing in substantial volumes."

Exam Probability: **Low**

52. *Answer choices:*

(see index for correct answer)

- a. Dryrock
- b. Raw material
- c. FDU materials
- d. Tensometer

Guidance: level 1

:: Marketing techniques ::

_____ is the activity of dividing a broad consumer or business market, normally consisting of existing and potential customers, into sub-groups of consumers based on some type of shared characteristics. In dividing or segmenting markets, researchers typically look for common characteristics such as shared needs, common interests, similar lifestyles or even similar demographic profiles. The overall aim of segmentation is to identify high yield segments – that is, those segments that are likely to be the most profitable or that have growth potential – so that these can be selected for special attention.

Exam Probability: **High**

53. *Answer choices:*

(see index for correct answer)

- a. Trailer
- b. Unique selling proposition
- c. Microsegment
- d. Market segmentation

Guidance: level 1

:: Commercial item transport and distribution ::

In commerce, supply-chain management, the management of the flow of goods and services, involves the movement and storage of raw materials, of work-in-process inventory, and of finished goods from point of origin to point of consumption. Interconnected or interlinked networks, channels and node businesses combine in the provision of products and services required by end customers in a supply chain. Supply-chain management has been defined as the "design, planning, execution, control, and monitoring of supply-chain activities with the objective of creating net value, building a competitive infrastructure, leveraging worldwide logistics, synchronizing supply with demand and measuring performance globally." SCM practice draws heavily from the areas of industrial engineering, systems engineering, operations management, logistics, procurement, information technology, and marketing and strives for an integrated approach. Marketing channels play an important role in supply-chain management. Current research in supply-chain management is concerned with topics related to sustainability and risk management, among others. Some suggest that the "people dimension" of SCM, ethical issues, internal integration, transparency/visibility, and human capital/talent management are topics that have, so far, been underrepresented on the research agenda.

Exam Probability: **Low**

54. *Answer choices:*

(see index for correct answer)

- a. Cargo airline
- b. Supply chain management
- c. Pipeline transport
- d. Pallet

Guidance: level 1

:: Debt ::

_____ , in finance and economics, is payment from a borrower or deposit-taking financial institution to a lender or depositor of an amount above repayment of the principal sum , at a particular rate. It is distinct from a fee which the borrower may pay the lender or some third party. It is also distinct from dividend which is paid by a company to its shareholders from its profit or reserve, but not at a particular rate decided beforehand, rather on a pro rata basis as a share in the reward gained by risk taking entrepreneurs when the revenue earned exceeds the total costs.

Exam Probability: **High**

55. *Answer choices:*

(see index for correct answer)

- a. Extendible bond
- b. Student debt
- c. Interest
- d. Borrowing base

Guidance: level 1

:: Logistics ::

_____ is generally the detailed organization and implementation of a complex operation. In a general business sense, _____ is the management of the flow of things between the point of origin and the point of consumption in order to meet requirements of customers or corporations. The resources managed in _____ may include tangible goods such as materials, equipment, and supplies, as well as food and other consumable items. The _____ of physical items usually involves the integration of information flow, materials handling, production, packaging, inventory, transportation, warehousing, and often security.

Exam Probability: **Low**

56. *Answer choices:*

(see index for correct answer)

- a. Phase jitter modulation
- b. Design for availability
- c. Logistics center
- d. Menlo Worldwide Logistics

Guidance: level 1

:: Management ::

A _____ is a comprehensive document or blueprint that outlines the advertising and marketing efforts for the coming year. It describes business activities involved in accomplishing specific marketing objectives within a set time frame. A _____ also includes a description of the current marketing position of a business, a discussion of the target market and a description of the marketing mix that a business will use to achieve their marketing goals. A _____ has a formal structure, but can be used as a formal or informal document which makes it very flexible. It contains some historical data, future predictions, and methods or strategies to achieve the marketing objectives. _____s start with the identification of customer needs through a market research and how the business can satisfy these needs while generating an acceptable return. This includes processes such as market situation analysis, action programs, budgets, sales forecasts, strategies and projected financial statements. A _____ can also be described as a technique that helps a business to decide on the best use of its resources to achieve corporate objectives. It can also contain a full analysis of the strengths and weaknesses of a company, its organization and its products.

Exam Probability: **High**

57. *Answer choices:*

(see index for correct answer)

- a. Business rule
- b. Crisis plan
- c. Libertarian management
- d. Marketing plan

Guidance: level 1

In financial markets, a share is a unit used as mutual funds, limited partnerships, and real estate investment trusts. The owner of _____ in the corporation/company is a shareholder of the corporation. A share is an indivisible unit of capital, expressing the ownership relationship between the company and the shareholder. The denominated value of a share is its face value, and the total of the face value of issued _____ represent the capital of a company, which may not reflect the market value of those _____ .

Exam Probability: **Low**

58. *Answer choices:*

(see index for correct answer)

- a. Character
- b. Shares
- c. deep-level diversity
- d. Sarbanes-Oxley act of 2002

Guidance: level 1

:: Industrial design ::

In physics and mathematics, the _____ of a mathematical space is informally defined as the minimum number of coordinates needed to specify any point within it. Thus a line has a _____ of one because only one coordinate is needed to specify a point on it for example, the point at 5 on a number line. A surface such as a plane or the surface of a cylinder or sphere has a _____ of two because two coordinates are needed to specify a point on it for example, both a latitude and longitude are required to locate a point on the surface of a sphere. The inside of a cube, a cylinder or a sphere is three-_____ al because three coordinates are needed to locate a point within these spaces.

Exam Probability: **Low**

59. *Answer choices:*

(see index for correct answer)

- a. The Design of Everyday Things
- b. Concept art
- c. Flip
- d. Dimension

Guidance: level 1

Manufacturing

Manufacturing is the production of merchandise for use or sale using labor and machines, tools, chemical and biological processing, or formulation. The term may refer to a range of human activity, from handicraft to high tech, but is most commonly applied to industrial design , in which raw materials are transformed into finished goods on a large scale. Such finished goods may be sold to other manufacturers for the production of other, more complex products, such as aircraft, household appliances, furniture, sports equipment or automobiles, or sold to wholesalers, who in turn sell them to retailers, who then sell them to end users and consumers.

:: Natural materials ::

_____ is a finely-grained natural rock or soil material that combines one or more _____ minerals with possible traces of quartz, metal oxides and organic matter. Geologic _____ deposits are mostly composed of phyllosilicate minerals containing variable amounts of water trapped in the mineral structure. _____s are plastic due to particle size and geometry as well as water content, and become hard, brittle and non–plastic upon drying or firing. Depending on the soil's content in which it is found, _____ can appear in various colours from white to dull grey or brown to deep orange-red.

Exam Probability: **High**

1. *Answer choices:*

(see index for correct answer)

- a. Armenian bole
- b. Arizona flagstone
- c. Clay
- d. Pebble

Guidance: level 1

:: ::

In production, research, retail, and accounting, a _____ is the value of money that has been used up to produce something or deliver a service, and hence is not available for use anymore. In business, the _____ may be one of acquisition, in which case the amount of money expended to acquire it is counted as _____. In this case, money is the input that is gone in order to acquire the thing. This acquisition _____ may be the sum of the _____ of production as incurred by the original producer, and further _____s of transaction as incurred by the acquirer over and above the price paid to the producer. Usually, the price also includes a mark-up for profit over the _____ of production.

Exam Probability: **Medium**

2. *Answer choices:*

(see index for correct answer)

- a. levels of analysis
- b. hierarchical perspective
- c. open system
- d. Cost

Guidance: level 1

:: Quality assurance ::

The _____ is a United States-based nonprofit tax-exempt 501 organization that accredits more than 21,000 US health care organizations and programs. The international branch accredits medical services from around the world. A majority of US state governments recognize _____ accreditation as a condition of licensure for the receipt of Medicaid and Medicare reimbursements.

Exam Probability: **Medium**

3. *Answer choices:*

(see index for correct answer)

- a. DNV Healthcare
- b. Static testing
- c. Health Information and Quality Authority
- d. Joint Commission

Guidance: level 1

:: Gas technologies ::

A _____ is a device used to transfer heat between two or more fluids. _____ s are used in both cooling and heating processes. The fluids may be separated by a solid wall to prevent mixing or they may be in direct contact. They are widely used in space heating, refrigeration, air conditioning, power stations, chemical plants, petrochemical plants, petroleum refineries, natural-gas processing, and sewage treatment. The classic example of a _____ is found in an internal combustion engine in which a circulating fluid known as engine coolant flows through radiator coils and air flows past the coils, which cools the coolant and heats the incoming air. Another example is the heat sink, which is a passive _____ that transfers the heat generated by an electronic or a mechanical device to a fluid medium, often air or a liquid coolant.

Exam Probability: **Low**

4. *Answer choices:*

(see index for correct answer)

- a. The Oval Gasholders
- b. Heat exchanger
- c. Compressed air filters
- d. Chemical oxygen generator

Guidance: level 1

:: Project management ::

In general usage, a _____ is a comprehensive evaluation of an individual's current pay and future financial state by using current known variables to predict future income, asset values and withdrawal plans. This often includes a budget which organizes an individual's finances and sometimes includes a series of steps or specific goals for spending and saving in the future. This plan allocates future income to various types of expenses, such as rent or utilities, and also reserves some income for short-term and long-term savings. A _____ is sometimes referred to as an investment plan, but in personal finance a _____ can focus on other specific areas such as risk management, estates, college, or retirement.

Exam Probability: **Low**

5. *Answer choices:*

_(see index for correct answer)

- a. Project anatomy
- b. Scope creep
- c. PRINCE2
- d. Vertical slice

Guidance: level 1

:: Supply chain management ::

_____ is a core supply chain function and includes supply chain planning and supply chain execution capabilities. Specifically, _____ is the capability firms use to plan total material requirements. The material requirements are communicated to procurement and other functions for sourcing. _____ is also responsible for determining the amount of material to be deployed at each stocking location across the supply chain, establishing material replenishment plans, determining inventory levels to hold for each type of inventory, and communicating information regarding material needs throughout the extended supply chain.

Exam Probability: **Low**

6. *Answer choices:*

(see index for correct answer)

- a. Supply chain management software
- b. Transactional IT
- c. Supply chain engineering
- d. Vendor-managed inventory

Guidance: level 1

:: ::

Some scenarios associate "this kind of planning" with learning "life skills". Schedules are necessary, or at least useful, in situations where individuals need to know what time they must be at a specific location to receive a specific service, and where people need to accomplish a set of goals within a set time period.

Exam Probability: **Medium**

7. *Answer choices:*

(see index for correct answer)

- a. Scheduling
- b. corporate values
- c. surface-level diversity
- d. levels of analysis

Guidance: level 1

:: Time management ::

_____ is the process of planning and exercising conscious control of time spent on specific activities, especially to increase effectiveness, efficiency, and productivity. It involves a juggling act of various demands upon a person relating to work, social life, family, hobbies, personal interests and commitments with the finiteness of time. Using time effectively gives the person "choice" on spending/managing activities at their own time and expediency.

Exam Probability: **Medium**

8. *Answer choices:*

(see index for correct answer)

- a. Getting Things Done

- b. waiting room
- c. Time allocation
- d. Time management

Guidance: level 1

:: Management accounting ::

_____ are costs that are not directly accountable to a cost object . _____ may be either fixed or variable. _____ include administration, personnel and security costs. These are those costs which are not directly related to production. Some _____ may be overhead. But some overhead costs can be directly attributed to a project and are direct costs.

Exam Probability: **Medium**

9. *Answer choices:*
(see index for correct answer)

- a. Activity-based management
- b. Indirect costs
- c. Construction accounting
- d. Responsibility center

Guidance: level 1

:: Production and manufacturing ::

_____ is a concept in purchasing and project management for securing the quality and timely delivery of goods and components.

Exam Probability: **High**

10. *Answer choices:*

(see index for correct answer)

- a. Enterprise control
- b. Reverse engineering
- c. Mockup
- d. Expediting

Guidance: level 1

:: Retailing ::

_____ is the process of selling consumer goods or services to customers through multiple channels of distribution to earn a profit. _____ ers satisfy demand identified through a supply chain. The term "_____ er" is typically applied where a service provider fills the small orders of a large number of individuals, who are end-users, rather than large orders of a small number of wholesale, corporate or government clientele. Shopping generally refers to the act of buying products. Sometimes this is done to obtain final goods, including necessities such as food and clothing; sometimes it takes place as a recreational activity. Recreational shopping often involves window shopping and browsing: it does not always result in a purchase.

Exam Probability: **Low**

11. *Answer choices:*

(see index for correct answer)

- a. Flea market
- b. Retail
- c. Scrapstore
- d. Video game store

Guidance: level 1

:: Accounting source documents ::

A _____ is a commercial document and first official offer issued by a buyer to a seller indicating types, quantities, and agreed prices for products or services. It is used to control the purchasing of products and services from external suppliers. _____s can be an essential part of enterprise resource planning system orders.

Exam Probability: **Medium**

12. *Answer choices:*

(see index for correct answer)

- a. Bank statement
- b. Banknote
- c. Air waybill
- d. Credit memo

Guidance: level 1

:: Gas technologies ::

A _____ is a rotary mechanical device that extracts energy from a fluid flow and converts it into useful work. The work produced by a _____ can be used for generating electrical power when combined with a generator. A _____ is a turbomachine with at least one moving part called a rotor assembly, which is a shaft or drum with blades attached. Moving fluid acts on the blades so that they move and impart rotational energy to the rotor. Early _____ examples are windmills and waterwheels.

Exam Probability: **Low**

13. *Answer choices:*

(see index for correct answer)

- a. Oxygen tank
- b. Turbine
- c. Air horn
- d. Absorption

Guidance: level 1

:: Inventory ::

The _____ is the level of inventory which triggers an action to replenish that particular inventory stock. It is a minimum amount of an item which a firm holds in stock, such that, when stock falls to this amount, the item must be reordered. It is normally calculated as the forecast usage during the replenishment lead time plus safety stock. In the EOQ model, it was assumed that there is no time lag between ordering and procuring of materials. Therefore the _____ for replenishing the stocks occurs at that level when the inventory level drops to zero and because instant delivery by suppliers, the stock level bounce back.

Exam Probability: **High**

14. *Answer choices:*

(see index for correct answer)

- a. Spare part
- b. Periodic inventory
- c. Reorder point
- d. Lower of cost or market

Guidance: level 1

:: Water ::

_____ is a transparent, tasteless, odorless, and nearly colorless chemical substance, which is the main constituent of Earth's streams, lakes, and oceans, and the fluids of most living organisms. It is vital for all known forms of life, even though it provides no calories or organic nutrients. Its chemical formula is H2O, meaning that each of its molecules contains one oxygen and two hydrogen atoms, connected by covalent bonds. _____ is the name of the liquid state of H2O at standard ambient temperature and pressure. It forms precipitation in the form of rain and aerosols in the form of fog. Clouds are formed from suspended droplets of _____ and ice, its solid state. When finely divided, crystalline ice may precipitate in the form of snow. The gaseous state of _____ is steam or _____ vapor. _____ moves continually through the _____ cycle of evaporation, transpiration, condensation, precipitation, and runoff, usually reaching the sea.

Exam Probability: **High**

15. *Answer choices:*

(see index for correct answer)

- a. Seiche
- b. Flownet

- c. Rain chain
- d. Water

Guidance: level 1

:: Semiconductor companies ::

_____ Corporation is a Japanese multinational conglomerate corporation headquartered in Konan, Minato, Tokyo. Its diversified business includes consumer and professional electronics, gaming, entertainment and financial services. The company owns the largest music entertainment business in the world, the largest video game console business and one of the largest video game publishing businesses, and is one of the leading manufacturers of electronic products for the consumer and professional markets, and a leading player in the film and television entertainment industry. _____ was ranked 97th on the 2018 Fortune Global 500 list.

Exam Probability: **Medium**

16. *Answer choices:*

(see index for correct answer)

- a. VeriSilicon
- b. Renesas Electronics
- c. Maxim Integrated
- d. EM Microelectronic-Marin

Guidance: level 1

:: Supply chain management ::

_____ is the process of finding and agreeing to terms, and acquiring goods, services, or works from an external source, often via a tendering or competitive bidding process. _____ is used to ensure the buyer receives goods, services, or works at the best possible price when aspects such as quality, quantity, time, and location are compared. Corporations and public bodies often define processes intended to promote fair and open competition for their business while minimizing risks such as exposure to fraud and collusion.

Exam Probability: **High**

17. *Answer choices:*

(see index for correct answer)

- a. Procurement
- b. Revenue Technology Services
- c. Supply-chain operations reference
- d. Supply chain cyber security

Guidance: level 1

:: ::

A _____ or till is a mechanical or electronic device for registering and calculating transactions at a point of sale. It is usually attached to a drawer for storing cash and other valuables. A modern _____ is usually attached to a printer that can print out receipts for record-keeping purposes.

Exam Probability: **High**

18. *Answer choices:*

(see index for correct answer)

- a. empathy
- b. cultural
- c. interpersonal communication
- d. Cash register

Guidance: level 1

:: Information technology management ::

_____ within quality management systems and information technology systems is a process—either formal or informal—used to ensure that changes to a product or system are introduced in a controlled and coordinated manner. It reduces the possibility that unnecessary changes will be introduced to a system without forethought, introducing faults into the system or undoing changes made by other users of software. The goals of a _____ procedure usually include minimal disruption to services, reduction in back-out activities, and cost-effective utilization of resources involved in implementing change.

Exam Probability: **Medium**

19. *Answer choices:*

(see index for correct answer)

- a. Information protection policy
- b. Change control
- c. Service catalog
- d. Skills Framework for the Information Age

Guidance: level 1

:: Monopoly (economics) ::

_____ are "efficiencies formed by variety, not volume". For example, a gas station that sells gasoline can sell soda, milk, baked goods, etc through their customer service representatives and thus achieve gasoline companies _____ .

Exam Probability: **High**

20. *Answer choices:*

(see index for correct answer)

- a. Motion Picture Patents Company
- b. Economies of scope
- c. Natural monopoly

- d. Third-party access

Guidance: level 1

:: Production and manufacturing ::

> _____ is a theory of management that analyzes and synthesizes workflows. Its main objective is improving economic efficiency, especially labor productivity. It was one of the earliest attempts to apply science to the engineering of processes and to management. _____ is sometimes known as Taylorism after its founder, Frederick Winslow Taylor.

Exam Probability: **High**

21. *Answer choices:*

(see index for correct answer)

- a. Scientific management
- b. ORiN
- c. Fab lab
- d. Transfer cars

Guidance: level 1

:: Information technology management ::

_____ is the discipline of engineering concerned with the principles and practice of product and service quality assurance and control. In the software development, it is the management, development, operation and maintenance of IT systems and enterprise architectures with a high quality standard.

Exam Probability: **Medium**

22. *Answer choices:*

(see index for correct answer)

- a. IT Project Coordinator
- b. People Capability Maturity Model
- c. Storage hypervisor
- d. EDIFACT

Guidance: level 1

:: Quality control tools ::

A _____ is a type of diagram that represents an algorithm, workflow or process. _____ can also be defined as a diagramatic representation of an algorithm .

Exam Probability: **Medium**

23. *Answer choices:*

(see index for correct answer)

- a. CUSUM
- b. C-chart
- c. Cause-and-effect diagram
- d. Flowchart

Guidance: level 1

:: Production and manufacturing ::

> Automatic _____ in continuous production processes is a combination of control engineering and chemical engineering disciplines that uses industrial control systems to achieve a production level of consistency, economy and safety which could not be achieved purely by human manual control. It is implemented widely in industries such as oil refining, pulp and paper manufacturing, chemical processing and power generating plants.

Exam Probability: **Medium**

24. *Answer choices:*

(see index for correct answer)

- a. Equipment service management and rental
- b. Bill of materials
- c. Hydrosila
- d. Process control

Guidance: level 1

:: Project management ::

A _____ is a team whose members usually belong to different groups, functions and are assigned to activities for the same project. A team can be divided into sub-teams according to need. Usually _____ s are only used for a defined period of time. They are disbanded after the project is deemed complete. Due to the nature of the specific formation and disbandment, _____ s are usually in organizations.

Exam Probability: **Low**

25. *Answer choices:*

(see index for correct answer)

- a. Association for Project Management
- b. Outcome mapping
- c. Punch list
- d. Project charter

Guidance: level 1

:: Teams ::

A _____ usually refers to a group of individuals who work together from different geographic locations and rely on communication technology such as email, FAX, and video or voice conferencing services in order to collaborate. The term can also refer to groups or teams that work together asynchronously or across organizational levels. Powell, Piccoli and Ives define _____ s as "groups of geographically, organizationally and/or time dispersed workers brought together by information and telecommunication technologies to accomplish one or more organizational tasks." According to Ale Ebrahim et. al. , _____ s can also be defined as "small temporary groups of geographically, organizationally and/or time dispersed knowledge workers who coordinate their work predominantly with electronic information and communication technologies in order to accomplish one or more organization tasks."

Exam Probability: **Medium**

26. *Answer choices:*

(see index for correct answer)

- a. Team-building
- b. Virtual team

Guidance: level 1

:: Manufacturing ::

_____ or lean production, often simply "lean", is a systematic method for the minimization of waste within a manufacturing system without sacrificing productivity, which can cause problems. Lean also takes into account waste created through overburden and waste created through unevenness in work loads. Working from the perspective of the client who consumes a product or service, "value" is any action or process that a customer would be willing to pay for.

Exam Probability: **Medium**

27. *Answer choices:*

(see index for correct answer)

- a. Machine coordinate system
- b. Lean manufacturing
- c. Manufacturing Readiness Level
- d. Single-Minute Exchange of Die

Guidance: level 1

:: Natural resources ::

_____ s are resources that exist without actions of humankind. This includes all valued characteristics such as magnetic, gravitational, electrical properties and forces etc. On Earth it includes sunlight, atmosphere, water, land along with all vegetation, crops and animal life that naturally subsists upon or within the heretofore identified characteristics and substances.

Exam Probability: **High**

28. *Answer choices:*

(see index for correct answer)

- a. Asteroid mining
- b. Natural Resources Acts
- c. Exploitation of natural resources
- d. Natural resource

Guidance: level 1

:: ::

_____ is the quantity of three-dimensional space enclosed by a closed surface, for example, the space that a substance or shape occupies or contains. _____ is often quantified numerically using the SI derived unit, the cubic metre. The _____ of a container is generally understood to be the capacity of the container; i. e., the amount of fluid that the container could hold, rather than the amount of space the container itself displaces. Three dimensional mathematical shapes are also assigned _____ s. _____ s of some simple shapes, such as regular, straight-edged, and circular shapes can be easily calculated using arithmetic formulas. _____ s of complicated shapes can be calculated with integral calculus if a formula exists for the shape's boundary. One-dimensional figures and two-dimensional shapes are assigned zero _____ in the three-dimensional space.

Exam Probability: **High**

29. *Answer choices:*

(see index for correct answer)

- a. Sarbanes-Oxley act of 2002
- b. hierarchical
- c. interpersonal communication
- d. personal values

Guidance: level 1

:: Process management ::

_____ is a statistics package developed at the Pennsylvania State University by researchers Barbara F. Ryan, Thomas A. Ryan, Jr., and Brian L. Joiner in 1972. It began as a light version of OMNITAB 80, a statistical analysis program by NIST. Statistical analysis software such as _____ automates calculations and the creation of graphs, allowing the user to focus more on the analysis of data and the interpretation of results. It is compatible with other _____ , Inc. software.

Exam Probability: **Low**

30. *Answer choices:*

(see index for correct answer)

- a. Turnaround
- b. P and R measures
- c. Minitab

- d. Process performance index

Guidance: level 1

:: Evaluation ::

_____ is a way of preventing mistakes and defects in manufactured products and avoiding problems when delivering products or services to customers; which ISO 9000 defines as "part of quality management focused on providing confidence that quality requirements will be fulfilled". This defect prevention in _____ differs subtly from defect detection and rejection in quality control and has been referred to as a shift left since it focuses on quality earlier in the process .

Exam Probability: **High**

31. *Answer choices:*

(see index for correct answer)

- a. Quality assurance
- b. Ecological indicator
- c. Formative assessment
- d. Joint Committee on Standards for Educational Evaluation

Guidance: level 1

:: Procurement ::

Purchasing is the formal process of buying goods and services. The _____ can vary from one organization to another, but there are some common key elements.

Exam Probability: **Medium**

32. *Answer choices:*

(see index for correct answer)

- a. Purchasing process
- b. Inverted Sourcing
- c. Collateral Billing number
- d. Initial operating capability

Guidance: level 1

:: Casting (manufacturing) ::

A _____ is a regularity in the world, man-made design, or abstract ideas. As such, the elements of a _____ repeat in a predictable manner. A geometric _____ is a kind of _____ formed of geometric shapes and typically repeated like a wallpaper design.

Exam Probability: **Medium**

33. *Answer choices:*

(see index for correct answer)

- a. Chill
- b. Investment casting
- c. Pattern
- d. Lost-foam casting

Guidance: level 1

:: Business process ::

A _____ or business method is a collection of related, structured activities or tasks by people or equipment which in a specific sequence produce a service or product for a particular customer or customers. _____ es occur at all organizational levels and may or may not be visible to the customers. A _____ may often be visualized as a flowchart of a sequence of activities with interleaving decision points or as a process matrix of a sequence of activities with relevance rules based on data in the process. The benefits of using _____ es include improved customer satisfaction and improved agility for reacting to rapid market change. Process-oriented organizations break down the barriers of structural departments and try to avoid functional silos.

Exam Probability: **High**

34. *Answer choices:*

(see index for correct answer)

- a. Business process outsourcing
- b. Extended Enterprise Modeling Language

- c. Business process outsourcing to India
- d. Software Ideas Modeler

Guidance: level 1

:: Sampling (statistics) ::

_____ uses statistical sampling to determine whether to accept or reject a production lot of material. It has been a common quality control technique used in industry. It is usually done as products leaves the factory, or in some cases even within the factory. Most often a producer supplies a consumer a number of items and a decision to accept or reject the items is made by determining the number of defective items in a sample from the lot. The lot is accepted if the number of defects falls below where the acceptance number or otherwise the lot is rejected.

Exam Probability: **Low**

35. *Answer choices:*
(see index for correct answer)

- a. Sampling frame
- b. Acceptance sampling
- c. Sampling error
- d. Expander walk sampling

Guidance: level 1

:: Management ::

A process is a unique combination of tools, materials, methods, and people engaged in producing a measurable output; for example a manufacturing line for machine parts. All processes have inherent statistical variability which can be evaluated by statistical methods.

Exam Probability: **Medium**

36. *Answer choices:*

(see index for correct answer)

- a. Linear scheduling method
- b. Line management
- c. Economic order quantity
- d. Process capability

Guidance: level 1

:: Production economics ::

In economics and related disciplines, a _____ is a cost in making any economic trade when participating in a market.

Exam Probability: **High**

37. Answer choices:

(see index for correct answer)

- a. Transaction cost
- b. Productivity Alpha
- c. Limiting factor
- d. Capitalist mode of production

Guidance: level 1

:: ::

_____ is a kind of action that occur as two or more objects have an effect upon one another. The idea of a two-way effect is essential in the concept of _____, as opposed to a one-way causal effect. A closely related term is interconnectivity, which deals with the _____ s of _____ s within systems: combinations of many simple _____ s can lead to surprising emergent phenomena. _____ has different tailored meanings in various sciences. Changes can also involve _____ .

Exam Probability: **Low**

38. Answer choices:

(see index for correct answer)

- a. hierarchical
- b. Interaction
- c. interpersonal communication

- d. Character

Guidance: level 1

:: Waste ::

_____ are unwanted or unusable materials. _____ is any substance which is discarded after primary use, or is worthless, defective and of no use. A by-product by contrast is a joint product of relatively minor economic value. A _____ product may become a by-product, joint product or resource through an invention that raises a _____ product's value above zero.

Exam Probability: **High**

39. *Answer choices:*

(see index for correct answer)

- a. Coal combustion products
- b. Wood ash
- c. Waste
- d. Biodegradable waste

Guidance: level 1

:: Management ::

_____, also known as natural process limits, are horizontal lines drawn on a statistical process control chart, usually at a distance of ±3 standard deviations of the plotted statistic from the statistic's mean.

Exam Probability: **Medium**

40. *Answer choices:*

(see index for correct answer)

- a. Managerialism
- b. Authoritarian leadership style
- c. Control limits
- d. Corporate foresight

Guidance: level 1

:: Direct marketing ::

_____ Inc. is an American privately owned multi-level marketing company. According to Direct Selling News, _____ was the sixth largest network marketing company in the world in 2018, with a wholesale volume of US$3.25 billion. _____ is based in Addison, Texas, outside Dallas. The company was founded by _____ Ash in 1963. Richard Rogers, _____'s son, is the chairman, and David Holl is president and was named CEO in 2006.

Exam Probability: **Medium**

41. *Answer choices:*

(see index for correct answer)

- a. Mary Kay
- b. A Common Reader
- c. Publishers Clearing House
- d. Warm market

Guidance: level 1

:: Debt ::

> _____ is the trust which allows one party to provide money or resources to another party wherein the second party does not reimburse the first party immediately , but promises either to repay or return those resources at a later date. In other words, _____ is a method of making reciprocity formal, legally enforceable, and extensible to a large group of unrelated people.

Exam Probability: **High**

42. *Answer choices:*

(see index for correct answer)

- a. Bailout
- b. Cessio bonorum
- c. Credit crunch
- d. Credit

Guidance: level 1

:: E-commerce ::

_____ is the activity of buying or selling of products on online services or over the Internet. Electronic commerce draws on technologies such as mobile commerce, electronic funds transfer, supply chain management, Internet marketing, online transaction processing, electronic data interchange , inventory management systems, and automated data collection systems.

Exam Probability: **Medium**

43. *Answer choices:*

(see index for correct answer)

- a. E-commerce
- b. Computer reservations system
- c. Alternative currency
- d. SMS banking

Guidance: level 1

:: Marketing techniques ::

A _____ is an award to be given to a person, a group of people like a sports team, or organization to recognise and reward actions or achievements. Official _____s often involve monetary rewards as well as the fame that comes with them. Some _____s are also associated with extravagant awarding ceremonies, such as the Academy Awards.

Exam Probability: **High**

44. *Answer choices:*

(see index for correct answer)

- a. Celebrity branding
- b. Continuity marketing
- c. Virtual event
- d. Prize

Guidance: level 1

:: Industrial design ::

In physics and mathematics, the _____ of a mathematical space is informally defined as the minimum number of coordinates needed to specify any point within it. Thus a line has a _____ of one because only one coordinate is needed to specify a point on it for example, the point at 5 on a number line. A surface such as a plane or the surface of a cylinder or sphere has a _____ of two because two coordinates are needed to specify a point on it for example, both a latitude and longitude are required to locate a point on the surface of a sphere. The inside of a cube, a cylinder or a sphere is three-_____ al because three coordinates are needed to locate a point within these spaces.

Exam Probability: **Low**

45. *Answer choices:*

(see index for correct answer)

- a. Core77
- b. International Archive of Women in Architecture
- c. Aeolipile
- d. 3D printing

Guidance: level 1

:: Sensitivity analysis ::

_____ is the study of how the uncertainty in the output of a mathematical model or system can be divided and allocated to different sources of uncertainty in its inputs. A related practice is uncertainty analysis, which has a greater focus on uncertainty quantification and propagation of uncertainty; ideally, uncertainty and _____ should be run in tandem.

Exam Probability: **Low**

46. *Answer choices:*

(see index for correct answer)

- a. Elementary effects method
- b. Variance-based sensitivity analysis
- c. Fourier amplitude sensitivity testing
- d. Tornado diagram

Guidance: level 1

:: Production and manufacturing ::

_____ is the process of determining the production capacity needed by an organization to meet changing demands for its products. In the context of _____ , design capacity is the maximum amount of work that an organization is capable of completing in a given period. Effective capacity is the maximum amount of work that an organization is capable of completing in a given period due to constraints such as quality problems, delays, material handling, etc.

Exam Probability: **Medium**

47. Answer choices:

(see index for correct answer)

- a. Piece work
- b. Capacity planning
- c. Experience curve
- d. Production engineering

Guidance: level 1

:: Building materials ::

_____ is an alloy of iron and carbon, and sometimes other elements. Because of its high tensile strength and low cost, it is a major component used in buildings, infrastructure, tools, ships, automobiles, machines, appliances, and weapons.

Exam Probability: **High**

48. Answer choices:

(see index for correct answer)

- a. Bungaroosh
- b. Ferrocement
- c. Jesmonite
- d. Steel

Guidance: level 1

:: Production and manufacturing ::

_____ is a production planning, scheduling, and inventory control system used to manage manufacturing processes. Most MRP systems are software-based, but it is possible to conduct MRP by hand as well.

Exam Probability: **Medium**

49. *Answer choices:*

(see index for correct answer)

- a. DeviceNet
- b. Workmanship
- c. Material requirements planning
- d. Order to cash

Guidance: level 1

:: Costs ::

In microeconomic theory, the _____, or alternative cost, of making a particular choice is the value of the most valuable choice out of those that were not taken. In other words, opportunity that will require sacrifices.

Exam Probability: **High**

50. *Answer choices:*

(see index for correct answer)

- a. Manufacturing cost
- b. Direct labor cost
- c. Cost per paper
- d. Opportunity cost

Guidance: level 1

:: Data interchange standards ::

_____ is the concept of businesses electronically communicating information that was traditionally communicated on paper, such as purchase orders and invoices. Technical standards for EDI exist to facilitate parties transacting such instruments without having to make special arrangements.

Exam Probability: **High**

51. *Answer choices:*

(see index for correct answer)

- a. Interaction protocol
- b. Domain Application Protocol
- c. Electronic data interchange

- d. Common Alerting Protocol

Guidance: level 1

:: Production and manufacturing ::

> A BOM can define products as they are designed, as they are ordered, as they are built, or as they are maintained. The different types of BOMs depend on the business need and use for which they are intended. In process industries, the BOM is also known as the formula, recipe, or ingredients list. The phrase "bill of material" is frequently used by engineers as an adjective to refer not to the literal bill, but to the current production configuration of a product, to distinguish it from modified or improved versions under study or in test.

Exam Probability: **High**

52. *Answer choices:*

(see index for correct answer)

- a. Production part approval process
- b. Bill of materials
- c. Expediting
- d. production control

Guidance: level 1

:: Asset ::

In financial accounting, an _____ is any resource owned by the business. Anything tangible or intangible that can be owned or controlled to produce value and that is held by a company to produce positive economic value is an _____ . Simply stated, _____ s represent value of ownership that can be converted into cash . The balance sheet of a firm records the monetary value of the _____ s owned by that firm. It covers money and other valuables belonging to an individual or to a business.

Exam Probability: **Medium**

53. *Answer choices:*

(see index for correct answer)

- a. Asset
- b. Current asset

Guidance: level 1

:: Management ::

_____ is a method of quality control which employs statistical methods to monitor and control a process. This helps to ensure that the process operates efficiently, producing more specification-conforming products with less waste . SPC can be applied to any process where the "conforming product" output can be measured. Key tools used in SPC include run charts, control charts, a focus on continuous improvement, and the design of experiments. An example of a process where SPC is applied is manufacturing lines.

Exam Probability: **Low**

54. *Answer choices:*

(see index for correct answer)

- a. Value migration
- b. Business rule
- c. Iterative and incremental development
- d. Statistical process control

Guidance: level 1

:: Management ::

> A supply-chain network is an evolution of the basic supply chain. Due to rapid technological advancement, organisations with a basic supply chain can develop this chain into a more complex structure involving a higher level of interdependence and connectivity between more organisations, this constitutes a supply-chain network.

Exam Probability: **Low**

55. *Answer choices:*

(see index for correct answer)

- a. Supply chain network
- b. Personal offshoring

- c. Strategic management
- d. Jarratt report

Guidance: level 1

:: ::

A _____ consists of an orchestrated and repeatable pattern of business activity enabled by the systematic organization of resources into processes that transform materials, provide services, or process information. It can be depicted as a sequence of operations, the work of a person or group, the work of an organization of staff, or one or more simple or complex mechanisms.

Exam Probability: **Low**

56. *Answer choices:*

(see index for correct answer)

- a. information systems assessment
- b. interpersonal communication
- c. Character
- d. open system

Guidance: level 1

:: Management ::

_____ is a formal technique useful where many possible courses of action are competing for attention. In essence, the problem-solver estimates the benefit delivered by each action, then selects a number of the most effective actions that deliver a total benefit reasonably close to the maximal possible one.

Exam Probability: **High**

57. *Answer choices:*

(see index for correct answer)

- a. Complementary assets
- b. Managerial hubris
- c. Pareto analysis
- d. Adhocracy

Guidance: level 1

:: Management ::

_____ is the discipline of strategically planning for, and managing, all interactions with third party organizations that supply goods and/or services to an organization in order to maximize the value of those interactions. In practice, SRM entails creating closer, more collaborative relationships with key suppliers in order to uncover and realize new value and reduce risk of failure.

Exam Probability: **Medium**

58. Answer choices:

(see index for correct answer)

- a. Business rule
- b. Cross ownership
- c. Integrated master plan
- d. Communications management

Guidance: level 1

:: Project management ::

A _____ is a type of bar chart that illustrates a project schedule, named after its inventor, Henry Gantt, who designed such a chart around the years 1910–1915. Modern _____ s also show the dependency relationships between activities and current schedule status.

Exam Probability: **High**

59. Answer choices:

(see index for correct answer)

- a. Changes clause
- b. Outcome mapping
- c. Gantt chart
- d. Elemental cost planning

Guidance: level 1

Commerce

Commerce relates to "the exchange of goods and services, especially on a large scale." It includes legal, economic, political, social, cultural and technological systems that operate in any country or internationally.

:: ::

_____ is the social science that studies the production, distribution, and consumption of goods and services.

Exam Probability: **Medium**

1. *Answer choices:*

(see index for correct answer)

- a. similarity-attraction theory
- b. cultural
- c. process perspective
- d. hierarchical perspective

Guidance: level 1

:: ::

The _____ is a U.S. business-focused, English-language international daily newspaper based in New York City. The Journal, along with its Asian and European editions, is published six days a week by Dow Jones & Company, a division of News Corp. The newspaper is published in the broadsheet format and online. The Journal has been printed continuously since its inception on July 8, 1889, by Charles Dow, Edward Jones, and Charles Bergstresser.

Exam Probability: **High**

2. *Answer choices:*

(see index for correct answer)

- a. imperative
- b. functional perspective
- c. cultural
- d. similarity-attraction theory

Guidance: level 1

:: Marketing analytics ::

_____ is a long-term, forward-looking approach to planning with the fundamental goal of achieving a sustainable competitive advantage. Strategic planning involves an analysis of the company's strategic initial situation prior to the formulation, evaluation and selection of market-oriented competitive position that contributes to the company's goals and marketing objectives.

Exam Probability: **Medium**

3. *Answer choices:*

(see index for correct answer)

- a. Marketing strategy
- b. Mission-driven marketing
- c. Marketing accountability
- d. Return on marketing investment

Guidance: level 1

:: Computer access control ::

_____ is the act of confirming the truth of an attribute of a single piece of data claimed true by an entity. In contrast with identification, which refers to the act of stating or otherwise indicating a claim purportedly attesting to a person or thing's identity, _____ is the process of actually confirming that identity. It might involve confirming the identity of a person by validating their identity documents, verifying the authenticity of a website with a digital certificate, determining the age of an artifact by carbon dating, or ensuring that a product is what its packaging and labeling claim to be. In other words, _____ often involves verifying the validity of at least one form of identification.

Exam Probability: **Medium**

4. *Answer choices:*

(see index for correct answer)

- a. Login manager
- b. Role hierarchy
- c. Initiative For Open Authentication
- d. Identity driven networking

Guidance: level 1

:: International trade ::

In finance, an _____ is the rate at which one currency will be exchanged for another. It is also regarded as the value of one country's currency in relation to another currency. For example, an interbank _____ of 114 Japanese yen to the United States dollar means that ¥114 will be exchanged for each US$1 or that US$1 will be exchanged for each ¥114. In this case it is said that the price of a dollar in relation to yen is ¥114, or equivalently that the price of a yen in relation to dollars is $1/114.

Exam Probability: **High**

5. *Answer choices:*

(see index for correct answer)

- a. Oriental Development Company
- b. Exchange rate
- c. International Trade Awards
- d. Regional integration

Guidance: level 1

:: Manufacturing ::

A _____ is an object used to extend the ability of an individual to modify features of the surrounding environment. Although many animals use simple _____ s, only human beings, whose use of stone _____ s dates back hundreds of millennia, use _____ s to make other _____ s. The set of _____ s needed to perform different tasks that are part of the same activity is called gear or equipment.

Exam Probability: **High**

6. *Answer choices:*

(see index for correct answer)

- a. Fixture
- b. Maquila Decree
- c. Tool
- d. Toolroom

Guidance: level 1

:: ::

> An _____ is an area of the production, distribution, or trade, and consumption of goods and services by different agents. Understood in its broadest sense, 'The _____ is defined as a social domain that emphasize the practices, discourses, and material expressions associated with the production, use, and management of resources`. Economic agents can be individuals, businesses, organizations, or governments. Economic transactions occur when two parties agree to the value or price of the transacted good or service, commonly expressed in a certain currency. However, monetary transactions only account for a small part of the economic domain.

Exam Probability: **Low**

7. *Answer choices:*

(see index for correct answer)

- a. co-culture
- b. levels of analysis
- c. Character
- d. Economy

Guidance: level 1

:: ::

In law, a _____ is a coming together of parties to a dispute, to present information in a tribunal, a formal setting with the authority to adjudicate claims or disputes. One form of tribunal is a court. The tribunal, which may occur before a judge, jury, or other designated trier of fact, aims to achieve a resolution to their dispute.

Exam Probability: **High**

8. *Answer choices:*

(see index for correct answer)

- a. cultural
- b. interpersonal communication
- c. similarity-attraction theory
- d. empathy

Guidance: level 1

:: Project management ::

Contemporary business and science treat as a _____ any undertaking, carried out individually or collaboratively and possibly involving research or design, that is carefully planned to achieve a particular aim.

Exam Probability: **Medium**

9. *Answer choices:*

(see index for correct answer)

- a. Market requirements document
- b. Project
- c. Outcome mapping
- d. Lean project management

Guidance: level 1

:: Supply chain management terms ::

In business and finance, _____ is a system of organizations, people, activities, information, and resources involved in moving a product or service from supplier to customer. _____ activities involve the transformation of natural resources, raw materials, and components into a finished product that is delivered to the end customer. In sophisticated _____ systems, used products may re-enter the _____ at any point where residual value is recyclable. _____ s link value chains.

Exam Probability: **Medium**

10. *Answer choices:*

(see index for correct answer)

- a. Cool Chain Quality Indicator
- b. Capital spare
- c. Direct shipment
- d. Supply chain

Guidance: level 1

:: Decision theory ::

A _____ is a deliberate system of principles to guide decisions and achieve rational outcomes. A _____ is a statement of intent, and is implemented as a procedure or protocol. Policies are generally adopted by a governance body within an organization. Policies can assist in both subjective and objective decision making. Policies to assist in subjective decision making usually assist senior management with decisions that must be based on the relative merits of a number of factors, and as a result are often hard to test objectively, e.g. work-life balance _____. In contrast policies to assist in objective decision making are usually operational in nature and can be objectively tested, e.g. password _____.

Exam Probability: **Medium**

11. *Answer choices:*

(see index for correct answer)

- a. Policy
- b. Action axiom
- c. Seven Management and Planning Tools
- d. Expected value of sample information

Guidance: level 1

:: ::

_____ is the collaborative effort of a team to achieve a common goal or to complete a task in the most effective and efficient way. This concept is seen within the greater framework of a team, which is a group of interdependent individuals who work together towards a common goal. Basic requirements for effective _____ are an adequate team size , available resources for the team to make use of , and clearly defined roles within the team in order for everyone to have a clear purpose. _____ is present in any context where a group of people are working together to achieve a common goal. These contexts include an industrial organization , athletics , a school , and the healthcare system . In each of these settings, the level of _____ and interdependence can vary from low , to intermediate , to high , depending on the amount of communication, interaction, and collaboration present between team members.

Exam Probability: **Low**

12. *Answer choices:*

(see index for correct answer)

- a. similarity-attraction theory
- b. corporate values

- c. deep-level diversity
- d. information systems assessment

Guidance: level 1

:: Cryptography ::

In cryptography, _____ is the process of encoding a message or information in such a way that only authorized parties can access it and those who are not authorized cannot. _____ does not itself prevent interference, but denies the intelligible content to a would-be interceptor. In an _____ scheme, the intended information or message, referred to as plaintext, is encrypted using an _____ algorithm – a cipher – generating ciphertext that can be read only if decrypted. For technical reasons, an _____ scheme usually uses a pseudo-random _____ key generated by an algorithm. It is in principle possible to decrypt the message without possessing the key, but, for a well-designed _____ scheme, considerable computational resources and skills are required. An authorized recipient can easily decrypt the message with the key provided by the originator to recipients but not to unauthorized users.

Exam Probability: **Medium**

13. *Answer choices:*

(see index for correct answer)

- a. Electronic Signature
- b. backdoor
- c. ciphertext
- d. Encryption

Guidance: level 1

:: Management ::

> The term _____ refers to measures designed to increase the degree of autonomy and self-determination in people and in communities in order to enable them to represent their interests in a responsible and self-determined way, acting on their own authority. It is the process of becoming stronger and more confident, especially in controlling one's life and claiming one's rights.
> _____ as action refers both to the process of self-_____ and to professional support of people, which enables them to overcome their sense of powerlessness and lack of influence, and to recognize and use their resources. To do work with power.

Exam Probability: **Low**

14. *Answer choices:*

(see index for correct answer)

- a. Empowerment
- b. Strategic lenses
- c. Public sector consulting
- d. Design leadership

Guidance: level 1

:: International trade ::

An _____ is a good brought into a jurisdiction, especially across a national border, from an external source. The party bringing in the good is called an _____ er. An _____ in the receiving country is an export from the sending country. _____ ation and exportation are the defining financial transactions of international trade.

Exam Probability: **Low**

15. *Answer choices:*

(see index for correct answer)

- a. Asian Clearing Union
- b. Import
- c. Global financial system
- d. Authorized economic operator

Guidance: level 1

:: ::

_____ is the amount of time someone works beyond normal working hours. The term is also used for the pay received for this time. Normal hours may be determined in several ways.

Exam Probability: **Medium**

16. *Answer choices:*

(see index for correct answer)

- a. Overtime
- b. corporate values
- c. information systems assessment
- d. process perspective

Guidance: level 1

:: Statutory law ::

_____ or statute law is written law set down by a body of legislature or by a singular legislator. This is as opposed to oral or customary law; or regulatory law promulgated by the executive or common law of the judiciary. Statutes may originate with national, state legislatures or local municipalities.

Exam Probability: **Medium**

17. *Answer choices:*
(see index for correct answer)

- a. Statutory law
- b. ratification
- c. Statute of repose
- d. incorporation by reference

Guidance: level 1

:: Industry ::

_____ , also known as flow production or continuous production, is the production of large amounts of standardized products, including and especially on assembly lines. Together with job production and batch production, it is one of the three main production methods.

Exam Probability: **Low**

18. *Answer choices:*

(see index for correct answer)

- a. Mass production
- b. Industrial safety system
- c. Industrial district
- d. Productivity

Guidance: level 1

:: Credit cards ::

The _____ Company, also known as Amex, is an American multinational financial services corporation headquartered in Three World Financial Center in New York City. The company was founded in 1850 and is one of the 30 components of the Dow Jones Industrial Average. The company is best known for its charge card, credit card, and traveler's cheque businesses.

Exam Probability: **Medium**

19. *Answer choices:*

(see index for correct answer)

- a. Japan Credit Bureau
- b. Visa Inc.
- c. Credit card debt
- d. Palladium Card

Guidance: level 1

:: E-commerce ::

The phrase _____ was originally coined in 1997 by Kevin Duffey at the launch of the Global _____ Forum, to mean "the delivery of electronic commerce capabilities directly into the consumer's hand, anywhere, via wireless technology." Many choose to think of _____ as meaning "a retail outlet in your customer's pocket."

Exam Probability: **Low**

20. *Answer choices:*

(see index for correct answer)

- a. Advance ship notice
- b. United Nations Convention on the Use of Electronic Communications in International Contracts
- c. Mobile commerce
- d. ROPO

Guidance: level 1

:: Direct marketing ::

_____ is a form of advertising where organizations communicate directly to customers through a variety of media including cell phone text messaging, email, websites, online adverts, database marketing, fliers, catalog distribution, promotional letters, targeted television, newspapers, magazine advertisements, and outdoor advertising. Among practitioners, it is also known as direct response marketing.

Exam Probability: **High**

21. *Answer choices:*

(see index for correct answer)

- a. Arthur Schiff
- b. Colony Brands
- c. Alticor

- d. The Cobra Group

Guidance: level 1

:: Production economics ::

In economics, _____ is the change in the total cost that arises when the quantity produced is incremented by one unit; that is, it is the cost of producing one more unit of a good. Intuitively, _____ at each level of production includes the cost of any additional inputs required to produce the next unit. At each level of production and time period being considered, _____ s include all costs that vary with the level of production, whereas other costs that do not vary with production are fixed and thus have no _____ . For example, the _____ of producing an automobile will generally include the costs of labor and parts needed for the additional automobile but not the fixed costs of the factory that have already been incurred. In practice, marginal analysis is segregated into short and long-run cases, so that, over the long run, all costs become marginal. Where there are economies of scale, prices set at _____ will fail to cover total costs, thus requiring a subsidy. _____ pricing is not a matter of merely lowering the general level of prices with the aid of a subsidy; with or without subsidy it calls for a drastic restructuring of pricing practices, with opportunities for very substantial improvements in efficiency at critical points.

Exam Probability: **High**

22. *Answer choices:*
(see index for correct answer)

- a. Marginal cost

- b. Multifactor productivity
- c. Foundations of Economic Analysis
- d. Peer production

Guidance: level 1

:: Customs duties ::

A _____ is a tax on imports or exports between sovereign states. It is a form of regulation of foreign trade and a policy that taxes foreign products to encourage or safeguard domestic industry. _____ s are the simplest and oldest instrument of trade policy. Traditionally, states have used them as a source of income. Now, they are among the most widely used instruments of protection, along with import and export quotas.

Exam Probability: **Medium**

23. *Answer choices:*

(see index for correct answer)

- a. Specific rate duty
- b. Tariff
- c. Customs area
- d. Carnet de Passages

Guidance: level 1

In financial markets, a share is a unit used as mutual funds, limited partnerships, and real estate investment trusts. The owner of _____ in the corporation/company is a shareholder of the corporation. A share is an indivisible unit of capital, expressing the ownership relationship between the company and the shareholder. The denominated value of a share is its face value, and the total of the face value of issued _____ represent the capital of a company, which may not reflect the market value of those _____ .

Exam Probability: **Medium**

24. *Answer choices:*

(see index for correct answer)

- a. information systems assessment
- b. deep-level diversity
- c. imperative
- d. process perspective

Guidance: level 1

In Western musical notation, the staff or stave is a set of five horizontal lines and four spaces that each represent a different musical pitch or in the case of a percussion staff, different percussion instruments. Appropriate music symbols, depending on the intended effect, are placed on the staff according to their corresponding pitch or function. Musical notes are placed by pitch, percussion notes are placed by instrument, and rests and other symbols are placed by convention.

Exam Probability: **High**

25. *Answer choices:*

(see index for correct answer)

- a. Staff position
- b. interpersonal communication
- c. co-culture
- d. open system

Guidance: level 1

:: Auctioneering ::

_____ are electronic auctions, which can be used by sellers to sell their items to many potential buyers. Sellers and buyers can be individuals, organizations etc.

Exam Probability: **Medium**

26. Answer choices:

(see index for correct answer)

- a. Wine auction
- b. Forward auction
- c. World Livestock Auctioneer Championship
- d. Japanese auction

Guidance: level 1

:: Market research ::

_____ is an organized effort to gather information about target markets or customers. It is a very important component of business strategy. The term is commonly interchanged with marketing research; however, expert practitioners may wish to draw a distinction, in that marketing research is concerned specifically about marketing processes, while _____ is concerned specifically with markets.

Exam Probability: **Low**

27. Answer choices:

(see index for correct answer)

- a. CoolBrands
- b. Charles Coolidge Parlin
- c. National Analysts
- d. CRISIL

Guidance: level 1

:: Consortia ::

A _____ is an association of two or more individuals, companies, organizations or governments with the objective of participating in a common activity or pooling their resources for achieving a common goal.

Exam Probability: **High**

28. *Answer choices:*

(see index for correct answer)

- a. Builder homesite
- b. Consortium
- c. Centre for Ultrahigh Bandwidth Devices for Optical Systems
- d. RapidIO

Guidance: level 1

:: Retailing ::

A _____ or trolley, also known by a variety of other names, is a cart supplied by a shop, especially supermarkets, for use by customers inside the shop for transport of merchandise to the checkout counter during shopping. In many cases customers can then also use the cart to transport their purchased goods to their vehicles, but some carts are designed to prevent them from leaving the shop.

Exam Probability: **High**

29. *Answer choices:*

(see index for correct answer)

- a. Confectionery store
- b. Gondola
- c. Shopping cart
- d. Planogram

Guidance: level 1

:: Minimum wage ::

A _____ is the lowest remuneration that employers can legally pay their workers—the price floor below which workers may not sell their labor. Most countries had introduced _____ legislation by the end of the 20th century.

Exam Probability: **High**

30. *Answer choices:*

(see index for correct answer)

- a. Working poor
- b. Minimum wage in the United States
- c. Minimum Wage Fairness Act
- d. Guaranteed minimum income

Guidance: level 1

:: Service industries ::

_____ is travel for pleasure or business; also the theory and practice of touring, the business of attracting, accommodating, and entertaining tourists, and the business of operating tours. _____ may be international, or within the traveller's country. The World _____ Organization defines _____ more generally, in terms which go "beyond the common perception of _____ as being limited to holiday activity only", as people "traveling to and staying in places outside their usual environment for not more than one consecutive year for leisure and not less than 24 hours, business and other purposes".

Exam Probability: **Medium**

31. *Answer choices:*

(see index for correct answer)

- a. Financial services in South Korea
- b. Financial services in Japan

- c. Inn sign
- d. Tourism

Guidance: level 1

:: ::

A _____ manages, commands, directs, or regulates the behavior of other devices or systems using control loops. It can range from a single home heating controller using a thermostat controlling a domestic boiler to large Industrial _____ s which are used for controlling processes or machines.

Exam Probability: **Medium**

32. *Answer choices:*

(see index for correct answer)

- a. Sarbanes-Oxley act of 2002
- b. information systems assessment
- c. imperative
- d. similarity-attraction theory

Guidance: level 1

:: Stock market ::

___ is freedom from, or resilience against, potential harm caused by others. Beneficiaries of ___ may be of persons and social groups, objects and institutions, ecosystems or any other entity or phenomenon vulnerable to unwanted change by its environment.

Exam Probability: **High**

33. *Answer choices:*

(see index for correct answer)

- a. Penny stock
- b. Security
- c. Common ordinary equity
- d. Prime Standard

Guidance: level 1

:: Industry ::

___ describes various measures of the efficiency of production. Often , a ___ measure is expressed as the ratio of an aggregate output to a single input or an aggregate input used in a production process, i.e. output per unit of input. Most common example is the labour ___ measure, e.g., such as GDP per worker. There are many different definitions of ___ and the choice among them depends on the purpose of the ___ measurement and/or data availability. The key source of difference between various ___ measures is also usually related to how the outputs and the inputs are aggregated into scalars to obtain such a ratio-type measure of ___ .

Exam Probability: **Medium**

34. *Answer choices:*

(see index for correct answer)

- a. Pareto priority index
- b. Reindustrialization
- c. Industrial robot
- d. Tertiary sector of the economy

Guidance: level 1

:: ::

A _____ is a structured form of play, usually undertaken for enjoyment and sometimes used as an educational tool. _____ s are distinct from work, which is usually carried out for remuneration, and from art, which is more often an expression of aesthetic or ideological elements. However, the distinction is not clear-cut, and many _____ s are also considered to be work or art.

Exam Probability: **Medium**

35. *Answer choices:*

(see index for correct answer)

- a. personal values
- b. co-culture

- c. Game
- d. corporate values

Guidance: level 1

:: ::

A _____ is a sworn body of people convened to render an impartial verdict officially submitted to them by a court, or to set a penalty or judgment. Modern juries tend to be found in courts to ascertain the guilt or lack thereof in a crime. In Anglophone jurisdictions, the verdict may be guilty or not guilty. The old institution of grand juries still exists in some places, particularly the United States, to investigate whether enough evidence of a crime exists to bring someone to trial.

Exam Probability: **Low**

36. *Answer choices:*

(see index for correct answer)

- a. Jury
- b. open system
- c. Character
- d. surface-level diversity

Guidance: level 1

:: ::

Advertising is a marketing communication that employs an openly sponsored, non-personal message to promote or sell a product, service or idea. Sponsors of advertising are typically businesses wishing to promote their products or services. Advertising is differentiated from public relations in that an advertiser pays for and has control over the message. It differs from personal selling in that the message is non-personal, i.e., not directed to a particular individual. Advertising is communicated through various mass media, including traditional media such as newspapers, magazines, television, radio, outdoor advertising or direct mail; and new media such as search results, blogs, social media, websites or text messages. The actual presentation of the message in a medium is referred to as an _____ , or "ad" or advert for short.

Exam Probability: **Medium**

37. *Answer choices:*

(see index for correct answer)

- a. corporate values
- b. open system
- c. interpersonal communication
- d. Sarbanes-Oxley act of 2002

Guidance: level 1

:: Land value taxation ::

_____, sometimes referred to as dry _____, is the solid surface of Earth that is not permanently covered by water. The vast majority of human activity throughout history has occurred in _____ areas that support agriculture, habitat, and various natural resources. Some life forms have developed from predecessor species that lived in bodies of water.

Exam Probability: **High**

38. *Answer choices:*

(see index for correct answer)

- a. Prosper Australia
- b. Land
- c. Harry Gunnison Brown
- d. Henry George

Guidance: level 1

:: Supply chain management ::

_____ is the process of finding and agreeing to terms, and acquiring goods, services, or works from an external source, often via a tendering or competitive bidding process. _____ is used to ensure the buyer receives goods, services, or works at the best possible price when aspects such as quality, quantity, time, and location are compared. Corporations and public bodies often define processes intended to promote fair and open competition for their business while minimizing risks such as exposure to fraud and collusion.

39. *Answer choices:*

(see index for correct answer)

- a. Dealer Business System
- b. Procurement
- c. Global supply-chain finance
- d. Helveta

Guidance: level 1

:: ::

_____ is an emotion involving pleasure, , or anxiety in considering or awaiting an expected event.

Exam Probability: **Low**

40. *Answer choices:*

(see index for correct answer)

- a. co-culture
- b. cultural
- c. surface-level diversity
- d. Anticipation

Guidance: level 1

:: Supply chain management ::

A _____ is a type of auction in which the traditional roles of buyer and seller are reversed. Thus, there is one buyer and many potential sellers. In an ordinary auction, buyers compete to obtain goods or services by offering increasingly higher prices. In contrast, in a _____ , the sellers compete to obtain business from the buyer and prices will typically decrease as the sellers underbid each other.

Exam Probability: **Medium**

41. *Answer choices:*

(see index for correct answer)

- a. Demand Solutions
- b. ERFx
- c. Suppliers and Parts database
- d. Irancode

Guidance: level 1

:: Commerce ::

_____ relates to "the exchange of goods and services, especially on a large scale". It includes legal, economic, political, social, cultural and technological systems that operate in a country or in international trade.

Exam Probability: **High**

42. *Answer choices:*

(see index for correct answer)

- a. Uttarapatha
- b. Commercialization of space
- c. Bill of sale
- d. Commerce

Guidance: level 1

:: Trading posts of the Hanseatic League ::

_____ is a city and unitary authority area in North _____ shire, England, with a population of 208,200 as of 2017. Located at the confluence of the Rivers Ouse and Foss, it is the county town of the historic county of _____ shire and was the home of the House of _____ throughout its existence. The city is known for its famous historical landmarks such as _____ Minster and the city walls, as well as a variety of cultural and sporting activities, which makes it a popular tourist destination in England. The local authority is the City of _____ Council, a single tier governing body responsible for providing all local services and facilities throughout the city. The City of _____ local government district includes rural areas beyond the old city boundaries.

Exam Probability: **Low**

43. *Answer choices:*

(see index for correct answer)

- a. Novgorod Republic
- b. York
- c. Pskov
- d. Kaunas

Guidance: level 1

:: Evaluation ::

_____ is a way of preventing mistakes and defects in manufactured products and avoiding problems when delivering products or services to customers; which ISO 9000 defines as "part of quality management focused on providing confidence that quality requirements will be fulfilled". This defect prevention in _____ differs subtly from defect detection and rejection in quality control and has been referred to as a shift left since it focuses on quality earlier in the process.

Exam Probability: **Low**

44. *Answer choices:*

(see index for correct answer)

- a. Cryptographic Module Testing Laboratory

- b. Review
- c. Continuous assessment
- d. American Evaluation Association

Guidance: level 1

:: ::

Competition law is a law that promotes or seeks to maintain market competition by regulating anti-competitive conduct by companies. Competition law is implemented through public and private enforcement. Competition law is known as "_____ law" in the United States for historical reasons, and as "anti-monopoly law" in China and Russia. In previous years it has been known as trade practices law in the United Kingdom and Australia. In the European Union, it is referred to as both _____ and competition law.

Exam Probability: **Medium**

45. *Answer choices:*
(see index for correct answer)

- a. Antitrust
- b. corporate values
- c. similarity-attraction theory
- d. Character

Guidance: level 1

:: Payments ::

A _____ or government incentive is a form of financial aid or support extended to an economic sector generally with the aim of promoting economic and social policy. Although commonly extended from government, the term _____ can relate to any type of support – for example from NGOs or as implicit subsidies. Subsidies come in various forms including: direct and indirect .

Exam Probability: **Medium**

46. *Answer choices:*

(see index for correct answer)

- a. Direct Payments
- b. Incentive payments
- c. Subsidy
- d. Market transition payments

Guidance: level 1

:: Scientific method ::

In the social sciences and life sciences, a _____ is a research method involving an up-close, in-depth, and detailed examination of a subject of study , as well as its related contextual conditions.

Exam Probability: **Medium**

47. *Answer choices:*

(see index for correct answer)

- a. explanatory research
- b. pilot project
- c. Case study
- d. Causal research

Guidance: level 1

:: ::

_____ is the study and management of exchange relationships. _____ is the business process of creating relationships with and satisfying customers. With its focus on the customer, _____ is one of the premier components of business management.

Exam Probability: **Medium**

48. *Answer choices:*

(see index for correct answer)

- a. empathy
- b. deep-level diversity
- c. process perspective

- d. co-culture

Guidance: level 1

:: ::

> _____ are electronic transfer of money from one bank account to another, either within a single financial institution or across multiple institutions, via computer-based systems, without the direct intervention of bank staff.

Exam Probability: **Low**

49. *Answer choices:*

(see index for correct answer)

- a. personal values
- b. Electronic funds transfer
- c. hierarchical perspective
- d. levels of analysis

Guidance: level 1

:: ::

_____ is the principled guide to action taken by the administrative executive branches of the state with regard to a class of issues, in a manner consistent with law and institutional customs.

Exam Probability: **Medium**

50. *Answer choices:*

(see index for correct answer)

- a. interpersonal communication
- b. Public policy
- c. co-culture
- d. Sarbanes-Oxley act of 2002

Guidance: level 1

:: Banking ::

A _____ is a financial institution that accepts deposits from the public and creates credit. Lending activities can be performed either directly or indirectly through capital markets. Due to their importance in the financial stability of a country, _____ s are highly regulated in most countries. Most nations have institutionalized a system known as fractional reserve _____ ing under which _____ s hold liquid assets equal to only a portion of their current liabilities. In addition to other regulations intended to ensure liquidity, _____ s are generally subject to minimum capital requirements based on an international set of capital standards, known as the Basel Accords.

Exam Probability: **Medium**

51. *Answer choices:*

(see index for correct answer)

- a. Commercial finance advisor
- b. Bank
- c. Refinancing risk
- d. Origination fee

Guidance: level 1

:: ::

_____ is a qualitative measure used to relate the quality of motor vehicle traffic service. LOS is used to analyze roadways and intersections by categorizing traffic flow and assigning quality levels of traffic based on performance measure like vehicle speed, density, congestion, etc.

Exam Probability: **Low**

52. *Answer choices:*

(see index for correct answer)

- a. process perspective
- b. personal values
- c. corporate values

- d. hierarchical perspective

Guidance: level 1

:: ::

_____s is the linguistic and philosophical study of meaning, in language, programming languages, formal logics, and semiotics. It is concerned with the relationship between signifiers—like words, phrases, signs, and symbols—and what they stand for in reality, their denotation.

Exam Probability: **High**

53. *Answer choices:*

(see index for correct answer)

- a. process perspective
- b. imperative
- c. Semantic
- d. open system

Guidance: level 1

:: E-commerce ::

_____ is the activity of buying or selling of products on online services or over the Internet. Electronic commerce draws on technologies such as mobile commerce, electronic funds transfer, supply chain management, Internet marketing, online transaction processing, electronic data interchange , inventory management systems, and automated data collection systems.

Exam Probability: **Low**

54. *Answer choices:*

(see index for correct answer)

- a. Cleaning card
- b. DVD-by-mail
- c. Online savings account
- d. GS1 Sweden

Guidance: level 1

:: Business law ::

The _____ , first published in 1952, is one of a number of Uniform Acts that have been established as law with the goal of harmonizing the laws of sales and other commercial transactions across the United States of America through UCC adoption by all 50 states, the District of Columbia, and the Territories of the United States.

Exam Probability: **Medium**

55. Answer choices:

(see index for correct answer)

- a. Unfair Commercial Practices Directive
- b. Forged endorsement
- c. Uniform Commercial Code
- d. Undervalue transaction

Guidance: level 1

:: International trade ::

> _____ involves the transfer of goods or services from one person or entity to another, often in exchange for money. A system or network that allows _____ is called a market.

Exam Probability: **High**

56. Answer choices:

(see index for correct answer)

- a. Public international law
- b. Hilton Quota
- c. Banana Framework Agreement
- d. Trade Act

Guidance: level 1

:: Marketing ::

_____ comes from the Latin neg and otsia referring to businessmen who, unlike the patricians, had no leisure time in their industriousness; it held the meaning of business until the 17th century when it took on the diplomatic connotation as a dialogue between two or more people or parties intended to reach a beneficial outcome over one or more issues where a conflict exists with respect to at least one of these issues. Thus, _____ is a process of combining divergent positions into a joint agreement under a decision rule of unanimity.

Exam Probability: **Low**

57. *Answer choices:*

(see index for correct answer)

- a. Target market
- b. Negotiation
- c. Industrial marketing
- d. Bass diffusion model

Guidance: level 1

:: ::

> Competition arises whenever at least two parties strive for a goal which cannot be shared: where one's gain is the other's loss.

Exam Probability: **Medium**

58. *Answer choices:*

(see index for correct answer)

- a. Competitor
- b. Character
- c. Sarbanes-Oxley act of 2002
- d. personal values

Guidance: level 1

:: ::

> A _____ is any person who contracts to acquire an asset in return for some form of consideration.

Exam Probability: **Low**

59. *Answer choices:*

(see index for correct answer)

- a. functional perspective

- b. levels of analysis
- c. empathy
- d. open system

Guidance: level 1

Business ethics

Business ethics (also known as corporate ethics) is a form of applied ethics or professional ethics, that examines ethical principles and moral or ethical problems that can arise in a business environment. It applies to all aspects of business conduct and is relevant to the conduct of individuals and entire organizations. These ethics originate from individuals, organizational statements or from the legal system. These norms, values, ethical, and unethical practices are what is used to guide business. They help those businesses maintain a better connection with their stakeholders.

:: Nepotism ::

_____ is the granting of favour to relatives in various fields, including business, politics, entertainment, sports, religion and other activities. The term originated with the assignment of nephews to important positions by Catholic popes and bishops. Trading parliamentary employment for favors is a modern-day example of _____ . Criticism of _____, however, can be found in ancient Indian texts such as the Kural literature.

Exam Probability: **Low**

1. *Answer choices:*

(see index for correct answer)

- a. Nepotism
- b. Crachach
- c. Cronyism
- d. Cardinal-nephew

Guidance: level 1

:: Labour law ::

An _____ is special or specified circumstances that partially or fully exempt a person or organization from performance of a legal obligation so as to avoid an unreasonable or disproportionate burden or obstacle.

Exam Probability: **Low**

2. *Answer choices:*

(see index for correct answer)

- a. Non-disclosure agreement
- b. Undue hardship
- c. Individual capacity
- d. Occupational exposure limit

Guidance: level 1

:: Business ethics ::

_____ is a persistent pattern of mistreatment from others in the workplace that causes either physical or emotional harm. It can include such tactics as verbal, nonverbal, psychological, physical abuse and humiliation. This type of workplace aggression is particularly difficult because, unlike the typical school bully, workplace bullies often operate within the established rules and policies of their organization and their society. In the majority of cases, bullying in the workplace is reported as having been by someone who has authority over their victim. However, bullies can also be peers, and occasionally subordinates. Research has also investigated the impact of the larger organizational context on bullying as well as the group-level processes that impact on the incidence and maintenance of bullying behaviour. Bullying can be covert or overt. It may be missed by superiors; it may be known by many throughout the organization. Negative effects are not limited to the targeted individuals, and may lead to a decline in employee morale and a change in organizational culture. It can also take place as overbearing supervision, constant criticism, and blocking promotions.

Exam Probability: **Low**

3. *Answer choices:*

(see index for correct answer)

- a. Workplace bullying
- b. Sherpa
- c. Financial privacy
- d. The FCPA Blog

Guidance: level 1

:: United Kingdom labour law ::

The _____ was a series of programs, public work projects, financial reforms, and regulations enacted by President Franklin D. Roosevelt in the United States between 1933 and 1936. It responded to needs for relief, reform, and recovery from the Great Depression. Major federal programs included the Civilian Conservation Corps, the Civil Works Administration, the Farm Security Administration, the National Industrial Recovery Act of 1933 and the Social Security Administration. They provided support for farmers, the unemployed, youth and the elderly. The _____ included new constraints and safeguards on the banking industry and efforts to re-inflate the economy after prices had fallen sharply. _____ programs included both laws passed by Congress as well as presidential executive orders during the first term of the presidency of Franklin D. Roosevelt.

Exam Probability: **Medium**

4. *Answer choices:*

(see index for correct answer)

- a. Collective action in the United Kingdom
- b. Eleventh and Final Report of the Royal Commissioners appointed to Inquire into the Organization and Rules of Trades Unions and Other Associations
- c. New Deal
- d. Employment Protection Act 1975

Guidance: level 1

:: False advertising law ::

The Lanham Act is the primary federal trademark statute of law in the United States. The Act prohibits a number of activities, including trademark infringement, trademark dilution, and false advertising.

Exam Probability: **Low**

5. *Answer choices:*

(see index for correct answer)

- a. Rebecca Tushnet
- b. POM Wonderful LLC v. Coca-Cola Co.

Guidance: level 1

:: Criminal law ::

_____ is the body of law that relates to crime. It proscribes conduct perceived as threatening, harmful, or otherwise endangering to the property, health, safety, and moral welfare of people inclusive of one's self. Most _____ is established by statute, which is to say that the laws are enacted by a legislature. _____ includes the punishment and rehabilitation of people who violate such laws. _____ varies according to jurisdiction, and differs from civil law, where emphasis is more on dispute resolution and victim compensation, rather than on punishment or rehabilitation. Criminal procedure is a formalized official activity that authenticates the fact of commission of a crime and authorizes punitive or rehabilitative treatment of the offender.

Exam Probability: **Medium**

6. *Answer choices:*

(see index for correct answer)

- a. Self-incrimination
- b. Criminal law
- c. Mala in se
- d. Mala prohibita

Guidance: level 1

:: Writs ::

In common law, a writ of _____ is a writ whereby a private individual who assists a prosecution can receive all or part of any penalty imposed. Its name is an abbreviation of the Latin phrase _____ pro domino rege quam pro se ipso in hac parte sequitur, meaning "[he] who sues in this matter for the king as well as for himself."

Exam Probability: **Medium**

7. *Answer choices:*

(see index for correct answer)

- a. Qui tam
- b. Writ of assistance

Guidance: level 1

:: Auditing ::

_____, as defined by accounting and auditing, is a process for assuring of an organization's objectives in operational effectiveness and efficiency, reliable financial reporting, and compliance with laws, regulations and policies. A broad concept, _____ involves everything that controls risks to an organization.

Exam Probability: **Low**

8. *Answer choices:*

(see index for correct answer)

- a. Internal control
- b. Recovery Auditing
- c. Mazars
- d. Performance audit

Guidance: level 1

:: ::

A _____ is a form of business network, for example, a local organization of businesses whose goal is to further the interests of businesses. Business owners in towns and cities form these local societies to advocate on behalf of the business community. Local businesses are members, and they elect a board of directors or executive council to set policy for the chamber. The board or council then hires a President, CEO or Executive Director, plus staffing appropriate to size, to run the organization.

Exam Probability: **High**

9. *Answer choices:*

(see index for correct answer)

- a. Character
- b. Chamber of Commerce
- c. personal values
- d. deep-level diversity

Guidance: level 1

:: Corporations law ::

A normal _____ consists of various departments that contribute to the company's overall mission and goals. Common departments include Marketing, [Finance, [[Operations managementOperations, Human Resource, and IT. These five divisions represent the major departments within a publicly traded company, though there are often smaller departments within autonomous firms. There is typically a CEO, and Board of Directors composed of the directors of each department. There are also company presidents, vice presidents, and CFOs. There is a great diversity in corporate forms as enterprises may range from single company to multi-corporate conglomerate. The four main _____ s are Functional, Divisional, Geographic, and the Matrix.Realistically, most corporations tend to have a "hybrid" structure, which is a combination of different models with one dominant strategy.

Exam Probability: **High**

10. *Answer choices:*

(see index for correct answer)

- a. Non-stock corporation
- b. Corporate structure
- c. Prest v Petrodel Resources Ltd
- d. Direct debit dividend contributions

Guidance: level 1

:: ::

_____ is the introduction of contaminants into the natural environment that cause adverse change. _____ can take the form of chemical substances or energy, such as noise, heat or light. Pollutants, the components of _____ , can be either foreign substances/energies or naturally occurring contaminants. _____ is often classed as point source or nonpoint source _____ .In 2015, _____ killed 9 million people in the world.

Exam Probability: **Medium**

11. *Answer choices:*

(see index for correct answer)

- a. Pollution
- b. personal values
- c. surface-level diversity
- d. levels of analysis

Guidance: level 1

:: Hazard analysis ::

Broadly speaking, a _____ is the combined effort of 1. identifying and analyzing potential events that may negatively impact individuals, assets, and/or the environment ; and 2. making judgments "on the tolerability of the risk on the basis of a risk analysis" while considering influencing factors . Put in simpler terms, a _____ analyzes what can go wrong, how likely it is to happen, what the potential consequences are, and how tolerable the identified risk is. As part of this process, the resulting determination of risk may be expressed in a quantitative or qualitative fashion. The _____ is an inherent part of an overall risk management strategy, which attempts to, after a _____ , "introduce control measures to eliminate or reduce" any potential risk-related consequences.

Exam Probability: **Medium**

12. *Answer choices:*
(see index for correct answer)

- a. Hazard
- b. Hazardous Materials Identification System
- c. Swiss cheese model
- d. Hazard identification

Guidance: level 1

:: Fraud ::

In the United States, _____ is the claiming of Medicare health care reimbursement to which the claimant is not entitled. There are many different types of _____ , all of which have the same goal: to collect money from the Medicare program illegitimately.

Exam Probability: **High**

13. *Answer choices:*

(see index for correct answer)

- a. Accreditation mill
- b. Control fraud
- c. Medicare fraud
- d. Virginity fraud

Guidance: level 1

:: Corporate scandals ::

Exxon Mobil Corporation, doing business as _____ , is an American multinational oil and gas corporation headquartered in Irving, Texas. It is the largest direct descendant of John D. Rockefeller's Standard Oil Company, and was formed on November 30, 1999 by the merger of Exxon and Mobil . _____ 's primary brands are Exxon, Mobil, Esso, and _____ Chemical.

Exam Probability: **Low**

14. *Answer choices:*

(see index for correct answer)

- a. Xybernaut
- b. Adelphia Communications Corporation
- c. Harken Energy scandal
- d. ExxonMobil

Guidance: level 1

:: ::

A _____ is a problem offering two possibilities, neither of which is unambiguously acceptable or preferable. The possibilities are termed the horns of the _____ , a clichéd usage, but distinguishing the _____ from other kinds of predicament as a matter of usage.

Exam Probability: **Low**

15. *Answer choices:*

(see index for correct answer)

- a. functional perspective
- b. open system
- c. corporate values
- d. information systems assessment

Guidance: level 1

:: Advertising techniques ::

The _____ is a story from the Trojan War about the subterfuge that the Greeks used to enter the independent city of Troy and win the war. In the canonical version, after a fruitless 10-year siege, the Greeks constructed a huge wooden horse, and hid a select force of men inside including Odysseus. The Greeks pretended to sail away, and the Trojans pulled the horse into their city as a victory trophy. That night the Greek force crept out of the horse and opened the gates for the rest of the Greek army, which had sailed back under cover of night. The Greeks entered and destroyed the city of Troy, ending the war.

Exam Probability: **Low**

16. *Answer choices:*

(see index for correct answer)

- a. Hard sell
- b. Unipole sign
- c. Trojan horse
- d. Two Cunts in a Kitchen

Guidance: level 1

:: Business ethics ::

The _____ are the names of two corporate codes of conduct, developed by the African-American preacher Rev. Leon Sullivan, promoting corporate social responsibility.

Exam Probability: **Low**

17. *Answer choices:*

(see index for correct answer)

- a. United Nations Global Compact
- b. Contingent work
- c. Wheelmen
- d. Enron Code of Ethics

Guidance: level 1

:: ::

_____ is an eight-block-long street running roughly northwest to southeast from Broadway to South Street, at the East River, in the Financial District of Lower Manhattan in New York City. Over time, the term has become a metonym for the financial markets of the United States as a whole, the American financial services industry, or New York–based financial interests.

Exam Probability: **High**

18. *Answer choices:*

(see index for correct answer)

- a. co-culture
- b. interpersonal communication
- c. Wall Street
- d. process perspective

Guidance: level 1

:: ::

The _____ is an American stock exchange located at 11 Wall Street, Lower Manhattan, New York City, New York. It is by far the world's largest stock exchange by market capitalization of its listed companies at US$30.1 trillion as of February 2018. The average daily trading value was approximately US$169 billion in 2013. The NYSE trading floor is located at 11 Wall Street and is composed of 21 rooms used for the facilitation of trading. A fifth trading room, located at 30 Broad Street, was closed in February 2007. The main building and the 11 Wall Street building were designated National Historic Landmarks in 1978.

Exam Probability: **Medium**

19. *Answer choices:*

(see index for correct answer)

- a. imperative
- b. New York Stock Exchange
- c. co-culture

- d. levels of analysis

Guidance: level 1

:: ::

The _____ , founded in 1912, is a private, nonprofit organization whose self-described mission is to focus on advancing marketplace trust, consisting of 106 independently incorporated local BBB organizations in the United States and Canada, coordinated under the Council of _____ s in Arlington, Virginia.

Exam Probability: **Low**

20. *Answer choices:*

(see index for correct answer)

- a. hierarchical
- b. process perspective
- c. deep-level diversity
- d. Better Business Bureau

Guidance: level 1

:: ::

The _____, the Calvinist work ethic or the Puritan work ethic is a work ethic concept in theology, sociology, economics and history that emphasizes that hard work, discipline and frugality are a result of a person's subscription to the values espoused by the Protestant faith, particularly Calvinism. The phrase was initially coined in 1904–1905 by Max Weber in his book The Protestant Ethic and the Spirit of Capitalism.

Exam Probability: **Low**

21. *Answer choices:*

(see index for correct answer)

- a. Protestant work ethic
- b. corporate values
- c. similarity-attraction theory
- d. process perspective

Guidance: level 1

:: Decentralization ::

_____ or sub _____ mainly refers to the unrestricted growth in many urban areas of housing, commercial development, and roads over large expanses of land, with little concern for urban planning. In addition to describing a particular form of urbanization, the term also relates to the social and environmental consequences associated with this development. In Continental Europe the term "peri-urbanisation" is often used to denote similar dynamics and phenomena, although the term _____ is currently being used by the European Environment Agency. There is widespread disagreement about what constitutes sprawl and how to quantify it. For example, some commentators measure sprawl only with the average number of residential units per acre in a given area. But others associate it with decentralization, discontinuity, segregation of uses, and so forth.

Exam Probability: **Medium**

22. *Answer choices:*

(see index for correct answer)

- a. Regions of Morocco
- b. Local government in the Philippines
- c. Jos Chathukulam
- d. Republics of the Soviet Union

Guidance: level 1

:: Confidence tricks ::

A _____ is a business model that recruits members via a promise of payments or services for enrolling others into the scheme, rather than supplying investments or sale of products. As recruiting multiplies, recruiting becomes quickly impossible, and most members are unable to profit; as such, _____ s are unsustainable and often illegal.

Exam Probability: **Medium**

23. *Answer choices:*

(see index for correct answer)

- a. Domain name scams
- b. Pyramid scheme
- c. Vanity gallery
- d. White van speaker scam

Guidance: level 1

:: ::

A _____ is the ability to carry out a task with determined results often within a given amount of time, energy, or both. _____ s can often be divided into domain-general and domain-specific _____ s. For example, in the domain of work, some general _____ s would include time management, teamwork and leadership, self-motivation and others, whereas domain-specific _____ s would be used only for a certain job. _____ usually requires certain environmental stimuli and situations to assess the level of _____ being shown and used.

Exam Probability: **Medium**

24. *Answer choices:*

(see index for correct answer)

- a. levels of analysis
- b. Skill
- c. Sarbanes-Oxley act of 2002
- d. open system

Guidance: level 1

:: ::

_____ is a private Dominican liberal arts college in Madison, Wisconsin. The college occupies a 55 acres campus overlooking the shores of Lake Wingra.

Exam Probability: **Low**

25. *Answer choices:*

(see index for correct answer)

- a. Edgewood College
- b. hierarchical perspective
- c. corporate values
- d. cultural

Guidance: level 1

____ is a bundle of characteristics, including ways of thinking, feeling, and acting, which humans are said to have naturally. The term is often regarded as capturing what it is to be human, or the essence of humanity. The term is controversial because it is disputed whether or not such an essence exists. Arguments about ____ have been a mainstay of philosophy for centuries and the concept continues to provoke lively philosophical debate. The concept also continues to play a role in science, with neuroscientists, psychologists and social scientists sometimes claiming that their results have yielded insight into ____. ____ is traditionally contrasted with characteristics that vary among humans, such as characteristics associated with specific cultures. Debates about ____ are related to, although not the same as, debates about the comparative importance of genes and environment in development.

Exam Probability: **Medium**

26. *Answer choices:*

(see index for correct answer)

- a. imperative
- b. open system
- c. deep-level diversity
- d. empathy

Guidance: level 1

:: Business ethics ::

_____ is a type of international private business self-regulation. While once it was possible to describe CSR as an internal organisational policy or a corporate ethic strategy, that time has passed as various international laws have been developed and various organisations have used their authority to push it beyond individual or even industry-wide initiatives. While it has been considered a form of corporate self-regulation for some time, over the last decade or so it has moved considerably from voluntary decisions at the level of individual organisations, to mandatory schemes at regional, national and even transnational levels.

Exam Probability: **High**

27. *Answer choices:*
(see index for correct answer)

- a. Corporate social responsibility
- b. Corruption of Foreign Public Officials Act
- c. Contingent work
- d. Being Globally Responsible Conference

Guidance: level 1

:: ::

MCI, Inc. was an American telecommunication corporation, currently a subsidiary of Verizon Communications, with its main office in Ashburn, Virginia. The corporation was formed originally as a result of the merger of _____ and MCI Communications corporations, and used the name MCI _____, succeeded by _____, before changing its name to the present version on April 12, 2003, as part of the corporation's ending of its bankruptcy status. The company traded on NASDAQ as WCOM and MCIP. The corporation was purchased by Verizon Communications with the deal finalizing on January 6, 2006, and is now identified as that company's Verizon Enterprise Solutions division with the local residential divisions being integrated slowly into local Verizon subsidiaries.

Exam Probability: **High**

28. *Answer choices:*

(see index for correct answer)

- a. WorldCom
- b. functional perspective
- c. open system
- d. imperative

Guidance: level 1

:: ::

A _____ is an astronomical body orbiting a star or stellar remnant that is massive enough to be rounded by its own gravity, is not massive enough to cause thermonuclear fusion, and has cleared its neighbouring region of _____ esimals.

Exam Probability: **High**

29. *Answer choices:*

(see index for correct answer)

- a. Planet
- b. process perspective
- c. personal values
- d. information systems assessment

Guidance: level 1

:: Corporate scandals ::

The _____ was a privately held international group of financial services companies controlled by Allen Stanford, until it was seized by United States authorities in early 2009. Headquartered in the Galleria Tower II in Uptown Houston, Texas, it had 50 offices in several countries, mainly in the Americas, included the Stanford International Bank, and said it managed US$8.5 billion of assets for more than 30,000 clients in 136 countries on six continents. On February 17, 2009, U.S. Federal agents placed the company into receivership due to charges of fraud. Ten days later, the U.S. Securities and Exchange Commission amended its complaint to accuse Stanford of turning the company into a "massive Ponzi scheme".

Exam Probability: **Medium**

30. *Answer choices:*

(see index for correct answer)

- a. Enron scandal
- b. Harken Energy scandal
- c. Stanford Financial Group
- d. Eurest Support Services

Guidance: level 1

:: Labor rights ::

The _____ is the concept that people have a human _____, or engage in productive employment, and may not be prevented from doing so. The _____ is enshrined in the Universal Declaration of Human Rights and recognized in international human rights law through its inclusion in the International Covenant on Economic, Social and Cultural Rights, where the _____ emphasizes economic, social and cultural development.

Exam Probability: **High**

31. *Answer choices:*

(see index for correct answer)

- a. China Labour Bulletin
- b. Kate Mullany House

- c. The Hyatt 100
- d. China Labor Watch

Guidance: level 1

:: Price fixing convictions ::

> _____ AG is a German multinational conglomerate company headquartered in Berlin and Munich and the largest industrial manufacturing company in Europe with branch offices abroad.

Exam Probability: **Medium**

32. *Answer choices:*
(see index for correct answer)

- a. Siemens
- b. Archer Daniels Midland
- c. Heineken International
- d. ThyssenKrupp

Guidance: level 1

:: Separation of investment and commercial banking ::

The _____ refers to § 619 of the Dodd–Frank Wall Street Reform and Consumer Protection Act. The rule was originally proposed by American economist and former United States Federal Reserve Chairman Paul Volcker to restrict United States banks from making certain kinds of speculative investments that do not benefit their customers. Volcker argued that such speculative activity played a key role in the financial crisis of 2007–2008. The rule is often referred to as a ban on proprietary trading by commercial banks, whereby deposits are used to trade on the bank's own accounts, although a number of exceptions to this ban were included in the Dodd-Frank law.

Exam Probability: **Low**

33. *Answer choices:*

(see index for correct answer)

- a. Volcker Rule
- b. Merchant bank
- c. investment bank
- d. GLBA

Guidance: level 1

:: ::

In ecology, a _____ is the type of natural environment in which a particular species of organism lives. It is characterized by both physical and biological features. A species' _____ is those places where it can find food, shelter, protection and mates for reproduction.

Exam Probability: **High**

34. *Answer choices:*

(see index for correct answer)

- a. deep-level diversity
- b. similarity-attraction theory
- c. surface-level diversity
- d. functional perspective

Guidance: level 1

:: Cultural appropriation ::

_____ is a social and economic order that encourages the acquisition of goods and services in ever-increasing amounts. With the industrial revolution, but particularly in the 20th century, mass production led to an economic crisis: there was overproduction—the supply of goods would grow beyond consumer demand, and so manufacturers turned to planned obsolescence and advertising to manipulate consumer spending. In 1899, a book on _____ published by Thorstein Veblen, called The Theory of the Leisure Class, examined the widespread values and economic institutions emerging along with the widespread "leisure time" in the beginning of the 20th century. In it Veblen "views the activities and spending habits of this leisure class in terms of conspicuous and vicarious consumption and waste. Both are related to the display of status and not to functionality or usefulness."

Exam Probability: **Medium**

35. Answer choices:

(see index for correct answer)

- a. Coon Chicken Inn
- b. Consumerism
- c. Blackface
- d. Imaging Blackness

Guidance: level 1

:: ::

A _____ is a proceeding by a party or parties against another in the civil court of law. The archaic term "suit in law" is found in only a small number of laws still in effect today. The term "_____" is used in reference to a civil action brought in a court of law in which a plaintiff, a party who claims to have incurred loss as a result of a defendant's actions, demands a legal or equitable remedy. The defendant is required to respond to the plaintiff's complaint. If the plaintiff is successful, judgment is in the plaintiff's favor, and a variety of court orders may be issued to enforce a right, award damages, or impose a temporary or permanent injunction to prevent an act or compel an act. A declaratory judgment may be issued to prevent future legal disputes.

Exam Probability: **Medium**

36. Answer choices:

(see index for correct answer)

- a. imperative
- b. Lawsuit
- c. interpersonal communication
- d. cultural

Guidance: level 1

:: ::

> Competition law is a law that promotes or seeks to maintain market competition by regulating anti-competitive conduct by companies. Competition law is implemented through public and private enforcement. Competition law is known as "_____ law" in the United States for historical reasons, and as "anti-monopoly law" in China and Russia. In previous years it has been known as trade practices law in the United Kingdom and Australia. In the European Union, it is referred to as both _____ and competition law.

Exam Probability: **Medium**

37. *Answer choices:*

(see index for correct answer)

- a. interpersonal communication
- b. Sarbanes-Oxley act of 2002
- c. imperative
- d. levels of analysis

Guidance: level 1

:: White-collar criminals ::

_____ refers to financially motivated, nonviolent crime committed by businesses and government professionals. It was first defined by the sociologist Edwin Sutherland in 1939 as "a crime committed by a person of respectability and high social status in the course of their occupation". Typical _____ s could include wage theft, fraud, bribery, Ponzi schemes, insider trading, labor racketeering, embezzlement, cybercrime, copyright infringement, money laundering, identity theft, and forgery. Lawyers can specialize in _____ .

Exam Probability: **High**

38. *Answer choices:*

(see index for correct answer)

- a. Du Jun
- b. Tongsun Park

Guidance: level 1

:: ::

_____ , O.S.A. was a German professor of theology, composer, priest, monk, and a seminal figure in the Protestant Reformation.

Exam Probability: **High**

39. *Answer choices:*

(see index for correct answer)

- a. Martin Luther
- b. information systems assessment
- c. empathy
- d. interpersonal communication

Guidance: level 1

:: ::

_____ is a region of India consisting of the Indian states of Bihar, Jharkhand, West Bengal, Odisha and also the union territory Andaman and Nicobar Islands. West Bengal's capital Kolkata is the largest city of this region. The Kolkata Metropolitan Area is the country's third largest.

Exam Probability: **High**

40. *Answer choices:*

(see index for correct answer)

- a. Character
- b. interpersonal communication
- c. East India

- d. information systems assessment

Guidance: level 1

:: ::

Oriental Nicety, formerly _____, Exxon Mediterranean, SeaRiver Mediterranean, S/R Mediterranean, Mediterranean, and Dong Fang Ocean, was an oil tanker that gained notoriety after running aground in Prince William Sound spilling hundreds of thousands of barrels of crude oil in Alaska. On March 24, 1989, while owned by the former Exxon Shipping Company, and captained by Joseph Hazelwood and First Mate James Kunkel bound for Long Beach, California, the vessel ran aground on the Bligh Reef resulting in the second largest oil spill in United States history. The size of the spill is estimated to have been 40,900 to 120,000 m3 , or 257,000 to 750,000 barrels. In 1989, the _____ oil spill was listed as the 54th largest spill in history.

Exam Probability: **Low**

41. *Answer choices:*

(see index for correct answer)

- a. hierarchical
- b. surface-level diversity
- c. levels of analysis
- d. Exxon Valdez

Guidance: level 1

:: Business law ::

A _____ is an arrangement where parties, known as partners, agree to cooperate to advance their mutual interests. The partners in a _____ may be individuals, businesses, interest-based organizations, schools, governments or combinations. Organizations may partner to increase the likelihood of each achieving their mission and to amplify their reach. A _____ may result in issuing and holding equity or may be only governed by a contract.

Exam Probability: **Low**

42. *Answer choices:*

(see index for correct answer)

- a. Partnership
- b. Enhanced use lease
- c. Process agent
- d. Certificate of incorporation

Guidance: level 1

:: Minimum wage ::

A _____ is the lowest remuneration that employers can legally pay their workers—the price floor below which workers may not sell their labor. Most countries had introduced _____ legislation by the end of the 20th century.

Exam Probability: **Medium**

43. *Answer choices:*

(see index for correct answer)

- a. Minimum wage
- b. Minimum wage in the United States
- c. Minimum Wage Fairness Act
- d. Working poor

Guidance: level 1

:: Statutory law ::

_____ or statute law is written law set down by a body of legislature or by a singular legislator . This is as opposed to oral or customary law; or regulatory law promulgated by the executive or common law of the judiciary. Statutes may originate with national, state legislatures or local municipalities.

Exam Probability: **High**

44. *Answer choices:*

(see index for correct answer)

- a. ratification
- b. incorporation by reference

- c. statute law
- d. Statute of repose

Guidance: level 1

:: ::

_____ is "property consisting of land and the buildings on it, along with its natural resources such as crops, minerals or water; immovable property of this nature; an interest vested in this an item of real property, buildings or housing in general. Also: the business of _____ ; the profession of buying, selling, or renting land, buildings, or housing." It is a legal term used in jurisdictions whose legal system is derived from English common law, such as India, England, Wales, Northern Ireland, United States, Canada, Pakistan, Australia, and New Zealand.

Exam Probability: **Low**

45. *Answer choices:*
(see index for correct answer)

- a. empathy
- b. personal values
- c. process perspective
- d. Real estate

Guidance: level 1

_____ ism is a form of government characterized by strong central power and limited political freedoms. Individual freedoms are subordinate to the state and there is no constitutional accountability and rule of law under an _____ regime. _____ regimes can be autocratic with power concentrated in one person or it can be more spread out between multiple officials and government institutions. Juan Linz's influential 1964 description of _____ ism characterized _____ political systems by four qualities.

Exam Probability: **High**

46. *Answer choices:*

(see index for correct answer)

- a. interpersonal communication
- b. cultural
- c. Authoritarian
- d. corporate values

Guidance: level 1

:: Environmental economics ::

_____ is an institutional arrangement designed to help producers in developing countries achieve better trading conditions. Members of the _____ movement advocate the payment of higher prices to exporters, as well as improved social and environmental standards. The movement focuses in particular on commodities, or products which are typically exported from developing countries to developed countries, but also consumed in domestic markets most notably handicrafts, coffee, cocoa, wine, sugar, fresh fruit, chocolate, flowers and gold. The movement seeks to promote greater equity in international trading partnerships through dialogue, transparency, and respect. It promotes sustainable development by offering better trading conditions to, and securing the rights of, marginalized producers and workers in developing countries. _____ is grounded in three core beliefs; first, producers have the power to express unity with consumers. Secondly, the world trade practices that currently exist promote the unequal distribution of wealth between nations. Lastly, buying products from producers in developing countries at a fair price is a more efficient way of promoting sustainable development than traditional charity and aid.

Exam Probability: **Medium**

47. *Answer choices:*

(see index for correct answer)

- a. Material Flow Cost Accounting
- b. Fair trade
- c. Natural resource economics
- d. Resource intensity

Guidance: level 1

:: Labour relations ::

_____ is a field of study that can have different meanings depending on the context in which it is used. In an international context, it is a subfield of labor history that studies the human relations with regard to work – in its broadest sense – and how this connects to questions of social inequality. It explicitly encompasses unregulated, historical, and non-Western forms of labor. Here, _____ define "for or with whom one works and under what rules. These rules determine the type of work, type and amount of remuneration, working hours, degrees of physical and psychological strain, as well as the degree of freedom and autonomy associated with the work."

Exam Probability: **Medium**

48. *Answer choices:*

(see index for correct answer)

- a. Passfield Memorandum
- b. Eurocadres
- c. Whipsaw strike
- d. Labor relations

Guidance: level 1

:: Social philosophy ::

The _____ describes the unintended social benefits of an individual's self-interested actions. Adam Smith first introduced the concept in The Theory of Moral Sentiments, written in 1759, invoking it in reference to income distribution. In this work, however, the idea of the market is not discussed, and the word "capitalism" is never used.

Exam Probability: **Medium**

49. *Answer choices:*

(see index for correct answer)

- a. Freedom to contract
- b. Societal attitudes towards abortion
- c. Veil of Ignorance
- d. vacancy chain

Guidance: level 1

:: ::

_____ was a philosopher during the Classical period in Ancient Greece, the founder of the Lyceum and the Peripatetic school of philosophy and Aristotelian tradition. Along with his teacher Plato, he is considered the "Father of Western Philosophy". His writings cover many subjects – including physics, biology, zoology, metaphysics, logic, ethics, aesthetics, poetry, theatre, music, rhetoric, psychology, linguistics, economics, politics and government. _____ provided a complex synthesis of the various philosophies existing prior to him, and it was above all from his teachings that the West inherited its intellectual lexicon, as well as problems and methods of inquiry. As a result, his philosophy has exerted a unique influence on almost every form of knowledge in the West and it continues to be a subject of contemporary philosophical discussion.

Exam Probability: **Medium**

50. *Answer choices:*

(see index for correct answer)

- a. interpersonal communication
- b. Aristotle
- c. Sarbanes-Oxley act of 2002
- d. personal values

Guidance: level 1

:: Confidence tricks ::

A _____ is a form of fraud that lures investors and pays profits to earlier investors with funds from more recent investors. The scheme leads victims to believe that profits are coming from product sales or other means, and they remain unaware that other investors are the source of funds. A _____ can maintain the illusion of a sustainable business as long as new investors contribute new funds, and as long as most of the investors do not demand full repayment and still believe in the non-existent assets they are purported to own.

Exam Probability: **High**

51. *Answer choices:*

(see index for correct answer)

- a. Technical support scam
- b. Strip search phone call scam

- c. The switch
- d. Miracle cars scam

Guidance: level 1

:: Coal ::

_____ is a combustible black or brownish-black sedimentary rock, formed as rock strata called _____ seams. _____ is mostly carbon with variable amounts of other elements; chiefly hydrogen, sulfur, oxygen, and nitrogen. _____ is formed if dead plant matter decays into peat and over millions of years the heat and pressure of deep burial converts the peat into _____ . Vast deposits of _____ originates in former wetlands—called _____ forests—that covered much of the Earth's tropical land areas during the late Carboniferous and Permian times.

Exam Probability: **High**

52. *Answer choices:*

(see index for correct answer)

- a. Chaldron
- b. Coal
- c. Coldry Process
- d. Black coal equivalent

Guidance: level 1

:: ::

_____ is a naturally occurring, yellowish-black liquid found in geological formations beneath the Earth's surface. It is commonly refined into various types of fuels. Components of _____ are separated using a technique called fractional distillation, i.e. separation of a liquid mixture into fractions differing in boiling point by means of distillation, typically using a fractionating column.

Exam Probability: **Medium**

53. *Answer choices:*

(see index for correct answer)

- a. deep-level diversity
- b. Petroleum
- c. open system
- d. hierarchical perspective

Guidance: level 1

:: Industry ::

_____ is the manner in which a given entity has decided to address issues of energy development including energy production, distribution and consumption. The attributes of _____ may include legislation, international treaties, incentives to investment, guidelines for energy conservation, taxation and other public policy techniques. Energy is a core component of modern economies. A functioning economy requires not only labor and capital but also energy, for manufacturing processes, transportation, communication, agriculture, and more.

Exam Probability: **Low**

54. *Answer choices:*

(see index for correct answer)

- a. Low carbon leakage
- b. Sexual division of labour
- c. Productivity
- d. Energy policy

Guidance: level 1

:: Timber industry ::

The _____ is an international non-profit, multi-stakeholder organization established in 1993 to promote responsible management of the world's forests. The FSC does this by setting standards on forest products, along with certifying and labeling them as eco-friendly.

Exam Probability: **Medium**

55. *Answer choices:*

(see index for correct answer)

- a. William Cameron Edwards
- b. Greenheart Group
- c. Timber recycling
- d. Brettstapel

Guidance: level 1

:: Anti-Revisionism ::

_____, officially the German Democratic Republic, was a country that existed from 1949 to 1990, when the eastern portion of Germany was part of the Eastern Bloc during the Cold War. It described itself as a socialist "workers' and peasants' state", and the territory was administered and occupied by Soviet forces at the end of World War II — the Soviet Occupation Zone of the Potsdam Agreement, bounded on the east by the Oder–Neisse line. The Soviet zone surrounded West Berlin but did not include it; as a result, West Berlin remained outside the jurisdiction of the GDR.

Exam Probability: **High**

56. *Answer choices:*

(see index for correct answer)

- a. Ho Chi Minh Thought
- b. Anti-Revisionism
- c. New Communist Movement
- d. East Germany

Guidance: level 1

:: Product certification ::

_____ is food produced by methods that comply with the standards of organic farming. Standards vary worldwide, but organic farming features practices that cycle resources, promote ecological balance, and conserve biodiversity. Organizations regulating organic products may restrict the use of certain pesticides and fertilizers in the farming methods used to produce such products. _____ s typically are not processed using irradiation, industrial solvents, or synthetic food additives.

Exam Probability: **Medium**

57. *Answer choices:*

(see index for correct answer)

- a. National Communications Commission
- b. Hardware certification
- c. Organic food
- d. Clerk of works

Guidance: level 1

:: Ethically disputed business practices ::

_____ is the trading of a public company's stock or other securities by individuals with access to nonpublic information about the company. In various countries, some kinds of trading based on insider information is illegal. This is because it is seen as unfair to other investors who do not have access to the information, as the investor with insider information could potentially make larger profits than a typical investor could make. The rules governing _____ are complex and vary significantly from country to country. The extent of enforcement also varies from one country to another. The definition of insider in one jurisdiction can be broad, and may cover not only insiders themselves but also any persons related to them, such as brokers, associates and even family members. A person who becomes aware of non-public information and trades on that basis may be guilty of a crime.

Exam Probability: **High**

58. *Answer choices:*

(see index for correct answer)

- a. Gaming the system
- b. Persuasive technology
- c. Insider trading
- d. Trademark troll

Guidance: level 1

:: Competition regulators ::

The _____ is an independent agency of the United States government, established in 1914 by the _____ Act. Its principal mission is the promotion of consumer protection and the elimination and prevention of anticompetitive business practices, such as coercive monopoly. It is headquartered in the _____ Building in Washington, D.C.

Exam Probability: **Low**

59. *Answer choices:*

(see index for correct answer)

- a. Competition Appeal Tribunal
- b. Federal Trade Commission
- c. Fair Trade Commission
- d. Federal Antimonopoly Service

Guidance: level 1

Accounting

Accounting or accountancy is the measurement, processing, and communication of financial information about economic entities such as businesses and corporations. The modern field was established by the Italian mathematician Luca Pacioli in 1494. Accounting, which has been called the "language of business", measures the results of an organization's economic activities and conveys this information to a variety of users, including investors, creditors, management, and regulators.

:: Real property law ::

_____ is the judicial process whereby a will is "proved" in a court of law and accepted as a valid public document that is the true last testament of the deceased, or whereby the estate is settled according to the laws of intestacy in the state of residence [or real property] of the deceased at time of death in the absence of a legal will.

Exam Probability: **Low**

1. *Answer choices:*

(see index for correct answer)

- a. Purveyance
- b. Quitclaim deed
- c. Land registration
- d. Sasine

Guidance: level 1

:: Financial accounting ::

In macroeconomics and international finance, the _____ is one of two primary components of the balance of payments, the other being the current account. Whereas the current account reflects a nation's net income, the _____ reflects net change in ownership of national assets.

Exam Probability: **Low**

2. *Answer choices:*

(see index for correct answer)

- a. Financial Condition Report
- b. Capital account
- c. Exit rate
- d. Mark-to-market accounting

Guidance: level 1

:: Organizational theory ::

> Decentralisation is the process by which the activities of an organization, particularly those regarding planning and decision making, are distributed or delegated away from a central, authoritative location or group. Concepts of _____ have been applied to group dynamics and management science in private businesses and organizations, political science, law and public administration, economics, money and technology.

Exam Probability: **Low**

3. *Answer choices:*

(see index for correct answer)

- a. Staff augmentation
- b. Solid line reporting
- c. Decentralization
- d. resource dependence

Guidance: level 1

:: Generally Accepted Accounting Principles ::

A _____ is a reduction of the recognized value of something. In accounting, this is a recognition of the reduced or zero value of an asset. In income tax statements, this is a reduction of taxable income, as a recognition of certain expenses required to produce the income.

Exam Probability: **Low**

4. *Answer choices:*

(see index for correct answer)

- a. Write-off
- b. Generally Accepted Accounting Practice
- c. Access to finance
- d. Net profit

Guidance: level 1

:: ::

_____ is the act of compensating someone for an out-of-pocket expense by giving them an amount of money equal to what was spent.

Exam Probability: **High**

5. *Answer choices:*

(see index for correct answer)

- a. similarity-attraction theory
- b. Reimbursement
- c. empathy
- d. information systems assessment

Guidance: level 1

:: ::

The _____ is a private, non-profit organization standard-setting body whose primary purpose is to establish and improve Generally Accepted Accounting Principles within the United States in the public's interest. The Securities and Exchange Commission designated the FASB as the organization responsible for setting accounting standards for public companies in the US. The FASB replaced the American Institute of Certified Public Accountants' Accounting Principles Board on July 1, 1973.

Exam Probability: **High**

6. *Answer choices:*

(see index for correct answer)

- a. Financial Accounting Standards Board

- b. surface-level diversity
- c. hierarchical perspective
- d. interpersonal communication

Guidance: level 1

:: Management ::

Business _____ is a discipline in operations management in which people use various methods to discover, model, analyze, measure, improve, optimize, and automate business processes. BPM focuses on improving corporate performance by managing business processes. Any combination of methods used to manage a company's business processes is BPM. Processes can be structured and repeatable or unstructured and variable. Though not required, enabling technologies are often used with BPM.

Exam Probability: **Low**

7. *Answer choices:*

(see index for correct answer)

- a. Work breakdown structure
- b. Productive efficiency
- c. Outrage constraint
- d. Line of business

Guidance: level 1

:: Financial ratios ::

_____ or interest coverage ratio is a measure of a company's ability to honor its debt payments. It may be calculated as either EBIT or EBITDA divided by the total interest payable.

Exam Probability: **High**

8. *Answer choices:*

(see index for correct answer)

- a. Sortino ratio
- b. Times interest earned
- c. Return on assets
- d. AlphaIC

Guidance: level 1

:: Business law ::

A _____ is a business entity created by two or more parties, generally characterized by shared ownership, shared returns and risks, and shared governance. Companies typically pursue _____ s for one of four reasons: to access a new market, particularly emerging markets; to gain scale efficiencies by combining assets and operations; to share risk for major investments or projects; or to access skills and capabilities.

Exam Probability: **Low**

9. *Answer choices:*

(see index for correct answer)

- a. Copyright transfer agreement
- b. Ordinary course of business
- c. Uniform Partnership Act
- d. Stick licensing

Guidance: level 1

:: Generally Accepted Accounting Principles ::

_____, or non-current liabilities, are liabilities that are due beyond a year or the normal operation period of the company. The normal operation period is the amount of time it takes for a company to turn inventory into cash. On a classified balance sheet, liabilities are separated between current and _____ to help users assess the company's financial standing in short-term and long-term periods. _____ give users more information about the long-term prosperity of the company, while current liabilities inform the user of debt that the company owes in the current period. On a balance sheet, accounts are listed in order of liquidity, so _____ come after current liabilities. In addition, the specific long-term liability accounts are listed on the balance sheet in order of liquidity. Therefore, an account due within eighteen months would be listed before an account due within twenty-four months. Examples of _____ are bonds payable, long-term loans, capital leases, pension liabilities, post-retirement healthcare liabilities, deferred compensation, deferred revenues, deferred income taxes, and derivative liabilities.

Exam Probability: **Medium**

10. *Answer choices:*

(see index for correct answer)

- a. Liability
- b. Long-term liabilities
- c. Completed-contract method
- d. Gross sales

Guidance: level 1

:: Accounting journals and ledgers ::

The subledger, or _____ , provides details behind entries in the general ledger used in accounting. The subledger shows detail for part of the accounting records such as property and equipment, prepaid expenses, etc. The detail would include such items as date the item was purchased or expense incurred, a description of the item, the original balance, and the net book value. The total of the subledger would match the line item amount on the general ledger. This corresponding line item in the general ledger is referred to as the controlling account. The _____ balance is compared with its controlling account balance as part of the process of preparing a trial balance.

Exam Probability: **Low**

11. *Answer choices:*

(see index for correct answer)

- a. Cash receipts journal
- b. Subledger
- c. Subsidiary ledger
- d. Check register

Guidance: level 1

:: Business ethics ::

> In accounting and in most Schools of economic thought, _____ is a rational and unbiased estimate of the potential market price of a good, service, or asset. It takes into account such objectivity factors as.

Exam Probability: **Low**

12. *Answer choices:*
(see index for correct answer)

- a. Employee raiding
- b. Anti-sweatshop movement
- c. Fair value
- d. Journal of Business Ethics Education

Guidance: level 1

:: ::

_____ is the income that is gained by governments through taxation. Taxation is the primary source of income for a state. Revenue may be extracted from sources such as individuals, public enterprises, trade, royalties on natural resources and/or foreign aid. An inefficient collection of taxes is greater in countries characterized by poverty, a large agricultural sector and large amounts of foreign aid.

Exam Probability: **Low**

13. *Answer choices:*

(see index for correct answer)

- a. hierarchical
- b. interpersonal communication
- c. levels of analysis
- d. surface-level diversity

Guidance: level 1

:: Accounting organizations ::

The _____ promotes accounting education, research and practice. Founded in 1916 as the American Association of University Instructors in Accounting, its present name was adopted in 1936. The Association is a voluntary group of persons interested in accounting education and research.

Exam Probability: **Low**

14. Answer choices:

(see index for correct answer)

- a. Accounting Hall of Fame
- b. American Accounting Association
- c. Southern African Institute for Business Accountants
- d. Centre for Social and Environmental Accounting Research

Guidance: level 1

:: E-commerce ::

> A _____ is a plastic payment card that can be used instead of cash when making purchases. It is similar to a credit card, but unlike a credit card, the money is immediately transferred directly from the cardholder's bank account when performing a transaction.

Exam Probability: **High**

15. Answer choices:

(see index for correct answer)

- a. Digital certificate
- b. USAePay
- c. SAP Sourcing
- d. Debit card

Guidance: level 1

:: Management accounting ::

> _____ is a professional business study of Accounts and management in which we learn importance of accounts in our management system.

Exam Probability: **Medium**

16. *Answer choices:*

(see index for correct answer)

- a. Constraints accounting
- b. Inventory valuation
- c. Accounting management
- d. Average per-bit delivery cost

Guidance: level 1

:: Types of accounting ::

Various _____ systems are used by various public sector entities. In the United States, for instance, there are two levels of government which follow different accounting standards set forth by independent, private sector boards. At the federal level, the Federal Accounting Standards Advisory Board sets forth the accounting standards to follow. Similarly, there is the _____ Standards Board for state and local level government.

Exam Probability: **Medium**

17. *Answer choices:*

(see index for correct answer)

- a. Personal environmental impact accounting
- b. Product control
- c. Governmental accounting

Guidance: level 1

:: Financial accounting ::

In accounting, _____ is the value of an asset according to its balance sheet account balance. For assets, the value is based on the original cost of the asset less any depreciation, amortization or impairment costs made against the asset. Traditionally, a company's _____ is its total assets minus intangible assets and liabilities. However, in practice, depending on the source of the calculation, _____ may variably include goodwill, intangible assets, or both. The value inherent in its workforce, part of the intellectual capital of a company, is always ignored. When intangible assets and goodwill are explicitly excluded, the metric is often specified to be "tangible _____".

Exam Probability: **High**

18. *Answer choices:*

(see index for correct answer)

- a. Advance payment
- b. Mark-to-market accounting
- c. Book value
- d. Accounting identity

Guidance: level 1

:: Accounting terminology ::

_____ of something is, in finance, the adding together of interest or different investments over a period of time. It holds specific meanings in accounting, where it can refer to accounts on a balance sheet that represent liabilities and non-cash-based assets used in _____ -based accounting. These types of accounts include, among others, accounts payable, accounts receivable, goodwill, deferred tax liability and future interest expense.

Exam Probability: **Medium**

19. *Answer choices:*

(see index for correct answer)

- a. Impairment cost
- b. Accounting equation
- c. Adjusting entries
- d. Checkoff

Guidance: level 1

:: Accounting terminology ::

In management accounting or _____ , managers use the provisions of accounting information in order to better inform themselves before they decide matters within their organizations, which aids their management and performance of control functions.

Exam Probability: **Low**

20. Answer choices:

(see index for correct answer)

- a. outstanding balance
- b. Cash flow management
- c. Managerial accounting
- d. Double-entry accounting

Guidance: level 1

:: Generally Accepted Accounting Principles ::

> In accrual accounting, the revenue recognition principle states that expenses should be recorded during the period in which they are incurred, regardless of when the transfer of cash occurs. Conversely, cash basis accounting calls for the recognition of an expense when the cash is paid, regardless of when the expense was actually incurred.

Exam Probability: **Low**

21. Answer choices:

(see index for correct answer)

- a. Fin 48
- b. Construction in progress
- c. Net profit
- d. Matching principle

Guidance: level 1

:: Expense ::

An _____, operating expenditure, operational expense, operational expenditure or opex is an ongoing cost for running a product, business, or system. Its counterpart, a capital expenditure, is the cost of developing or providing non-consumable parts for the product or system. For example, the purchase of a photocopier involves capex, and the annual paper, toner, power and maintenance costs represents opex. For larger systems like businesses, opex may also include the cost of workers and facility expenses such as rent and utilities.

Exam Probability: **High**

22. *Answer choices:*

(see index for correct answer)

- a. Stock option expensing
- b. Momentem
- c. Freight expense
- d. Operating expense

Guidance: level 1

:: Taxation and efficiency ::

_____ is the legal usage of the tax regime in a single territory to one's own advantage to reduce the amount of tax that is payable by means that are within the law. Tax sheltering is very similar, although unlike _____ tax sheltering is not necessarily legal. Tax havens are jurisdictions which facilitate reduced taxes.

Exam Probability: **High**

23. *Answer choices:*

(see index for correct answer)

- a. Tax incentive
- b. Capital flight
- c. Excess burden of taxation
- d. Supply-side economics

Guidance: level 1

:: ::

_____ is a costing method that identifies activities in an organization and assigns the cost of each activity to all products and services according to the actual consumption by each. This model assigns more indirect costs into direct costs compared to conventional costing.

Exam Probability: **Low**

24. *Answer choices:*

(see index for correct answer)

- a. Activity-based costing
- b. similarity-attraction theory
- c. levels of analysis
- d. surface-level diversity

Guidance: level 1

:: Income ::

_____ is a ratio between the net profit and cost of investment resulting from an investment of some resources. A high ROI means the investment's gains favorably to its cost. As a performance measure, ROI is used to evaluate the efficiency of an investment or to compare the efficiencies of several different investments. In purely economic terms, it is one way of relating profits to capital invested. _____ is a performance measure used by businesses to identify the efficiency of an investment or number of different investments.

Exam Probability: **High**

25. *Answer choices:*

(see index for correct answer)

- a. Return on investment
- b. Total personal income

- c. Creative real estate investing
- d. Mandatory tipping

Guidance: level 1

:: Management accounting ::

A _____ is a part of a business which is expected to make an identifiable contribution to the organization's profits.

Exam Probability: **Medium**

26. *Answer choices:*

(see index for correct answer)

- a. Bridge life-cycle cost analysis
- b. Net present value
- c. Profit center
- d. Target income sales

Guidance: level 1

:: Credit cards ::

A _____ is a payment card issued to users to enable the cardholder to pay a merchant for goods and services based on the cardholder's promise to the card issuer to pay them for the amounts plus the other agreed charges. The card issuer creates a revolving account and grants a line of credit to the cardholder, from which the cardholder can borrow money for payment to a merchant or as a cash advance.

Exam Probability: **Medium**

27. *Answer choices:*

(see index for correct answer)

- a. North American Bancard
- b. Revolution Money
- c. Medi Script
- d. Credit card

Guidance: level 1

:: ::

_____ is a process whereby a person assumes the parenting of another, usually a child, from that person's biological or legal parent or parents. Legal _____ s permanently transfers all rights and responsibilities, along with filiation, from the biological parent or parents.

Exam Probability: **Low**

28. *Answer choices:*

(see index for correct answer)

- a. surface-level diversity
- b. hierarchical
- c. Adoption
- d. Character

Guidance: level 1

:: Commerce ::

A _____ , is a document acknowledging that a person has received money or property in payment following a sale or other transfer of goods or provision of a service. All _____ s must have the date of purchase on them. If the recipient of the payment is legally required to collect sales tax or VAT from the customer, the amount would be added to the _____ and the collection would be deemed to have been on behalf of the relevant tax authority. In many countries, a retailer is required to include the sales tax or VAT in the displayed price of goods sold, from which the tax amount would be calculated at point of sale and remitted to the tax authorities in due course. Similarly, amounts may be deducted from amounts payable, as in the case of wage withholding taxes. On the other hand, tips or other gratuities given by a customer, for example in a restaurant, would not form part of the payment amount or appear on the _____ .

Exam Probability: **High**

29. *Answer choices:*

(see index for correct answer)

- a. Custom house
- b. Perfect tender rule
- c. Commercialization of space
- d. Reseller

Guidance: level 1

:: ::

An _____ is an asset that lacks physical substance. It is defined in opposition to physical assets such as machinery and buildings. An _____ is usually very hard to evaluate. Patents, copyrights, franchises, goodwill, trademarks, and trade names. The general interpretation also includes software and other intangible computer based assets are all examples of _____ s. _____ s generally—though not necessarily—suffer from typical market failures of non-rivalry and non-excludability.

Exam Probability: **High**

30. *Answer choices:*

(see index for correct answer)

- a. open system
- b. Intangible asset
- c. process perspective
- d. empathy

Guidance: level 1

:: Generally Accepted Accounting Principles ::

An _____ or profit and loss account is one of the financial statements of a company and shows the company's revenues and expenses during a particular period.

Exam Probability: **Medium**

31. *Answer choices:*

(see index for correct answer)

- a. Income statement
- b. Access to finance
- c. Provision
- d. Historical cost

Guidance: level 1

:: Taxation in the United States ::

Basis, as used in United States tax law, is the original cost of property, adjusted for factors such as depreciation. When property is sold, the taxpayer pays/ taxes on a capital gain/ that equals the amount realized on the sale minus the sold property's basis.

Exam Probability: **Low**

32. *Answer choices:*

(see index for correct answer)

- a. Cost basis
- b. Tax accounting
- c. School Infrastructure Local Option
- d. Tax ladder

Guidance: level 1

:: Manufacturing ::

> _____ costs are all manufacturing costs that are related to the cost object but cannot be traced to that cost object in an economically feasible way.

Exam Probability: **Medium**

33. *Answer choices:*

(see index for correct answer)

- a. Clean Driving Zone
- b. Squeezeform
- c. Muda
- d. Manufacturing overhead

Guidance: level 1

:: Financial accounting ::

A _____ is an ownership interest in a corporation with enough voting stock shares to prevail in any stockholders' motion. A majority of voting shares is always a _____ . When a party holds less than the majority of the voting shares, other present circumstances can be considered to determine whether that party is still considered to hold a controlling ownership interest.

Exam Probability: **Low**

34. *Answer choices:*

(see index for correct answer)

- a. Holding gains
- b. Deferred financing cost
- c. Net worth
- d. Controlling interest

Guidance: level 1

:: Personal taxes ::

A _____ is the completion of documentation that calculates an entity's income earned with the amount of tax payable to the government, government organisations or to potential taxpayers.

Exam Probability: **Low**

35. *Answer choices:*

(see index for correct answer)

- a. Tithe
- b. Pay-as-you-earn tax
- c. Fiscus Judaicus
- d. Tax return

Guidance: level 1

:: Accounting source documents ::

An _____, bill or tab is a commercial document issued by a seller to a buyer, relating to a sale transaction and indicating the products, quantities, and agreed prices for products or services the seller had provided the buyer.

Exam Probability: **Medium**

36. *Answer choices:*

(see index for correct answer)

- a. Credit memorandum
- b. Parcel audit
- c. Remittance advice
- d. Banknote

Guidance: level 1

:: Management ::

_____ is the identification, evaluation, and prioritization of risks followed by coordinated and economical application of resources to minimize, monitor, and control the probability or impact of unfortunate events or to maximize the realization of opportunities.

Exam Probability: **Low**

37. *Answer choices:*

(see index for correct answer)

- a. Tacit knowledge
- b. PhD in management
- c. Project team builder
- d. Project management information system

Guidance: level 1

:: Stock market ::

A _____, equity market or share market is the aggregation of buyers and sellers of stocks, which represent ownership claims on businesses; these may include securities listed on a public stock exchange, as well as stock that is only traded privately. Examples of the latter include shares of private companies which are sold to investors through equity crowdfunding platforms. Stock exchanges list shares of common equity as well as other security types, e.g. corporate bonds and convertible bonds.

Exam Probability: **Medium**

38. *Answer choices:*

(see index for correct answer)

- a. Investor relations
- b. Stock Market
- c. CEE Stock Exchange Group
- d. Somalia Stock Exchange

Guidance: level 1

:: ::

_____ is the consumption and saving opportunity gained by an entity within a specified timeframe, which is generally expressed in monetary terms. For households and individuals, "_____ is the sum of all the wages, salaries, profits, interest payments, rents, and other forms of earnings received in a given period of time."

Exam Probability: **Low**

39. *Answer choices:*

(see index for correct answer)

- a. hierarchical perspective
- b. imperative
- c. deep-level diversity
- d. Income

Guidance: level 1

:: Information systems ::

An accounting as an information system is a system of collecting, storing and processing financial and accounting data that are used by decision makers. An _____ is generally a computer-based method for tracking accounting activity in conjunction with information technology resources. The resulting financial reports can be used internally by management or externally by other interested parties including investors, creditors and tax authorities. _____s are designed to support all accounting functions and activities including auditing, financial accounting & reporting, managerial/ management accounting and tax. The most widely adopted accounting information systems are auditing and financial reporting modules.

Exam Probability: **High**

40. *Answer choices:*

(see index for correct answer)

- a. Cold start
- b. Control flow diagram
- c. Vehicle Information and Communication System
- d. Accounting information system

Guidance: level 1

:: Generally Accepted Accounting Principles ::

_____ is all a person's receipts and gains from all sources, before any deductions. The adjective "gross", as opposed to "net", generally qualifies a word referring to an amount, value, weight, number, or the like, specifying that necessary deductions have not been taken into account.

Exam Probability: **Medium**

41. *Answer choices:*

(see index for correct answer)

- a. Deferral
- b. Gross income
- c. Generally Accepted Accounting Practice
- d. Deprival value

Guidance: level 1

:: Generally Accepted Accounting Principles ::

_____ is a measure of a fixed or current asset's worth when held in inventory, in the field of accounting. NRV is part of the Generally Accepted Accounting Principles and International Financial Reporting Standards that apply to valuing inventory, so as to not overstate or understate the value of inventory goods. _____ is generally equal to the selling price of the inventory goods less the selling costs . Therefore, it is expected sales price less selling costs . NRV prevents overstating or understating of an assets value. NRV is the price cap when using the Lower of Cost or Market Rule.

Exam Probability: **High**

42. *Answer choices:*

(see index for correct answer)

- a. Generally Accepted Accounting Practice
- b. Net realizable value
- c. Operating income before depreciation and amortization
- d. Depreciation

Guidance: level 1

:: Business law ::

A _____ is an arrangement where parties, known as partners, agree to cooperate to advance their mutual interests. The partners in a _____ may be individuals, businesses, interest-based organizations, schools, governments or combinations. Organizations may partner to increase the likelihood of each achieving their mission and to amplify their reach. A _____ may result in issuing and holding equity or may be only governed by a contract.

Exam Probability: **Low**

43. *Answer choices:*

(see index for correct answer)

- a. Partnership
- b. Law of agency
- c. Advertising regulation
- d. Industrial relations

Guidance: level 1

:: Costs ::

The _____ is computed by dividing the total cost of goods available for sale by the total units available for sale. This gives a weighted-average unit cost that is applied to the units in the ending inventory.

Exam Probability: **Medium**

44. *Answer choices:*
(see index for correct answer)

- a. Cost per paper
- b. Road Logistics Costing in South Africa
- c. Average cost
- d. labor cost

Guidance: level 1

:: Payment systems ::

A _____ is a bond of the redeemable transaction type which is worth a certain monetary value and which may be spent only for specific reasons or on specific goods. Examples include housing, travel, and food _____ s. The term _____ is also a synonym for receipt and is often used to refer to receipts used as evidence of, for example, the declaration that a service has been performed or that an expenditure has been made. _____ is a tourist guide for using services with a guarantee of payment by the agency.

Exam Probability: **Low**

45. *Answer choices:*

(see index for correct answer)

- a. RuPay
- b. Scrip
- c. Voucher
- d. Bad check restitution program

Guidance: level 1

:: Inventory ::

Costs are associated with particular goods using one of the several formulas, including specific identification, first-in first-out , or average cost. Costs include all costs of purchase, costs of conversion and other costs that are incurred in bringing the inventories to their present location and condition. Costs of goods made by the businesses include material, labor, and allocated overhead. The costs of those goods which are not yet sold are deferred as costs of inventory until the inventory is sold or written down in value.

Exam Probability: **High**

46. *Answer choices:*

(see index for correct answer)

- a. Order fulfillment

- b. Lower of cost or market
- c. Ending inventory
- d. Cost of goods sold

Guidance: level 1

:: Accounting systems ::

In accounting, a business or an organization and its owners are treated as two separately identifiable parties. This is called the _____ . The business stands apart from other organizations as a separate economic unit. It is necessary to record the business's transactions separately, to distinguish them from the owners' personal transactions. This helps to give a correct determination of the true financial condition of the business. This concept can be extended to accounting separately for the various divisions of a business in order to ascertain the financial results for each division. Under the business _____ , a business holds separate entity and distinct from its owners. "The entity view holds the business 'enterprise to be an institution in its own right separate and distinct from the parties who furnish the funds"

Exam Probability: **High**

47. *Answer choices:*

(see index for correct answer)

- a. Convention of consistency
- b. Installment sales method
- c. Dome Publishing
- d. Entity concept

Guidance: level 1

:: Finance ::

In accounting, _____ is the portion of a subsidiary corporation's stock that is not owned by the parent corporation. The magnitude of the _____ in the subsidiary company is generally less than 50% of outstanding shares, or the corporation would generally cease to be a subsidiary of the parent.

Exam Probability: **High**

48. *Answer choices:*

(see index for correct answer)

- a. Minority interest
- b. Performance attribution
- c. Due diligence
- d. Secured creditor

Guidance: level 1

:: Financial ratios ::

The _____ shows the percentage of how profitable a company's assets are in generating revenue.

Exam Probability: **Medium**

49. *Answer choices:*

(see index for correct answer)

- a. Return on assets
- b. Theoretical ex-rights price
- c. Sortino ratio
- d. Dividend yield

Guidance: level 1

:: Real estate ::

Amortisation is paying off an amount owed over time by making planned, incremental payments of principal and interest. To amortise a loan means "to kill it off". In accounting, amortisation refers to charging or writing off an intangible asset's cost as an operational expense over its estimated useful life to reduce a company's taxable income.

Exam Probability: **Medium**

50. *Answer choices:*

(see index for correct answer)

- a. Coving
- b. Deeds registration
- c. Rural land sales
- d. Amortization

Guidance: level 1

:: Banking ::

A _____ is a financial account maintained by a bank for a customer. A _____ can be a deposit account, a credit card account, a current account, or any other type of account offered by a financial institution, and represents the funds that a customer has entrusted to the financial institution and from which the customer can make withdrawals. Alternatively, accounts may be loan accounts in which case the customer owes money to the financial institution.

Exam Probability: **Low**

51. *Answer choices:*

(see index for correct answer)

- a. Bank account
- b. Universal bank
- c. Standing order
- d. Branch manager

Guidance: level 1

:: Management accounting ::

"_____ s are the structural determinants of the cost of an activity, reflecting any linkages or interrelationships that affect it". Therefore we could assume that the _____ s determine the cost behavior within the activities, reflecting the links that these have with other activities and relationships that affect them.

Exam Probability: **Low**

52. *Answer choices:*

(see index for correct answer)

- a. Profit center
- b. Direct material usage variance
- c. Fixed cost
- d. Certified Management Accountants of Canada

Guidance: level 1

:: Valuation (finance) ::

_____ refers to an assessment of the viability, stability, and profitability of a business, sub-business or project.

Exam Probability: **Medium**

53. *Answer choices:*

(see index for correct answer)

- a. Member of the Appraisal Institute
- b. Investment value
- c. Russian Society of Appraisers
- d. Financial analysis

Guidance: level 1

:: Generally Accepted Accounting Principles ::

_____ s is an accounting term that refers to groups of accounts serving to express the cost of goods and service allocatable within a business or manufacturing organization. The principle behind the pool is to correlate direct and indirect costs with a specified cost driver, so to find out the total sum of expenses related to the manufacture of a product.

Exam Probability: **Medium**

54. *Answer choices:*

(see index for correct answer)

- a. Contributed capital
- b. Depreciation

- c. Revenue
- d. Treasury stock

Guidance: level 1

:: United States Generally Accepted Accounting Principles ::

In a companies' financial reporting, _____ "includes all changes in equity during a period except those resulting from investments by owners and distributions to owners". Because that use excludes the effects of changing ownership interest, an economic measure of _____ is necessary for financial analysis from the shareholders' point of view

Exam Probability: **Low**

55. *Answer choices:*
(see index for correct answer)

- a. Accounting for leases in the United States
- b. Comprehensive income
- c. Comprehensive annual financial report
- d. GASB 45

Guidance: level 1

:: Generally Accepted Accounting Principles ::

A _____, in accrual accounting, is any account where the asset or liability is not realized until a future date, e.g. annuities, charges, taxes, income, etc. The deferred item may be carried, dependent on type of _____, as either an asset or liability. See also accrual.

Exam Probability: **Low**

56. *Answer choices:*

(see index for correct answer)

- a. Contributed capital
- b. Deferred income
- c. Deferral
- d. Earnings before interest, taxes and depreciation

Guidance: level 1

:: Accounting software ::

_____ is any item or verifiable record that is generally accepted as payment for goods and services and repayment of debts, such as taxes, in a particular country or socio-economic context. The main functions of _____ are distinguished as: a medium of exchange, a unit of account, a store of value and sometimes, a standard of deferred payment. Any item or verifiable record that fulfils these functions can be considered as _____.

Exam Probability: **Low**

57. Answer choices:

(see index for correct answer)

- a. Money
- b. Quicken
- c. E-accounting
- d. Chrysler Comprehensive Compensation System

Guidance: level 1

:: Value theory ::

> Within philosophy, it can be known as ethics or axiology. Early philosophical investigations sought to understand good and evil and the concept of "the good". Today, much of _____ aspires to the scientifically empirical, recording what people do value and attempting to understand why they value it in the context of psychology, sociology, and economics.

Exam Probability: **Medium**

58. Answer choices:

(see index for correct answer)

- a. Marginalism
- b. economic value
- c. Subjective theory of value
- d. Theory of imputation

Guidance: level 1

:: Financial statements ::

_____ s - are the "Financial statements of a group in which the assets, liabilities, equity, income, expenses and cash flows of the parent company and its subsidiaries are presented as those of a single economic entity", according to International Accounting Standard 27 "Consolidated and separate financial statements", and International Financial Reporting Standard 10 "_____ s".

Exam Probability: **Medium**

59. *Answer choices:*

(see index for correct answer)

- a. quarterly report
- b. Consolidated financial statement
- c. Balance sheet
- d. Emphasis of matter

Guidance: level 1

INDEX: Correct Answers

Foundations of Business

1. c: Budget

2. c: Cash

3. c: Alliance

4. a: Direct investment

5. a: Management system

6. a: Stock market

7. c: Need

8. d: Franchising

9. d: Review

10. c: Privacy

11. b: Industry

12. : Utility

13. b: Specification

14. a: Good

15. c: Competitive advantage

16. b: Negotiation

17. c: Inventory

18. c: Officer

19. b: Business model

20. : Sexual harassment

21. b: Business plan

22. a: Building

23. c: Document

24. a: Productivity

25. : Capital market

26. : Career

27. d: Goal

28. c: Strategy

29. c: Percentage

30. c: Six Sigma

31. c: Sony

32. b: Reputation

33. d: Organizational culture

34. a: Financial services

35. c: Partnership

36. c: Sharing

37. : Customs

38. b: Loan

39. b: Marketing research

40. : Market segmentation

41. c: Scheduling

42. c: Asset

43. : Question

44. d: Dividend

45. a: Contract

46. a: Image

47. : Fraud

48. : Interest rate

49. a: Case study

50. b: Balanced scorecard

51. c: Social responsibility

52. d: Project management

53. d: Subsidiary

54. d: Strategic planning

55. d: Gross domestic product

56. c: Risk management

57. c: Joint venture

58. b: Initiative

59. a: Size

Management

1. b: Supply chain management

2. d: Assessment center

3. : Total quality management

4. b: Workforce

5. : Job design

6. c: Trade agreement

7. c: Management

8. b: Strategic alliance

9. : Bargaining

10. a: Myers-Briggs type

11. c: Competitive advantage

12. d: Performance management

13. b: Asset

14. a: Certification

15. c: Overtime

16. a: Referent power

17. c: Cooperative

18. : Job satisfaction

19. d: Protection

20. c: Outsourcing

21. : Quality assurance

22. a: Career

23. b: Interview

24. a: Crisis

25. d: Free trade

26. c: Delegation

27. d: Decision-making

28. : Subsidiary

29. b: Resource allocation

30. c: Budget

31. b: Self-assessment

32. : Review

33. : Job analysis

34. : Sexual harassment

35. c: Firm

36. : Simulation

37. a: Decentralization

38. d: Committee

39. a: Interaction

40. a: Leadership

41. d: Balanced scorecard

42. c: Labor force

43. b: Negotiation

44. b: Export

45. c: Six Sigma

46. c: Benchmarking

47. b: Brainstorming

48. b: Board of directors

49. b: Performance appraisal

50. b: SWOT analysis

51. a: Reinforcement

52. : Supervisor

53. d: Cost

54. d: Globalization

55. b: Change management

56. c: Revenue

57. a: Perception

58. a: Information

59. d: Bias

Business law

1. a: Damages

2. : Arbitration

3. a: Wire fraud

4. c: Contributory negligence

5. d: Consumer Good

6. b: Economic Espionage Act

7. d: Authority

8. b: Income

9. b: Commercial speech

10. : Standing

11. d: Patent

12. d: Issuer

13. c: Surety

14. a: Sherman Act

15. b: Insider trading

16. b: Complaint

17. d: Puffery

18. c: Contract Clause

19. : Restraint of trade

20. a: Mens rea

21. a: Misdemeanor

22. d: Embezzlement

23. b: Foreclosure

24. : Employment law

25. : Negotiation

26. b: Creditor

27. : Substantive law

28. b: Collective bargaining

29. : Liquidation

30. b: Environmental Protection

31. c: Promissory note

32. c: Economy

33. d: Garnishment

34. c: Bad faith

35. : Personal property

36. c: Beneficiary

37. : Warehouse

38. a: Welfare

39. : Security

40. a: Reasonable person

41. : Ford

42. c: Acceleration clause

43. d: Interest

44. b: Deed

45. d: Rescind

46. c: Marketing

47. a: Unconscionability

48. a: Constitutional law

49. d: Testimony

50. a: Subrogation

51. a: Utilitarianism

52. a: Opening statement

53. : Voidable contract

54. b: Securities and Exchange Commission

55. d: Adverse possession

56. b: Free trade

57. a: Undue influence

58. d: Accord and satisfaction

59. c: Copyright

Finance

1. d: Selling

2. a: Annual report

3. a: Adjusting entries

4. b: Internal rate of return

5. d: Stock split

6. d: Indenture

7. b: Income statement

8. b: Contribution margin

9. : Amortization

10. b: Economy

11. c: Interest

12. : Write-off

13. d: Manufacturing overhead

14. b: Wall Street

15. d: Shareholder

16. b: Credit

17. d: Matching principle

18. b: Public company

19. : Financial ratio

20. a: Financial analysis

21. b: Board of directors

22. b: General journal

23. d: Financial Accounting Standards Board

24. c: Market price

25. b: Double taxation

26. c: Interest rate risk

27. d: Balanced scorecard

28. a: Schedule

29. c: Absorption costing

30. c: Commercial bank

31. b: Financial risk

32. a: Conservatism

33. c: Receipt

34. a: Taxation

35. d: Inventory turnover

36. b: Debit card

37. c: Finance

38. a: Put option

39. a: Corporate governance

40. c: Competition

41. a: Advertising

42. a: Cost object

43. d: Time value of money

44. b: Rate of return

45. a: Cost allocation

46. b: Sales

47. b: Variable Costing

48. b: Creditor

49. c: Capital lease

50. c: Incentive

51. : Free cash flow

52. a: Primary market

53. b: Debenture

54. d: Balance sheet

55. : Investor

56. : Income

57. c: Financial market

58. b: Market value

59. a: Indirect costs

Human resource management

1. c: Bureau of Labor Statistics

2. : Card check

3. b: Employee surveys

4. d: Job satisfaction

5. b: Supply chain

6. c: Organizational justice

7. d: Performance improvement

8. a: Golden parachute

9. b: Assessment center

10. c: Census

11. b: Material safety data sheet

12. d: Globalization

13. b: Bottom line

14. : Picketing

15. b: Independent contractor

16. d: Sick leave

17. d: Social contract

18. : Executive search

19. c: Recession

20. : Cost

21. a: Organizational chart

22. c: Bundy v. Jackson

23. d: Eustress

24. d: Affirmative action

25. d: Transformational leadership

26. c: Unfair labor practice

27. b: Delayering

28. a: Content validity

29. b: Performance measurement

30. d: Enforcement

31. a: Trade union

32. c: Decentralization

33. : Resource management

34. a: Business process outsourcing

35. : Executive officer

36. d: Employment

37. b: Restructuring

38. c: Self-actualization

39. a: Employee assistance program

40. a: Free Trade

41. : Peter Principle

42. a: Applicant tracking system

43. c: Information overload

44. : Management by objectives

45. c: Absenteeism

46. : Internship

47. b: Asset

48. a: Deferred compensation

49. b: National Institute for Occupational Safety and Health

50. : Love contract

51. a: National Association of Colleges and Employers

52. d: Predictive validity

53. : Cost of living

54. : Social networking

55. d: Goal setting

56. c: Halo effect

57. d: Questionnaire

58. a: Efficiency wage

59. c: Global workforce

Information systems

1. a: Intrusion detection system

2. d: Viral marketing

3. d: Census

4. c: Computer security

5. c: Payment card

6. b: Read-only memory

7. : Competitive advantage

8. : Domain name

9. : Debit card

10. a: Trojan horse

11. d: Total cost

12. a: Disaster recovery

13. : Tacit knowledge

14. : Reputation management

15. b: Security management

16. a: Keystroke dynamics

17. b: Network management

18. c: Enterprise information system

19. b: Virtual team

20. d: Strategic information system

21. a: Disaster recovery plan

22. b: Wiki

23. a: ICANN

24. a: Google Maps

25. c: Authentication

26. d: Knowledge management

27. c: Galileo

28. : Total cost of ownership

29. a: First mover advantage

30. : Cookie

31. d: Strategic planning

32. b: Picasa

33. c: M-Pesa

34. b: Peer production

35. a: One Laptop per Child

36. d: Subscription

37. b: Balanced scorecard

38. b: Chart

39. : Data element

40. a: Long tail

41. a: Data link

42. d: Supply chain

43. b: Metadata

44. : Non-repudiation

45. a: Data cleansing

46. c: Web server

47. a: Management information system

48. c: Extranet

49. : Clickstream

50. a: Business intelligence

51. a: Interactivity

52. d: Common Criteria

53. a: Economies of scale

54. d: Output device

55. : Data file

56. d: Data aggregator

57. b: Enterprise application

58. c: Worm

59. : Authorization

Marketing

1. c: Corporation

2. d: Planning

3. a: Mass customization

4. c: Star

5. a: Survey research

6. d: Direct selling

7. c: Strategic planning

8. : Coupon

9. a: Target audience

10. a: Contract

11. d: Brand image

12. b: Gross domestic product

13. d: Policy

14. a: Department store

15. : Committee

16. c: Brand loyalty

17. a: Need

18. b: Authority

19. d: Preference

20. b: Sherman Antitrust Act

21. b: Retail

22. b: Inflation

23. b: Viral marketing

24. a: Pricing

25. d: Nonprofit

26. c: Product development

27. c: Database marketing

28. c: Logo

29. c: New product development

30. : Insurance

31. c: Advertising campaign

32. c: Aid

33. a: Consultant

34. d: Bottom line

35. d: Loyalty program

36. : Data analysis

37. : Universal Product Code

38. : Retailing

39. b: Federal Trade Commission

40. c: Trademark

41. : Qualitative research

42. a: Innovation

43. c: E-commerce

44. a: Fixed cost

45. c: Manager

46. c: Relationship marketing

47. a: Product differentiation

48. b: Price

49. b: Trade association

50. a: Sales

51. : Business Week

52. b: Raw material

53. d: Market segmentation

54. b: Supply chain management

55. c: Interest

56. : Logistics

57. d: Marketing plan

58. b: Shares

59. d: Dimension

Manufacturing

1. c: Clay

2. d: Cost

3. d: Joint Commission

4. b: Heat exchanger

5. : Financial plan

6. : Materials management

7. a: Scheduling

8. d: Time management

9. b: Indirect costs

10. d: Expediting

11. b: Retail

12. : Purchase order

13. b: Turbine

14. c: Reorder point

15. d: Water

16. : Sony

17. a: Procurement

18. d: Cash register

19. b: Change control

20. b: Economies of scope

21. a: Scientific management

22. : Quality Engineering

23. d: Flowchart

24. d: Process control

25. : Project team

26. b: Virtual team

27. b: Lean manufacturing

28. d: Natural resource

29. : Volume

30. c: Minitab

31. a: Quality assurance

32. a: Purchasing process

33. c: Pattern

34. : Business process

35. b: Acceptance sampling

36. d: Process capability

37. a: Transaction cost

38. b: Interaction

39. c: Waste

40. c: Control limits

41. a: Mary Kay

42. d: Credit

43. a: E-commerce

44. d: Prize

45. : Dimension

46. : Sensitivity analysis

47. b: Capacity planning

48. d: Steel

49. c: Material requirements planning

50. d: Opportunity cost

51. c: Electronic data interchange

52. b: Bill of materials

53. a: Asset

54. d: Statistical process control

55. a: Supply chain network

56. : Workflow

57. c: Pareto analysis

58. : Supplier relationship management

59. c: Gantt chart

Commerce

1. : Economics

2. : Wall Street Journal

3. a: Marketing strategy

4. : Authentication

5. b: Exchange rate

6. c: Tool

7. d: Economy

8. : Trial

9. b: Project

10. d: Supply chain

11. a: Policy

12. : Teamwork

13. d: Encryption

14. a: Empowerment

15. b: Import

16. a: Overtime

17. a: Statutory law

18. a: Mass production

19. : American Express

20. c: Mobile commerce

21. : Direct marketing

22. a: Marginal cost

23. b: Tariff

24. : Shares

25. a: Staff position

26. b: Forward auction

27. : Market research

28. b: Consortium

29. c: Shopping cart

30. : Minimum wage

31. d: Tourism

32. : Control system

33. b: Security

34. : Productivity

35. c: Game

36. a: Jury

37. : Advertisement

38. b: Land

39. b: Procurement

40. d: Anticipation

41. : Reverse auction

42. d: Commerce

43. b: York

44. : Quality assurance

45. a: Antitrust

46. c: Subsidy

47. c: Case study

48. : Marketing

49. b: Electronic funds transfer

50. b: Public policy

51. b: Bank

52. : Level of service

53. c: Semantic

54. : E-commerce

55. c: Uniform Commercial Code

56. : Trade

57. b: Negotiation

58. a: Competitor

59. : Buyer

Business ethics

1. a: Nepotism

2. b: Undue hardship

3. a: Workplace bullying

4. c: New Deal

5. c: Lanham Act

6. b: Criminal law

7. a: Qui tam

8. a: Internal control

9. b: Chamber of Commerce

10. b: Corporate structure

11. a: Pollution

12. : Risk assessment

13. c: Medicare fraud

14. d: ExxonMobil

15. : Dilemma

16. c: Trojan horse

17. : Sullivan principles

18. c: Wall Street

19. b: New York Stock Exchange

20. d: Better Business Bureau

21. a: Protestant work ethic

22. : Urban sprawl

23. b: Pyramid scheme

24. b: Skill

25. a: Edgewood College

26. : Human nature

27. a: Corporate social responsibility

28. a: WorldCom

29. a: Planet

30. c: Stanford Financial Group

31. : Right to work

32. a: Siemens

33. a: Volcker Rule

34. : Habitat

35. b: Consumerism

36. b: Lawsuit

37. : Antitrust

38. c: White-collar crime

39. a: Martin Luther

40. c: East India

41. d: Exxon Valdez

42. a: Partnership

43. a: Minimum wage

44. : Statutory law

45. d: Real estate

46. c: Authoritarian

47. b: Fair trade

48. d: Labor relations

49. : Invisible hand

50. b: Aristotle

51. : Ponzi scheme

52. b: Coal

53. b: Petroleum

54. d: Energy policy

55. : Forest Stewardship Council

56. d: East Germany

57. c: Organic food

58. c: Insider trading

59. b: Federal Trade Commission

Accounting

1. : Probate

2. b: Capital account

3. c: Decentralization

4. a: Write-off

5. b: Reimbursement

6. a: Financial Accounting Standards Board

7. : Process Management

8. b: Times interest earned

9. : Joint venture

10. b: Long-term liabilities

11. c: Subsidiary ledger

12. c: Fair value

13. : Tax revenue

14. b: American Accounting Association

15. d: Debit card

16. c: Accounting management

17. c: Governmental accounting

18. c: Book value

19. : Accrual

20. c: Managerial accounting

21. d: Matching principle

22. d: Operating expense

23. : Tax avoidance

24. a: Activity-based costing

25. a: Return on investment

26. c: Profit center

27. d: Credit card

28. c: Adoption

29. : Receipt

30. b: Intangible asset

31. a: Income statement

32. a: Cost basis

33. d: Manufacturing overhead

34. d: Controlling interest

35. d: Tax return

36. : Invoice

37. : Risk management

38. b: Stock Market

39. d: Income

40. d: Accounting information system

41. b: Gross income

42. b: Net realizable value

43. a: Partnership

44. c: Average cost

45. c: Voucher

46. d: Cost of goods sold

47. d: Entity concept

48. a: Minority interest

49. a: Return on assets

50. d: Amortization

51. a: Bank account

52. : Cost driver

53. d: Financial analysis

54. : Cost pool

55. b: Comprehensive income

56. c: Deferral

57. a: Money

58. : Value theory

59. b: Consolidated financial statement

CPSIA information can be obtained
at www.ICGtesting.com
Printed in the USA
LVHW051306301019
635717LV00007B/809/P